It's a Crazy, Wonderful Life!

101 Brief Accounts
of the Crazy, Unusual,
Happy, Strange, Delightful,
Sometimes Dangerous
Things that Happened
on the Way to
My Grave

John Hartog II

Edited and expanded by
Martha Hartog

Order this book online at www.trafford.com
or email orders@trafford.com

Most Trafford titles are also available at major online book retailers.

© Copyright 2013 John Hartog II.
All rights reserved. No part of this publication may be reproduced, stored in a retrieval system, or transmitted, in any form or by any means, electronic, mechanical, photocopying, recording, or otherwise, without the written prior permission of the author.

Printed in the United States of America.

ISBN: 978-1-4269-0775-3 (sc)

Trafford rev. 05/07/2013

 www.trafford.com

North America & international
toll-free: 1 888 232 4444 (USA & Canada)
phone: 250 383 6864 ♦ fax: 812 355 4082

A Special Word of Thanks

These nine individuals helped make this book possible and deserve special mention and appreciation:

Liz Gifford waded through the first rough, rough draft. She was a brave pioneer.

Matthew Johnson, at a turning point, helped me keep the project alive by reading the rough draft and letting me know that the book was worth publishing.

Becki Lounsbrough also read the rough draft and reassured me that the would-be book had value. Her cheerfulness carried the manuscript another step ahead.

My sister Fran and her husband Bill read an updated version of the book and found it hilarious! This meant much to me at a difficult time.

Joel Graham, Eric Schnirring, and Lance Young. Their technological knowledge was invaluable in the production of this book.

My wife Martha spent *many* long months editing the book. Her goal was to ensure that the stories expressed accurately the events and my concurrent thoughts. Sometimes she succeeded, but sometimes . . . . You'll have to find out. Her sense of humor added "sugar & hot spice" to this book.

Thank you! Thank you! Thank you!
Thank you! Thank you! Thank you!
Thank you! Thank you! Thank you!

Dedication

This book is dedicated to my wife, Martha, and to me—to compensate for the times we looked within, laughed out loud, or pondered together. All these moments helped preserve our sanity during this project.

This book is also dedicated to our sons, John III and Paul Anthony. They thought we were crazy for thinking we could write it.

Finally, this book is dedicated to all my students, past and present. Their laughter at my illustrations, which I weaved through my lectures, motivated me to put these "rabbit trails" in a book. Often, after hearing my stories, my attentive students responded, "You should write a book!" They convinced me! And I did!

Disclaimer

Most of the stories in this book are amusing; others are simple accounts about everyday life; and a few depict problems we have experienced along the way.

Indeed, all of the stories are narratives about my *crazy, wonderful life*. So laugh when you can, or shed a tear when you must as your heart prompts you, because that is what life is all about.

Global Warming?

1936 was my birth year.

It was the **hottest year** ever in Iowa's History. 1936 set 21 new daily record highs for Des Moines. These records still stand at the time of this writing.

July 1936 was the **hottest month** of that year. During that month alone, 12 of its 31 days set new record highs that never have been broken. No other month has ever come close to that.

July 25, 1936, hit a stifling 110° actual temperature, and Iowa's **hottest day** ever.

1936, the year I was born, gave me an **extremely warm** welcome!

Laughter

"He who cannot laugh at himself is a most miserable person."—John Hartog II

"Of all the things God created, I am often most grateful He created laughter."—Charles Swindoll

"With the fearful strain that is on me night and day, if I did not laugh I should die."—Abraham Lincoln

"If both sides make you laugh, you are broad minded."—Author unknown

"I laugh, for hope hath happy place with me."—William Ellery Channing

"Laughter is to life what salt is to the egg."—Helen Valentine

"There is no jovial companionship equal to that where the jokes are rather small and the laughter abundant."—Washington Irving

"Laff every time you pheel tickled, and laff once in awhile enyhow."—Josh Billings

"Laff every tym u pheel tyckled, an laff wonce in awhyle inkneehow."—Revised ed., JH II

"No one is laughable who laughs at himself."—Seneca

"All of us need to laugh at ourselves once in a while—it is the most genuine form of laughter."—John Hartog II

Picture Locations

1. My Best Friend/Wife and I — 11
2. Me at Six Months with My Family — 17
3. The House on 2nd Street — 25
4. Courthouse, Sioux County, IA — 30
5. Second Grade Art Award — 33
6. Two Fawns and Blue Ribbon — 36
7. Trouble at Threshing Time — 43
8. Martha Squeezing into Married Life — 104
9. Lipscomb Telephone System — 133
10. Our 64½ Mustang, Martha, and Our Sons — 180
11. Martha Wearing Guatemalan Hat by a Homestead Flowering Bush — 241
12. Our Sons and Tar Baby — 261
13. My '72 Mustang — 282
14. Vinsy and Rex Resting on the Deck — 325
15. Oh, My Pawpaw Fruit — 345
16. Taking a Break at Machu Picchu — 372
17. Martha Socializing at Cusco — 378
18. Lucy, Desi, and Beula — 389
19. Itsy Bitsy's Gang with Martha — 394
20. Mother and I — 417

Facts about the Author

*When I was a child, a hatchery worker stuffed my pockets full of live baby chicks and sent me home.

*When I was a teenager taking care of my grand-father by myself, he set on fire the couch on which he was sitting.

*I was in kindergarten, first grade, and second grade, all in the same calendar year. Nine years later, I became a high school drop out. After high school, I attended school for seventeen years. In the process, I earned six academic degrees including two doctorates.

*On one occasion, a seminary classmate and I were famished, and the only food on hand was under dirt. To get through the day, we dug raw peanuts with our bare hands out of an already harvested field.

*To get married, I climbed a pole onto a roof, and my wife was shoved into the church through a window.

*The airline, which my wife and I flew on a South American trip, went bankrupt and left us stranded in a 1,200-foot-high-mountain city.

But all that is getting ahead of what you are about to read. All the incidents recorded in this book are true and are recorded to the best of my memory.

Sit back, grab a cup of tea,
and have a few laughs along the way because,
"A merry heart does good like medicine."
Proverbs 17:22 (NKJV ™)

My Best Friend/Wife and I

Contents

A Special Word of Thanks	5
Dedication & Disclaimer	6
Global Warming?	7
Laughter	8
Picture Index	9
Facts about the Author	10

Story		**Page**
1.	Seney	19
2.	That House on Second Street	22
3.	Growing Up Dutch	26
4.	The Budding Artist	32
5.	Under Cloud Nine	39
6.	A Chick-Chick Here And Chick-Chick There	45
7.	The Piggy-Back Ride	48
8.	When the Lights Went Out	50
9.	Achan Was Taken	52
10.	Upside Down or Downside up?	55
11.	The High School Dropout	58
12.	Grandpa on the Hot Seat	61
13.	Better Than on the Floor!	65
14.	I'll Never Teach Again!	68
15.	The Attack Cat	71
16.	A Case of Mistaken Identity	73
17.	Wake Up! Sleepy, Sleepy Head!	76
18.	The Oklahoma Peanut Farm	78
19.	Rats!	81
20.	Three + One + One Is a Crowd	84
21.	Drive, Baby, Drive!	86

22.	Westward Ho!	88
23.	The 4th of July Switcheroo	93
24.	Wedding Bells (part one)	95
25.	Wedding Bells (part two)	99
26.	Wedded Bliss	107
27.	Brother, Do You Have Ten Bucks?	111
28.	Wendy, the Educated Dog	115
29.	Mrs. Black	120
30.	A Hole in One	123
31.	Locked Jaw	128
32.	The Original "On-Line" Phone System	131
33.	The Musical Boy	135
34.	Murphy's Law on Wheels	137
35.	Our Fair Lady	143
36.	Rattlesnakes!	146
37.	Testing Time	149
38.	Penny Pinching	153
39.	One in a Hole	156
40.	Hold Your Tongue!	162
41.	The "Archeologist"	167
42.	"Those Amateurs!"	173
43.	Family Expansion!	177
44.	Lions and Tigers and Bears	183
45.	Apartment Living (part one)	187
46.	Apartment Living (part two)	191
47.	A Christmas to Remember	196
48.	The Black Out	201
49.	Horse Mountain	207
50.	Ditch all Your Belongings	210
51.	Just off the Road a Piece	215
52.	I Beg You, Have Mercy on Me!	219
53.	Where Has All My Honey Gone?	222
54.	Baby Sitter?	226
55.	Ichabod, the Oilaholic	230

56.	Far South of the Border (El Salvador)	235
57.	Far South of the Border (Guatemala)	239
58.	Of Diamonds and Gold	243
59.	Ice Fallies	247
60.	Hanging on for Dear Life	249
61.	That Low Sinking Feeling	251
62.	On a slippery slope	253
63.	Sunset Galloway Ranch	257
64.	Oh Where, Oh Where Has My Little Dog Gone?	260
65.	Pie in the Sky—and Everywhere Else!	263
66.	School in a Box	265
67.	Tar Baby and the Goose	269
68.	Few Bees or not Few Bees	271
69.	Our White House in the Woods	276
70.	Just a Matter of Time	280
71.	The Jaws of Death!	285
72.	Fire! Fire!	288
73.	Preach It, Brother!	291
74.	What's in a Name?	294
75.	The Raymore Police	297
76.	The Disappearing Act	302
77.	A Sign of the Times	305
78.	Hillbilly Bean Soup	308
79.	The Great Library Makeover	312
80.	Life in the Slow Lane	316
81.	Living with an Angel	321
82.	Rex	326
83.	Abraham	330
84.	The Silver Bullet	334
85.	An Unwanted Guest in the Coop	338
86.	Oh, Mi Pawpaw!	341
87.	The Day I Got "Nailed"	348
88.	"Only a Little Bit"	353
89.	Flying High (part one)	356

90.	Flying High (part two)	360
91.	Trujillo	365
92.	Urubamba/Machu Picchu	369
93.	Cusco	375
94.	Homeward Bound!	380
95.	It Was a Bloody Event!	384
96.	Granny, Get Your Gun!	387
97.	Itsy Bitsy and His Gang	392
98.	Edelweiss	396
99.	Are All Things Possible?	402
100.	All Things Are Possible!	406
101.	Rest in Peace	413
Appendix. Heaven is a wonderful place!		419

Me at Six Months Old with My Family

1

Seney

Orange City, Iowa, the county seat of Sioux, welcomed me into the world. My mother gave me birth in a big white house, turned into a hospital, as my father waited expectantly for the news in the "waiting room." He was delighted when the doctor came out and roared, "You have a boy!" I would carry on my parents' Dutch heritage, or so they thought!

After all, three of my grandparents (my paternal grandparents and maternal grandpa) immigrated from the Netherlands. My maternal grandma was born in America to a couple who had immigrated from the Netherlands a generation earlier. Before coming to America, my maternal great grandpa had been a sea captain. His world travels had enabled him to become fluent in seven languages. From him I inherited the fascination with foreign languages.

Though I was born in Orange City, I spent my first six years in Seney, a small Iowa village that had no paved roads or sidewalks. Our sidewalk was actually a boardwalk. We lived in a rented house that cost $10.00 a month. Uncle Jake and Aunt Anna also lived in Seney. Since their house was a little smaller than ours, their rent was only $8.00 a month. We had no running water; so we hauled water from a well using a hand powered pump, which froze sometimes in the winter.

My father was a wise entrepreneur who began a grain elevator business during the Great Depression—He started out with nothing. Through diligent work and prudent financial principles, he was able to buy an old, abandoned grain elevator in Seney. Father's business prospered under his guidance, and later he bought a second elevator in Granville, Iowa.

Of course, when they first began their endeavor, my parents experienced some financial hardships. One day, Father came home from work with a quart of milk, which was all he could afford to buy for supper. It was dark when he arrived home; and, when he set the jug on the kitchen counter, he did not realize that he had set it on the edge. The glass jug fell to the floor and broke! That night Mother and Father went to bed hungry.

The earliest recollection I have of my childhood happened on a fishing trip when I was about two and a half years old. On this occasion, our family and Aunt Nellie were on our way to the Lake of the Woods in northern Minnesota—my father's favorite fishing spot. Seated in the back seat next to Aunt Nellie, I was enjoying every bit of the beautiful scenery, especially the trees. They allured me, although I was so young.

The majestic evergreens parading by my window mesmerized me. Eventually, their rapid speed made me dizzy and weak. Aunt Nellie pinpointed the trouble the moment she saw the pale, sad-eyed little boy sitting beside her. She opened the rear window, grabbed me by my pants, and shoved me halfway out of the window. And I lost my dinner to the wind!

Another incident that is imprinted on my mind took place when I was five years old in kindergarten, which met in a two-room school house. The U.S. Department of Agriculture had a surplus of peanut butter, and the solution to their problem was to give it away. Thus, our school became the recipient of a government handout. We received peanut butter jars galore. Yummy!

The teacher gave each child a pint jar and told us to take it home and to lick the jar clean. I took her literally and ate peanut butter all afternoon, using my finger as a scoop. By the end of the day, the jar was as clean as a whistle. To this day, I can't believe I ate the whole thing!

A couple of months later on my sixth birthday, Mother gave me a bag of candy to take to school to share with my classmates. Excited about it, I arrived to school early. Since the doors were not opened yet, I stopped to play on the swing for a while and put the bag of candy on the grass near the swing set. When the school bell rang, I ran into the building and left the candy behind. Throughout the morning I kept thinking of the bag with the sweet, delicious candy.

At recess I raced to the swing set to pick up my candy, but it was not where I had left it. I searched everywhere but could not find it. When the teacher asked if anyone had seen it, an older boy said he had found it and had eaten all of it. The teacher gave him a harsh lecture for being so selfish. Unfortunately, I did not even get a taste of my birthday candy! To this day, I can't believe he ate the whole thing!

Some people bring happiness wherever they go.
Others whenever they go.

—Author unknown

2

That House on Second Street

Due to an injury that resulted in blood poisoning, my father passed away unexpectedly at the young age of thirty-six. Mother, who was twenty nine, was left with six small children between eight years old and two months old: Fran, Geri, me, Marj, Janice, and Paul. I had just turned six the month before father's death.

At that time, Social Security had no provision for helping widows with small children. Mother was left on her own with no outside help. Some people advised her to put up for adoption my brother Paul, who was only two months. Of course, Mother firmly rejected that idea. Instead, she determined to do whatever it took to keep the family together.

Since Father did not have a written will, the court made Mother sell the grain elevators and invest the proceeds in farmland. Also, she was able to buy a house on Second Street in Orange City. It was a well-built house with character and beauty, evidenced by its solid oak woodwork. It had all the luxuries that a house built in 1920 afforded, including central heat and a built-in central vacuum system. Mother loved that house and lived in it for sixty-six years, until right before the last few months of her life.

Of course, my siblings and I also cherished that house. In the cold winter months, we transformed the basement into our own skating rink. We used to skate round and round the furnace, which was in the middle of the basement.

During inclement weather in spring, summer, and fall we played in the attic that was accessible by a pull-down stairs. It had large gable windows on the north and south and a smaller gable window in the middle of the east side. It was a perfect playroom because it had a wood-covered floor; and its high ceiling made it possible for us to stand up and walk around in it, except at the east and west sides where the roof sloped down.

Our attic served many purposes. All of us liked to read. When we read mystery books, it was a quiet reading room where you could hear a pin drop. But it was a noisy reading room, alive with giggles, when we read our comic books. The girls practiced their home-making skills in their staked-out "houses." Since it had many crooks and crannies, our elevated playroom became a treasure chest where we stored toys and other precious goodies. One day, after visiting a pond at the edge of town, we came home with a bunch of cattails and took them up to the attic. We stored them in a corner where they kept well—nice and dry.

After several months had passed by, we were playing in the attic and spotted our precious cattails beckoning us to play with them. We picked them up and used them as swords in a dueling match. Soon, the whole attic looked like a football field in the midst of a thundering snow storm that was rumbling with the giggles and screams of children at play.

The duel ended with a messy draw—our bodies and attic covered with fuzz. Mother discovered the mess and ordered us to clean it up. The fun was over, but memories of that incident still bring me much joy!

Mother was a good housekeeper and kept the house spick-and-span. On the other hand, she also made certain that it was an enjoyable home for growing kids. She let us have house dogs, and every so often, I had rabbits and a few chickens in outside cages.

On Sundays, my hometown resonated with all the church bells calling the people to worship. Orange City burst at the seams as farmers from the nearby area joined the town worshippers. Our house became the after-church gathering place for our farm relatives; and our small kitchen was filled with the fragrance of brewed coffee and tea and freshly baked goodies.

With the uncles and aunts, and grandpa and grandma, the number of Sunday visitors easily could reach twenty-five to thirty or more! Mother came from a family of nine. One of her sisters had eleven children; another had ten; if we add the children of the rest of mother's siblings, the number of maternal cousins is truly great! To this number we must add all the cousins on my father's side. Thus in all, I have well over one hundred cousins; and most of them lived in the area.

A childhood memory is from World War II when the government rationed sugar. Mother was gone one early summer afternoon during rhubarb-picking time. The luscious rhubarb sparked an idea in Frances's head. Typical of her, she put a whole bunch of feet to her idea and marched my siblings and me to the house of a neighbor. Frances told her that mother wanted to borrow some sugar, and the generous neighbor lent us a cupful. We brought it home, picked some rhubarb, dipped it in the borrowed sugar, and relished every bite.

A few days later, our neighbor came to our house and asked mother to return the borrowed sugar. Mother had no idea what the lady was talking about and looked at us for a hint. It was time to confess! Thankfully, Mother took it all in stride. But we learned a lesson: "Be sure, your sins will find you out!"

The House on Second Street

3

Growing Up Dutch

Our move to Orange City two months after Father's death meant that we were returning to the town that welcomed both Mother and me into this world. Orange City became my hometown from the time I was six years old until I moved away to finish college as an eighteen-year-old.

Often, people ask me the source of my hometown's name. For sure, its name does not derive from the oranges that grow there, like in Orange City, Florida, which is named for the orange groves that cover its landscape. The only oranges that landscape Orange City, Iowa, are found piled up in the fruit bins of grocery stores. Northwest Iowa's cold winters make it impossible to grow citrus fruits. Nor does Orange City bear that name because all of its buildings are painted orange. The only structures painted a bright orange color are its water towers!

Orange City, Iowa, is named after William of Orange, ancestor of the royal family of the Netherlands. My hometown was founded in 1870 by sixty three pioneer families who left Pella, Iowa, and made the trek northwest in horse-drawn wagon trains. Pella was an earlier Dutch settlement southeast of Des Moines.

The original frontiersmen had selected Calliope as the county seat. Calliope is history, and Hawarden sits on its former site. Back then, Orange City was twenty miles east of Calliope. Though a newer settlement, Orange City had become the leading town in the county within two years of its existence. Of course, the Dutch wanted *their town* to be the seat of Sioux County.

The settlers of Calliope refused to go along with the Dutch because county seats generally grew faster; so the Dutch decided to take the matter into their own hands. They hitched their horses to wagons and went by night the twenty miles to Calliope. They broke into the "courthouse," grabbed the official documents, and hauled them off to Orange City. Because of the daring escapade of the stubborn Dutch, Orange City has been the county seat ever since.

When automobiles came on the scene, several businesses met their inevitable fate—they closed shop. For example, the old Tinch Hotel, the blacksmith shop, and the livery stable, which originally were located on the corner of Second and Main, were eventually torn down; and that block became Courthouse Square. Our house in Orange City was a block west of the county courthouse and two blocks west of Main Street.

During my childhood years, Orange City was still 99.44% pure Dutch. When I was in grade school, almost all of my relatives lived nearby in the northwestern part of the state. Mother's brother, Uncle Elmer, worked at the Sunrise Hatchery, which was the only hatchery in our town. Because I enjoyed seeing baby chicks when they first hatched, I often visited the hatchery, which turned into a visit to my uncle.

One day when I went to the hatchery, Uncle Elmer approached me with a handful of baby chicks. He stuffed them in my pockets and sent me home. Mother always seemed to roll with the punches and let me keep the chicks. Their peeping sounds echoed through our basement for a few days until I moved my fuzzy pets into the garage. Eventually, they ended up outside.

Orange City was clean and neat as a pin, except that cigarette wrappers sometimes littered its otherwise clean sidewalks. Almost all the men in town smoked, and often they threw their cigarette-pack wrappers on the sidewalk or street; but the trash did not remain there long. Ahead of their time, third and fourth grade boys recycled the trash and turned it into a work of art. The aluminum foil inner liners became shiny balls in the hands of the young sculptors, who brought them to school and competed in the game of "Who made the largest aluminum ball?"

Naturally, I joined the competition. After school I liked to wander around town. Since I lived close to down-town, I often found wrappers first. In time, I sculpted an aluminum ball as big as a large grapefruit. It may not have been the largest one ever, but it was the largest aluminum ball any one of us had ever seen!

As youngsters we also went to the courthouse at about nine o'clock on Saturday mornings. This was the time when the courthouse custodian went to the top of the tower to wind up the big clocks. He allowed only four or five children to go with him. The first few who lined up had the privilege to go up.

The clock room, large enough to hold a number of people at the same time, contained four clocks—one facing each direction: North, South, East, and West. The room one level down from the clocks had special "windows." Actually, these were only open spaces that began about four feet off the floor, to keep people from falling out, and went up another five or six feet. There were no bars for protection; but as far as I know, only one person ever fell out from one of these "windows." Since I left home, apart from the clock winder, no one has been allowed to go up to the tower.

The walk up to the clock room was a challenge because the courthouse was by far the tallest building in town. Therefore, we had to be old enough to climb that many steps, but it was worth it! The clocks had no back and were so big that a six-foot man could stand up inside of them. The kind custodian let us climb up and stand in the clocks. For youngsters like me, the room one level down was a wonderful place from which to survey the whole city. We could look out and see a long way beyond the city limits. From that vantage point, we had a clear view of our houses, all the stores up and down Main Street, the many churches in town, as well as the parks, and the farms beyond.

The clocks always chimed on the hour: once at one o'clock, twice at two o'clock, three times at three o'clock . . . and a dozen times at noon and midnight. Regardless of where we were, we could tell what time it was. Interestingly, we didn't hear the chimes after we went to bed. To this day, the majestic clocks boom their punctual chimes throughout my hometown.

A quarter block northeast of the courthouse is the county jail, which my buddies and I found intriguing. We visited it sometimes—voluntarily, of course. The sheriff gave us private tours, and he pointed out the jail cells, empty and forlorn, ready for some tenants. The jail seldom had a prisoner in it; and whenever we visited, we never saw anyone locked up in a cell.

Orange City was an extraordinarily religious town. During my boyhood days, it had a population of about 2,000; but on Sunday mornings, it increased to 5,000. Farm families from the surrounding area assembled in the churches interspersed within the city limits. I knew of only one man who did not attend church. When I asked my mother, "Why doesn't he go to church?" She said that something had happened at his church years before, which had offended him; and he had never gone back to church.

Sioux County Courthouse

Orange City, Iowa

Because everyone was a church member, everyone kept watch over everybody else. That was not all bad. We did not have to lock our house doors at night. We could leave our bikes out on the lawn or in front of the store, and no one stole them. A man's word and a handshake was as good as a notarized document is today. And the jail hardly ever had an inmate.

Growing up Dutch has had an influence on my life. I often heard the slogan the Dutch say with tongue in cheek "If you ain't Dutch you ain't much." My wife, who is Spanish, counters with one of her own: "If you ain't Spanish vanish!"

At one time in history, Spain owned the Netherlands. The Dutch revolted in 1568 and finally secured their freedom in 1648. Their quest for freedom is sometimes called the Eighty Years' War. The conflict finally ended when the Dutch and the Spanish signed a peace agreement some 360 years ago. Martha and I took it one step farther. We bound Dutch and Spanish into one family unit!

Today, a big highway sign welcomes visitors to Orange City with these words, "Discover the Dutch!" The first time Martha saw that sign, she turned to me and exclaimed proudly, "I did much better than that. I conquered a Dutchman!"

4

The Budding Artist

Drawing pictures was one of my favorite pastimes as a child—a hobby that was to come in handy in my adult years. A "Superior Award" became mine for a sketching project when I was six years old. Then, as an eight-year old, I won a blue ribbon at a county fair for a drawing of two fawns with the inscription, "You are a little deer." The year before, when I was seven years old, an event took place I will never forget, and which I was to experience in reverse as an adult. The particular incident back in grade school was related to my artistic endeavors. It was not first place in a drawing contest, but the potential of being the first student at school!

At that time, I was in third grade. My assigned seat was on the outside aisle close to a wall that was decorated with a picture of a vase with colorful flowers. During class hours, I often glanced over and stared at that lovely picture. One afternoon when the bell rang marking the end of the school day, I decided to reproduce the flower vase.

My teacher was staying after school to do some grading; so I began my work of art. About half an hour later, she got ready to leave; but I was still putting the finishing touches on my picture, and I asked her if I might stay and finish it. She gave me permission since the custodian was still working anyway, and he would lock the doors when he was through cleaning.

My teacher promised, "I'll talk to the custodian and ask him to let you know when he's ready to lock up."

Second Grade Art Award

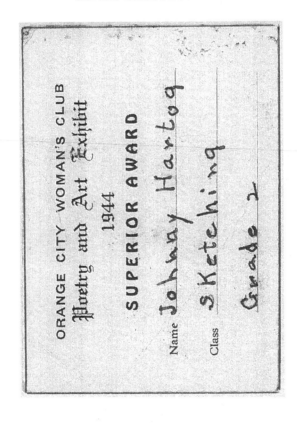

The vase and the variety of flowers were quite detailed, and it took me much longer than I had planned to finish my "work of art." I wanted it to be perfect! When it was completed, I put away my pencil and ran out of the room. I was eager to get home and show Mother the picture I had drawn for her.

No one was in the school; so I broke the rule and ran as fast as I could till I reached the outside door. It was locked! I called for the custodian, but there was no answer. I went around looking for him. But he was nowhere in sight! In those days, crash bars did not exist to open doors from the inside, and some doors would not have them even twenty years later! It took a key to open doors both from the inside and from the outside.

I thought, "I will leave by the fire escape door." And I ran to that door. But it was locked as well. I tried to open the windows, which were many, by pushing up firmly with my small arms and hands. But none of the windows dislodged at all. The building was old, and they were sealed shut with hundreds of coats of paint. I could not get out of school!

The only creative option I could think of was to draw more pictures until my teacher or the custodian returned and opened the front door for me. However, I felt no fear since I was in familiar surroundings. Also, it was still light outside, and the windows provided plenty of light inside for me to draw.

You may be wondering, "What about your mother?" I wondered the same thing and asked her about it—after the event, of course. At first, she did not think much about my not coming home at the regular time. The school was only a block and a half from our house, and we always walked to school. It was not as if I had missed the bus. Besides, the school playground had swings, teeter-totters, and merry-go rounds that lured children to play for a while before leaving school.

Sometimes after school, I stopped at grandma's place; it was only about three blocks away from our house. Other times

The Budding Artist

I went home with a classmate and played for a while before supper. More importantly, our town was safe in those days, and parents had no reason to worry about their children.

When six o'clock came around, mother began to get a little concerned because supper was always at six o'clock sharp. Everything was precise in our town. Sunday was church day, Monday was wash day, and so it went for the days of the week.

The days also were orderly: A day began with breakfast; then came morning lunch at 9:00 a.m. (if you were at home); dinner was at 12 noon; then 3:00 p.m. was time for the afternoon lunch (again this was for those at home or for farmers out in the fields); we ate supper at six o'clock p.m.; and we always had a bedtime snack. I often say, "When I grew up, we ate six meals a day!"

At home on that particular evening, mother was a little concerned but not worried since everybody knew everyone else in town. She thought that perhaps I was at a friend's house and had forgotten to look at the clock. However, locked inside the school, I kept looking at the clock and waited patiently for someone to show up. "It won't be long now," I thought, "and they will come for me so that I can go home for supper." But no one came.

By seven o'clock, mother began to worry. She called neighbors and relatives and asked them if they had seen me. All of their responses were discouraging.

Grandma said, "No! I have not seen him. He didn't stop by here."

"He did not come home with Georgie," Uncle Rich replied.

The owner of the Woudstra Meat Market informed mother, "He hasn't come by today." I often stopped there to watch the butchers slaughter animals.

Two Fawns and Blue Ribbon

When eight o'clock came around, mother was almost beside herself. She called the police and others to help her search for me. They checked the library. I was not there. They searched the city park. No little boy there. They called my teacher. She told mother that I had stayed a little longer than she had, and she did not know where I had gone after leaving the building.

This incident happened in early fall when the days were getting shorter. Moreover, the heat was always turned down lower at night. The school was heated by furnaces with floor grates, which were in the aisles and were warm but never too hot; people walked over them not concerned about getting burned.

As it got cooler and darker, I decided to lay my coat over the grate and go to sleep. There was nothing else I could do anyway. By now, I had concluded that my teacher and the custodian had forgotten me. But I was not worried. If I could not get out of the school, no one else could get in either!

Besides as an almost eight year-old optimist, I realized right away that I would be the first one at school the next morning. The prospect of being there even before my teacher was exhilarating! I curled up on my coat on the warm grate and fell asleep.

At nine o'clock, I woke up to the noise of a crowd chatting loudly outside. Like "Curious George," I decided to investigate the source of all that commotion. In the dark, I was able to find my way down to the first floor, and then to the front door where I saw the silhouette of a tall figure trying to unlock the door. When the door flew open, the silhouette became visibly clear. Standing in the doorway was a tall, husky policeman with a crowd of people behind him! Mother was there too!

As a last resort, someone had come up with the idea of checking the school, although most people were certain that no little boy would be in it. However, I was standing right before them—hungry and tired, and astonished at the sight of the policeman.

How did I end up locked up in the school? The custodian forgot that I was still in the room working on my drawing. I was so quiet that he had no reason to believe that anyone was still in the big, three-story school building. After finishing his cleaning tasks, he locked up all the doors behind him and went home.

My exciting plans to be the first one in school the next morning came to an abrupt end—much to the relief of Mother and the search team.

I don't know whatever happened to my hand-drawn "masterpiece." It disappeared in the midst of all the excitement. However, the picture of the vase with beautiful flowers becomes a reality every summer as I gaze with wonder at my colorful flowerbeds.

*Happiness is waking up to
Daffodils smiling in April.*

—Martha Hartog

5

Under Cloud Nine

The state of Iowa, a "bread basket" of America, is laid out pretty much in square miles; each square mile is called a section. In the days of family farms, a section usually contained four farms. A typical farm had one hundred and sixty acres, but some farms had half that many—only eighty acres. My mother grew up on one of those eighty-acre farms; it supported Grandpa and grandma and their nine children.

During the Great Depression, many farmers lost their farms; the banks foreclosed on the owners when they could not make payments on their loans. Since his banker was a close friend, Grandpa received a little leeway in making his payments. This enabled him to keep his farm.

Grandpa and the boys, my uncles, worked the farm. Their job was to plant and harvest the corn, hay, and oats. The men's chores also involved taking care of the cows and pigs. Grandma and the girls, my mother and her sisters, took care of the chickens and the garden.

The farm was virtually self-sufficient and provided the family's daily provisions. Cows supplied the family with fresh milk, which also could be made into tasty cheese or could be churned into butter by Grandma's strong, skilled hands. The open range-fed chickens laid "incredible, edible eggs" with bright yellow yokes. These eggs tasted good simply fried or scrambled, and they were, of course, an important ingredient in the scrumptious goodies that Grandma and the girls baked.

The ladies' painstaking labor in the garden and orchards yielded colorful vegetables and luscious fruit. Grandma was then able to serve delightful summer meals to the family. She also supervised the canning of the garden and orchard surplus. She made sure that each sealed glass jar was placed neatly along with the others on the pantry shelves. Throughout the cold Iowa winter, the family enjoyed the abundant produce of the ladies' summer efforts.

Grandpa's farm did not have electricity. In those days, almost no one living on farms in Iowa had electricity, unless the farm was right next to a town. Coleman lanterns and kerosene lamps supplied basic light for farmers. Kerosene lamps gave some light, but the Coleman lanterns gave much more light because they had little cloth bags that absorbed the kerosene. Before lighting a lantern, Grandpa pumped its pressure tank with a hand air-pump. When he lit the lantern, its kerosene-saturated-cloth bags gave out a bright light.

Grandpa and grandma were not Amish, but they farmed with horses. One of my childhood memories is the image of Grandpa's big, strong horses pulling heavy wagons loaded with hay or grain. Grandpa's hay crops fed the cows and horses. The hard-working horses also received oats as part of their daily diet.

Corn was the staple food for pigs and was also one of Grandpa's sources for cash. He sold corn to the elevator in return for cash, which he then applied to his farm loan at the bank. He also used some of the cash to buy sacks of ground-up feed for the animals. The feed sacks were made of heavy cloth with colorful prints. The ladies transformed these feed sacks into pretty dresses, blouses, and skirts, and even stylish shirts. Almost nothing went to waste on a family farm.

The ladies' sewing expertise also included making hand-sewn quilts and mending worn out, "holy socks." All these sewing activities—mending, quilting, and making clothes from empty feed sacks—provided great opportunities for the women to visit and listen to Grandma's common-sense solutions to daily problems, or what some people call "old-fashioned wisdom."

To plant corn, grandpa stretched long wires that spanned the field from one end to the other. The wires had knots in them every so often. When a knot went through the corn planter, the knot let a few kernels of corn fall into the ground.

In the fall when the corn was mature, the stalks and ears turned brown. Grandpa hitched the horses to a wagon, and the horses pulled the wagon up and down the field, next to the rows of corn. The ears did not fall automatically into the wagons. Someone had to pull them off the stalks.

Mother told us of the many grueling hours she and her siblings spent pulling the ears from the stalks and throwing them into the wagon, as the horses pulled it down the rows. Harvesting corn was strenuous and time consuming, but it kept many young people busy and out of trouble.

Eventually, Grandpa was able to buy a tractor. It had big wheels with "lugs" on them. The lugs were like iron triangles attached to the wheels. This prevented the tractor from getting stuck in the mud. The tractor came on the scene, but the family had to continue to trust God to provide needed strength and the right weather for sowing and reaping.

Although I grew up in town, I spent many summers on my uncles' farms; and I learned that life on the farm was never boring. Harvest time on small family farms brings back pleasant memories. It was a time when neighbors helped neighbors bring in the rewards of spring and summer's hard work; it was a time when all the farmers worked together. First they brought in the harvest at one farmer's place. Then, they moved on to another farm, and then to still another until all the farmers' grain crops were reaped.

My favorite was the oat harvest. The fields, which had been a luscious green through the summer, now shimmered with a golden hue. The farmers went through the fields with a binder that cut the oats and straw, tied them into bundles, and dropped them on the ground. The reapers then picked up the bundles, stacked them up together, and formed sheaves.

Next, the farmers loaded the sheaves into wagons, and brought these to a big threshing machine that had three identical giant spouts. To a child, that threshing machine looked like a huge, three-headed monster or a Dinosaur Rex with three long necks.

One spout blew the straw unto a straw stack that started out small, but grew higher and higher as the day wore on—often the straw pile became as tall as a farm building. A second spout sent the oats into a wagon, which the farmer hauled to the grain elevator for sale. However, he kept some oats in his granary to feed the horses and chickens. The third spout shot out the chaff to another wagon that resembled the grain wagon.

One day when I was about ten, I went to grandpa's place during harvest time. I saw an empty wagon and climbed into it. I waited for the grain to start coming in; so that I could catch handfuls of kernels shooting out from the threshing spout.

Instantly, I heard the loud roar of the big tractor engine start up; the long, wide belts from the tractor to the giant threshing machine started to turn; the black exhaust of the old tractor ascended heavenward; and the spout directed toward my wagon began to rattle. I became excited at the thought of the grain pouring into my wagon. I could picture myself walking in golden pebbles as it got fuller and fuller with the golden grain. In my mind, I envisioned a little boy prancing gleefully in pure gold!

Trouble at Threshing Time

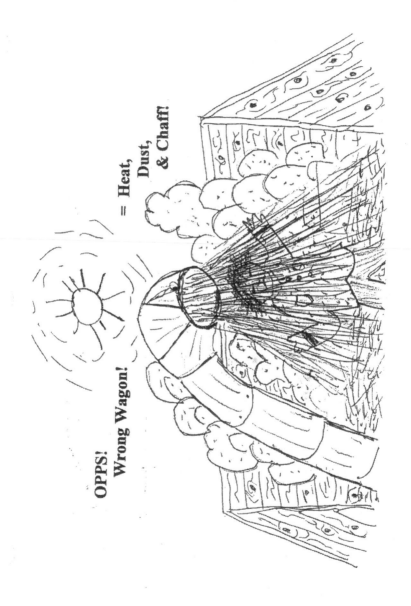

Suddenly, I was in the middle of a tremendously thick cloud of dust. I had climbed into the chaff wagon, not into the grain wagon! The moment the threshing machine started up, the chaff came pouring down on me! Instead of prancing in pure gold, I was choking in a dust storm that blotted out the sun!

When I staggered out of the wagon, I looked like a real-life version of Charlie Brown's pal, Pigpen!

To be happy, add not to your possessions
But subtract from your desires.

—Seneca

6

A Chick-Chick Here And Chick-Chick There

If a "farm gene" exists, undoubtedly, such a molecular unit is part of my DNA. My maternal grandparents were life-long farmers, and most of my uncles and aunts lived on farms. All agricultural activities fascinated me as a young boy, and nothing pleased me more than to hear my uncles ask me, "Do you want to help with the chores?" I was on my feet and ready to go! I rode with them on the tractor as they plowed the fields or mowed the hay. Since the old tractor did not have many cylinders, it made a deafening, popping sound as it went down the rows.

Spring was my favorite time to visit the farm. New life sprouted everywhere. Soon after birth, calves tried to stand up on wobbly legs but usually fell over on their first attempts. These calves, with their pure red and white colored hides, were a pretty sight to behold in the green pasture. A pen in the pig house was home to piglets. They flanked each other in perfect, pink formation, as they suckled ravenously from the sow. It was hard to resist the urge to hold them and stroke their soft skin; but they let out a loud, ear-piercing squeal whenever someone pulled them away from the sow.

The tops of straw and hay mounds became beds for cats nursing a batch of new little kittens, some of which seemed no bigger than little fat mice. At milking time, the cats appeared silently out of nowhere and stood by wide-eyed, hoping for a drink of fresh, warm milk. My cousins liked to squirt milk all over the face of a begging cat, which didn't mind the soaking at all! The cat simply put to work its rough, little tongue and licked off the streams of delicious milk as fast as it could.

The feline population was innumerable and came in all sizes, shapes, and colors; but they had a useful purpose in the farm: to keep under control the mice population, which outnumbered the felines by far! Their favorite pastime was to hunt mice and to serve the fuzzy, little pests for dinner to their kittens. Mama cats targeted mice but did not limit their hunting to these pesky creatures. Sometimes cats went after creatures bigger then themselves—wild rabbits!

The cats also helped to keep the farm rats in check, to some degree at least. These big rodents were a huge problem! They feasted on the corn that was stored in the corn crib; they chewed on the wooden walls; and they made tunnels under the wooden floors of the farm buildings. My uncles set big traps to catch the rats but never could get rid of all of them.

Spring time was also the time of the year when my uncles ordered new baby chicks from the mail-order hatcheries. The chicks were shipped in boxes with little round holes in the sides for air to get in. This prevented the chicks from suffocating. When the boxes arrived, they resounded with the loud peeping of hundreds of baby chicks that had hatched only the day before.

The brooder coop, especially furnished for day-old chicks, was their home for several weeks. The ground up cobs covering the floor came to life as the peeping chicks crowded around their food and water supply. They ate from little feeders full of Grape-Nuts-like feed, and they drank from small water fountains with shallow bases that prevented chicks from drowning.

The baby chicks also needed a warm place in order to survive; so the temperature in the coop, especially during the first week was set at about 95°. As the chicks grew, my uncles lowered the temperature week by week.

One spring day when I was twelve, I went to visit Uncle James' farm. As soon as I arrived, I asked him if I might visit the baby chicks; I knew they had arrived about three days before. He responded, "Sure! Let's go!" And he led me to the brooder coop. When we stepped in, the shrill, peeping sound of hundreds of baby chicks filled the hot coop. I looked down, and a horrible scene, too horrible for words, caught my eyes.

I shouted, "Look! Uncle James! Some of the chicks don't have legs!" Immediately, Uncle James bent down to take a closer look, and so did I. Bloody chicks were lying here and there with one leg or no legs at all. The rats had chewed holes in the floor, and had grabbed the chicks as they stepped over the holes. Uncle James told me to stay put; he rushed out to get some tin, a hammer, and nails to cover the holes.

As I stood still in that dreadfully hot brooder coop, my eyes glared at the poor, bloody, little chicks with no legs. Suddenly, I began to feel light-headed. Uncle James was not gone long, but the moment he opened the door and stepped inside, he spotted the problem: his young nephew was about to faint!

He hollered, "Go out and get some fresh air!" But it was too late! To his horror, I fainted instantly and fell flat, landing on the peeping chicks! When I woke up and opened my eyes, I was no longer in the coop. My uncle had hauled me into the house.

I'm not sure if on that day Uncle James lost more chicks to the rats or to me!

7

The Piggy-Back Ride

Although spring was my favorite time to visit the farm, summers were more special. Since school was out, my visits lasted longer and my cousins were there all day long. However, Uncle Art and Aunt Katherine, had only girls. When I visited their farm, I was pretty much on my own while the girls did their girl things.

As a twelve-year-old, I explored the farm looking for exciting adventures. Invariably, these explorations led me to the animals. They were not confined in the farm buildings all day long because it was summer.

For example, the full-grown sows were free to roam the pasture during the day; but at night, they went into the pig house. A long driveway lay between the pig house and the pasture. The sows' daily trek to and from the pasture did not involve a simple walk across the long driveway, but an agility course through a big culvert that ran under the driveway.

The pasture was on the side of a small hill; from the back of the pasture to the culvert it was down hill all the way. One summer, about the third day of my visit to Uncle Art's farm, I wandered into the pig pasture, walked to the top of the little hill, and noticed that most of the sows were up there.

Then something scared the pigs, and they all raced down the hill, dashed through the culvert, and scuttled into the pig house. The sight of the stampeding pigs reminded me of a herd

The Piggy-Back Ride

of wild mustangs galloping over the country side, rowdy and free.

The next day I went out and climbed the small hill, hoping to see the pigs again. Sure enough, most of them were at the top of the hill. An adventure was in the making! My imagination wheels started spinning, and I thought, "I wonder if I can ride a pig down the hill like cowboys ride horses."

I walked up to a pig that was busy eating grass, and it did not move as I approached it. I hopped on its back and was able to ride it a few feet before it threw me off and left me in the dust. I felt like a cowboy at a rodeo riding a bucking bronco. The fun had just begun!

I got up and straddled another pig and off we went! I rode it halfway down the hill before I fell off. Undaunted, I determined to ride a pig right through the culvert and into the pig house. It was tricky to hold onto a bare-back pig that was running full speed ahead in its agility race. After a few more failed attempts, I rode a big sow all the way down the hill, through the culvert, and into the pig house!

Unfortunately, even though I could not see him, my uncle's astute eyes saw the whole thing! That night he scolded me and told me not to ride the pigs again. His explanation made sense: Since the sows were so fat, they could have had a heart attack from running fast. Obviously, I was glad that our little adventure had not harmed any of the pigs.

Nevertheless, ignorance regarding the welfare of the pigs had made it possible for me to experience a thrilling adventure. It was just what a twelve-year-old boy needed during a week of wandering around alone on an all-girl farm!

8

When the Lights Went Out

That experience with the baby chicks, which lost their legs to the rats, had an adverse effect on my life. My body underwent syncope spells. That is, I suffered transient loss of consciousness and postural tone due to global cerebral hypoperfusion. Just in case you are wondering what all that means, simply put, I fainted!

This unpleasant outcome happened whenever I witnessed bloody incidents or heard someone telling gory, bloody stories in detail. Interestingly, I was able to butcher chickens and rabbits with no qualms what-soever. I also went deer hunting, degutted the kill on the field, and dressed it in my garage with great pride.

Evidently, my reaction was mainly associated with human blood—but not always! This physical and emotional nuisance continued to plague me for many years. Actually, it was the thought of suffering that went along with the sight of blood that triggered my fainting spells.

One day, I was working in the garden and a piece of glass slashed my finger; I ran into the house to wash it. As I sat on the edge of the tub next to the sink and rinsed my finger, I discovered that the nasty cut was deep. The water running off from it reminded me of the Nile River during the first of the Ten Plagues in Egypt. The next thing I knew, I was flat on my back looking up at two white walls; they were the sides of the bath tub. I had fainted and fallen into it! Thankfully, there was no water in it!

Another fainting incident happened when I was an eighth grader. An evangelist came into town for city-wide meetings—he was truly a courageous man! His amazingly dramatic presentations attracted many people, including me. The night I decided to attend the meetings, I followed the crowd into the city hall auditorium. Once inside, I scrutinized carefully the sitting areas. Then, I glanced upward and headed for the top row of the bleachers.

On this particular evening, the evangelist preached on the crucifixion of Christ. He dramatized the event by describing in detail the crown of thorns and the process of crucifixion in the Roman world. He explained the crucifixion so graphically, that I could picture the whole scene clearly in my mind. I sensed that I was about to suffer transient loss of consciousness and postural tone due to global cerebral hypoperfusion; so I got up to leave.

At the top of the aisle, it happened. I fainted! I was told that my body slid down the steps, step by step. In an instant, the people's attention turned from the amazing preacher to the remarkable spectacle of a boy apparently responding to the altar call, even before the preacher had given it!

Instead of walking down the isle, I had taken the bumpy road down to the altar! At least, that's what some people probably thought that night.

In God's presence is fullness of joy.

—Psalm 16:11a

9

Achan Was Taken

My high school *alma mater* was Northwestern Classical Academy. NCA was founded way back in 1882. The middle designation, "Classical," indicated that languages and liberal arts subjects were part and parcel of the core curriculum. Thus, Latin was one of the required classes, along with literature, history, algebra, chemistry, rhetoric, civics, and others.

"The Academy," as it was known by the students, was the older but much smaller sector of Northwestern Junior College in Orange City. The junior college had about one hundred and twenty-five students, but the Academy had forty to forty-five. Since we were such a small high school, we did not have a first-rate basketball team.

During one of the years I attended, our first-string players did not win even one game. However, toward the end of that year, our second-string team won a game. Our whole school was in such high spirits that we declared the next day, "Glory Day!" All classes were cancelled. We could celebrate our junior varsity team's great victory!

The record of our sports' teams left something to be desired, but our education was certainly top notch. Since the Academy was connected to the junior college, our high school teachers were college professors with advanced degrees.

Because we had so few students, everyone was required to be in the school choir. The freshmen began choir practice shortly after the fall semester started. I was a year younger than all the other freshmen because I was in kindergarten, first grade, and second grade within less than a year's time.

This is how it all happened: In September, I had entered kindergarten at the age of five. Then two and a half months later, on November 15, I turned six. On December 11, my father passed away—an event that devastated our family, but God upheld us. January began the second semester of my kindergarten year.

In March, mother gathered up her six children and moved to Orange City, where she had grown up.[1] Immediately, she enrolled the three oldest children in Orange City Christian School. Fran and Geri were able to continue in their current grades, but OCCS did not have kindergarten. I was promoted to the first grade!

Consequently, in February I was in Kindergarten, and in March I was a first grader. Two months later in May, the school year was over, and I was ready for a well-deserved summer vacation. When school started in the fall, I ended up in second grade. Thus, between February and September of 1943, I was in three grades: kindergarten, first grade, and second grade.

From that point on, I always was a year younger than my class mates. This age-difference posed some disadvantages. For instance, my classmates were able to get their drivers' licenses when they turned sixteen. That school year, I was the only one in my class who could not drive.

Now, that you've heard my driving sob story, let's get back to the singing subject. As I said, every student in the Academy was required to be in choir. The day of our first music class, the professor had the entire freshmen class, about sixteen of us, stand up and sing.

We had barely warmed up, when he stopped us and divided us into two sections. Then, he asked our half to sing. Again, he

---

[1] See "Growing up Dutch," story #3.

stopped us, this time before we had reached the end of the first stanza; and he split our group in two. Once more, my group of four got up to sing. We were no longer a choir, but a mixed quartet!

As the four of us stood straight and sang out with all our might, the teacher stepped closer towards us. With his hand cupped behind his right ear, he stopped in front of each of us and listened intently to our voices. We had not even sung one complete measure, when he signaled us to stop singing.

Then, he asked me to step forward and sing a solo—something I haven't done since that day! I sang a couple of measures loudly and clearly, and I didn't even have to look at the score. Due to all our "repeat performances," I knew the first measures of the song by heart. However, each time I sang it, the tune sounded just a tad different to me.

The music teacher did not appreciate my creative, off-key repertoire for the same song, whatsoever. After hearing me sing only a few notes of the same old song, he did what he had to do. He grimaced and dismissed me immediately.

For the rest of my four years at the Academy, I was the only one excused from choir! Like Achan, the biblical thief who was stoned to death,[2] I was singled out and separated from the rest of my peers. But at least *I* lived to write about it!

---

[2] Joshua 7:10-26.

10

Upside Down or Downside up?

To help my widowed mother with my personal expenses, I worked after school hours through my high school years. As a freshman, I landed a part-time job at the hatchery. My boss knew me from the visits I had paid to the baby chicks and Uncle Elmer when he worked there. My new job afforded me many "fowl" experiences. Usually the fowl were chickens, but occasionally ducks and turkeys showed up, and I had to learn how to take care of them, too.

I started out at the bottom of the "hatchery ladder" by making egg boxes. These came flattened out, and I had to assemble them into egg boxes one by one. They were large enough to hold about thirty dozen eggs each. My boss paid me by the box; the faster I put the boxes together, the more I earned per hour.

I also set eggs—not on them, but in the incubators! Each spring, the hatchery hatched about 100,000 baby chicks. The incubation period is three weeks. When the eggs hatched, the huge incubators came alive with the shrill peeping noise of chicks breaking out of their egg shells.

We could have been overwhelmed with thousands of chicks all at once, but my boss set one third of the eggs every week. At any given week, one third of the eggs had been in the incubators for three weeks, another third had been in for two weeks, and the other third, only for one week.

One day, a baby chick hatched equipped with four legs! My boss had been running the hatchery for about twenty years; in that time some two million chicks had hatched. He told me that this was only the second time a four-legged chick had emerged from an egg.

It was not a typical four-legged critter like a dog or a cow with two front legs and two hind legs. Rather, this chick had two normal legs underneath it like all other chicks; but it also had two legs that stuck straight up out of its back.

Since the first four-legged chick died shortly after it hatched, my boss was convinced that this one was destined to die before long as well. But, I didn't agree; so I asked him, "May I take the poor little thing home and give it a chance to live?"

He said, "Yes, but don't get too attached. It is bound to die soon."

Ignoring his warning, I grabbed the little chick and took it home. I was confident that this strange creature was meant to live. The chicken had to stay in a small cardboard box for a few days, until it moved into its cage. I built it much like a rabbit pen, and it kept my chicken safe and sound. My four-legged chick did survive! As it grew, all four of its legs grew as well. Over the summer quite a few people came by our yard to see my strange but content little fowl.

One of the questions people asked me most often was, "Can your chicken flip over and walk on the top two legs like it does on the bottom two?"

It was tempting to say things like, "He can walk upside down or down side up!"

Or, "He uses all four legs for walking through a low tunnel, the bottom two for the floor and the top two for the ceiling."

Or, "If he gets tired of walking on the bottom two legs, he just turns over and uses the top two."

But I would have to add, "Not really."

My fowl friend could not use its top two legs at all. They had no muscle and just stuck up on his back. Moreover, the extra legs were more of a problem than an advantage. Occasionally, they became tangled in the chicken wire that surrounded the cage.

The warm days of summer left as soon as they had come, and the green landscape changed from luscious green to brown and golden hues. Fall with its cool days had arrived! I could not keep my four-legged pet in its pen in my yard anymore. It needed a warm chicken coop or a barn to survive the winter. I asked an uncle if my chicken could stay at his farm, and he was happy to provide a home for it in his barn.

The first nine months worked out fine; but some time during the winter, a predator came into the barn and killed my extraordinary chicken. It met a tragic end but lived longer than expected. Most importantly, it taught me to care for a handicapped creature and to be compassionate to the helpless.

Happiness walks on busy feet.

—Kitte Turmell

11

The High School Dropout

Spring was in the air! It was the middle of my junior year at the Academy, and four of the guys in our class came down with "school fever!" They thought the cure was to stay away from demanding teachers and to breathe school-free air: No more verbs to parsley or nouns to incline; no dramatizing sentences, listening to "Madame Butterfingers," finding out the area of a trapeze, knowing the date of the Battle of the Bulges, or memorizing poems by a fellow named Long. None of these had anything to do with getting ahead in life!

The half-educated guys, determined to abandon the musty textbooks and to drop out of high school. On the march to their new-found freedom, they saw me, halted, and recruited me to join their forces. I was sixteen, working a part-time job in a chicken hatchery; School did not excite me; and the prospect of making more money was irresistible. Their resolve and well-thought-out argument convinced me that I could start climbing the "hatchery ladder" much faster.

Having made my decision, I made certain I was not left in the lurch! When I arrived at work that day, I approached my boss right away with the news that I was dropping out of school. I re-iterated the reasons my buddies had given me, and I put myself at his disposal for a full-time position.

The timing was perfect! Spring, the busiest time at the hatchery, was around the corner! We were already preparing to set thousands of eggs in the incubators. Soon, the hatchery would resound with the shrill peeping sound of one-day-old chicks. My resolve and well-thought-out argument convinced my boss to let me start climbing the "hatchery ladder." He hired me as a full-time worker, and he offered me sixty five cents an hour, which was not bad in those days.

With the financial matters settled, I went home and told Mother the good news: "I have a full-time job now, and I'm dropping out of school." Her countenance gave away her displeasure, but she did not try to force me to go back to school.

The Academy was a private, church-related school and was not free. Mother had paid the tuition for the first two years of my high school, just like she had done for my two older sisters, Fran and Geri. However, it was up to us to pay for the last two years.

Being wiser than Solomon of old, Mother came up with her own plan. She determined to have a parent to parent talk with my boss, who was a member of the Academy board. Mother and my board-member boss decided that if I did not go back to school in the fall, I would not have a job at the hatchery anymore—making my own way in life would be over at that point.

My boss sat down with me and laid out my options for the fall: (1) go back to school and have a part-time job or (2) not go to school and have no job at all. It was pretty obvious which option I decided to take. In the meantime, I determined to rake in the dough.

During that spring and summer, I worked forty hours a week in the daytime at the hatchery; and I also had night work: My boss owned a place for raising turkeys out at the edge of town. The turkey farm consisted of perhaps a dozen coops with attached outside runs for the birds to get fresh air as they grew.

My nighttime job was to check on the turkeys every two hours. If something scares turkeys, they pile up in a corner and end up smothering each other. My job went well for the first two months. Then one night, something scared the silly fowl. When I checked on them, they were piled up three feet deep in a corner. I ran straight for the pile and flung the frightened critters over my shoulders all over the coop. I had discovered the piled-up turkeys just in time—the ones in the bottom looked a little limp but were still breathing!

During the summer, I also became a first-responder for chicken emergencies. We eat chickens, but chickens eat one another. They are cannibals and evidence this trait the moment an opportunity arises. It takes only one chicken to start pecking and drawing blood, and the rest of the nasty foul follow suit. Soon, the coop becomes a bloody battlefield. The farmers then called us to the rescue. As soon as we arrived at the bloody field, we broke up the "Battle of the Beaks" by disarming the combatants: We cut the tips off their beaks. De-beaking is like trimming tough finger nails!

Toward the end of the summer, I was ready to go back to school. One of the professors allowed me to take an independent summer school class. Then in the fall, I was back in school and graduated with my class. Another of the "five dropouts" returned to school a year later, but the other three never finished high school.

Every so often, the halls of higher learning beckoned me back. Continuing my education resulted in six graduate degrees, including two doctorates.

My mother and my boss certainly outsmarted this high school dropout. Indeed, I am thankful. As for chickens, they are still part of my way of life. To this day, a small, colorful flock cackles in our back yard.

12

Grandpa on the Hot Seat

Like many of the European immigrants of the 1900's, my maternal Great-grandfather moved the family from the Netherlands to America with the hope of beginning a new life. The family settled on an Iowa farm, and all of them, including Grandpa, had to work doing manual labor. Labor-intensive farm work was a new venture for the family, and they had to adjust to it.

Shortly before moving, my relatives had lived in luxury. My great-grandfather owned much property in the Old Country, and the rental fees supplied above the family's needs. Their financial demise came about when my grandpa's older brother came to America, expecting to strike it rich himself. He had heard that America was the land of opportunity, and he crossed the Atlantic with visions of an affluent life.

The grandiose plans of Grandpa's brother went up in smoke, and he sent word back to Holland that he needed more money to make his dreams come true. Great Grandfather complied. The plea for money went out from America numerous times until the family back in the Netherlands lost everything. With the loss of his wealth, Great-grandfather also lost his standing in the community. He went from a prestigious position in the upper class to that of a laborer in the lower class. This also resulted in the loss of former friends.

The family moved away. Grandpa was a teenager when the family came to America. In time, Grandma and Grandpa met and got married; then, children came along. Grandpa farmed to support the family, but this was not by choice. It was not easy for him to make the adjustment from living in rich surroundings to working the rich-black, Iowa soil.

Grandma was a wonderfully efficient homemaker and gardener. She loved the farm with all its plants and animals. She especially enjoyed feeding her chickens! Her big garden, flowerbeds, and houseplants thrived and flourished under her green thumb; and they were a welcome sight to every visitor. Her gorgeous Christmas cacti never failed to bloom. She bequeathed me her green thumb and her love of plants.

When Grandpa and Grandma were old, they moved into town and lived a couple of blocks from us. After a few years, Grandpa suffered a stroke. He survived the stroke, but he never was the same again. For one thing, Grandpa forgot his English and spoke only Dutch. Naturally, it became difficult for us grandchildren to communicate with him since we knew little Dutch.

Also, after the stroke, grandpa became house bound, and somebody had to stay with him at all times. As a college freshman, I had the privilege of "grandpa sitting" on Sunday afternoons when Grandma went to church. Our church had three services: morning, afternoon, and evening. I went to the morning and evening services with Mother, and Grandma went to the afternoon service while I stayed with Grandpa.

One of my college classes that year was German. Since Dutch is a Germanic language, my German knowledge came in handy on Sunday afternoons. Though a bit on the rough edges, conversation was possible between Grandpa and me.

He spoke in Dutch and I answered him in German. Sometimes this worked like a charm; but at other times, my German was inadequate, and communication failed between us. When this happened, Grandpa, who had a bad temper, chewed me out in Dutch. I learned a few of those Dutch

Grandpa on the Hot Seat

words and asked my mother what they meant. With a shocked expression, she replied, "Those are not nice words. Don't ever use them!"

One of Grandpa's traits was the perpetual smoking pipe in his mouth, especially when he was sitting on the couch. One Sunday afternoon, he dropped his pipe, and the red-hot ashes burnt a hole in the couch. I tried to lift him up and move him to an easy chair, but he declined to do so—stubbornly!

At once, the Dutch colorful language began to flow like lava out of his mouth, and he raked me over the coals (figuratively speaking, not the hot ashes burning a hole in the couch!) I went to the kitchen, got a glass of water, and poured it on the spot where the pipe ashes were burning. I felt better about the whole situation, thinking the fire was quenched. But shortly, the smoldering fire came up in a different place. I scurried to the kitchen for more water and poured it on that spot. As I stood sizing up the incident, I noticed that the sneaky fire was playing "hide and peek" with me.

The fire had made its way into the deep parts of the couch and was making tunnels throughout it. Just when I thought I had it quenched, it suddenly came up again and showed its little red and gray face in another place.

Soon, Grandpa looked like he was sitting in a sauna-like couch, with dozens of little smoking pillars around him. That did not faze him at all! He sat nonchalantly with the pipe in his mouth. Each time the fire came up, I poured water on it. I never knew where a pillar of smoke was turning up next, and I wondered, "What would happen if the fire came up directly under Grandpa?" One thing for sure, That might get him off the couch!

My efforts to protect Grandpa from going up in smoke continued until the afternoon service was over. Grandma came home from church to "burnt couch." My aunts and uncles were with her, and they tried to coax Grandpa to stand up. True to his stubborn Dutch heritage, he refused to budge!

It took two of my husky uncles to lift him and set him down on an easy chair. Grandma's couch looked like someone had used it for target practice, using fire darts; it was peppered with little round, black holes. Before the whole living room went up in flames, my uncles grabbed the smoldering couch and hauled it outside. Then, they poured buckets of water on it and finally put out the fire.

Grandma forgot about Grandpa and focused on her loss. She did not appreciate it one bit that the men had drenched her couch. She scolded them, "You should have left it burn up! Then the insurance company would have given us money to buy a brand new one!"

All the while Grandpa sat on the easy chair, clearly unaffected by the fact that his favorite couch had gone up in smoke. In contrast to the commotion around him, Grandpa sat relaxed with a contended smile, smoking his pipe in his typical old way.

A happy face shows a glad heart.

—Author unknown

13

Better Than on the Floor!

Then, there was good old Prof. Vander Kamp—not his real name; but to protect his reputation I will use a Dutch sounding name. His former students will no doubt recognize our "ancient Prof." from his depiction in this chapter. Our Prof. had a two-fold responsibility at the Academy. He managed the bookstore, and he also taught a high school class in business or business law. I do not remember the exact title of the course. But I will never forget his annoying habit in the classroom and his connection with the bookstore.

When I was a student, Prof. Vander Kamp hired me as a bookstore clerk. The bookstore sold not only textbooks, but also candy bars, knick knacks, school supplies, sweaters with the school logo on them, and other school memorabilia. The students benefitted from this merchandize in one way or another. Sometimes Prof. Vander Kamp ordered school souvenirs that did not sell well. This was the case with an embossed button, which remained on the shelf for a number of years.

One day Prof. said to me, "If you sell all these buttons, I'll give you a candy bar." I am a chocoholic, and turning down such a challenge is something beyond my comprehension! Immediately, I devised a plan to render the shelf completely empty of its ugly buttons.

Right there on the spot, I replied with this request, "Besides my reward, I will need three free buttons and three free candy bars to get the sales going."

Prof. gladly granted my request. I was keenly aware of peer pressure and its powerful effect among high school students. I figured that if I gave free buttons to three of the most popular students in the school—along with a free candy bar for each of them if they wore the buttons for a week—the buttons might well sell like hot cakes! When I approached the students with my offer, all three agreed to it.

The next Monday, the three students showed up wearing the embossed buttons. Before long, a few other students came into the bookstore to buy a button like the ones worn by the "trend setters." The fad caught on like wild fire, and soon almost every high school student was wearing one. We sold every single button in the store in just a few days. Now the shelf was empty and ready to be re-stocked with other silly souvenirs.

I was also in Prof. Vander Kamp's business class. While he lectured, he always sat behind a small table. One day half-way through the class, two of the table legs fell off, and it collapsed. Several of the guys hollered, "We will fix it for you, Prof.!" They quickly got out of their seats, put the legs back on the table, and tightened the wing-nuts on the bolts.

Impressed with the students' helpful spirit, Prof. Vander Kamp responded in kind. "Stop by the bookstore," he told them, "and you'll get a free candy bar for your efforts."

Following that incident, I noticed that several of the guys regularly came to class five minutes before the good Prof. arrived. When they did, Prof's table mysteriously collapsed, and the "early birds" eagerly fixed it for him. After class, they marched grinning shamelessly to the bookstore for their treat.

The table never collapsed for any other professor who taught in that room. The students knew it was "a mere

Better Than on the Floor!

coincidence" that it always happened in business class with Prof. Vander Kamp. Nevertheless, he was thankful to have such helpful students.

It's a good thing that Prof. Vander Kamp was easy going, because he had a terribly, sickening, disgusting, unforgettable habit. While he lectured, he made a loud, rumbling, coughing, sound deep down in his throat. As we watched him in horror, knowing exactly what he was going to do next, he slowly pulled out his handkerchief from his pocket; and then he spit into it.

As if directed to do so, we all shouted in unison, "Ugh!" or "Yucky!" or "Icky!" or a similar descriptive exclamation.

To our outrage, Prof. always replied soberly and in a deep voice, "Better than on the floor!"

Not a class went by without our teacher coughing nosily and using his hankie as a receptacle for the gross contents from his throat. On some days, Prof. hacked and spit more than once during the class hour.

In time, "Better than on the floor!" became a byword among Prof. Vander Kamp's students.

Happiness is often overlooked
Just because it doesn't cost anything.

—Author unknown

14

I'll Never Teach Again!

All the way up through high school, I was an outgoing kid. While attending the Academy, I preached at one Northwestern College chapel, and I also spoke at the rescue mission in Sioux City. However, when I talked to young ladies, my personality changed: I became extremely shy, and I was at a loss for words. It was easier to preach to the inebriated homeless than to speak to young women.

Ever since I was a junior at the Academy, I have had to work and pay for my schooling, including all of my graduate education. While I was a student in Illinois, work and my problem with women collided.

As a Wheaton College student, I landed a job doing custodial work for a religious publishing company. I cleaned the offices at night after everyone else had left for the day. One Saturday, as I cleaned the office of an older lady employee, I found a note on her desk addressed to me. It stated that she was going to be out of town for two weeks, and she wanted me to teach her Sunday school class of college girls.

If she had asked me in person, I would have said, "Not me!" But she had already left town, and I had no way of reaching her. To make matters worse, she had not left any helpful Sunday school curriculum for me to follow. I knew that she taught from the Bible, but that was no comfort or help at that moment. Moreover, I was inexperienced in teaching, especially teaching college girls—of all things!

I went home and worked diligently to prepare a lesson. Sunday morning arrived sooner than expected, and I taught those girls. Yes, the lesson was boring, and it matched my dry mouth. Toward the end of the class, one of the girls contradicted me on something, and all of the girls burst out in a great fit of laughter. It was five minutes before the end of the class hour, but this was a good time to quit. Thus, I dismissed the class immediately. The whole thing had been a disaster!

That experience was bad enough, but I was scheduled to teach for two Sundays. The week that followed was one of the worst weeks in my whole life. How could I face those girls again? I had never been so humiliated. I did my best to prepare another lesson, but the thought of having to look into the faces of those girls scared me half to death!

My regular church ministry was to drive the church bus and pick up children whose parents did not go to church. When Sunday arrived, I started my bus route and picked up the children in plenty of time for them to get to Sunday school. But my mind, soul, and spirit were in turmoil at the thought of facing the girls.

I drove slowly, hoping not get to Sunday school any earlier than I had to. But as I drove, the image of me standing before those girls overwhelmed me; and I started driving in circles all over town. It seemed as if someone else was driving the bus. Finally the bus pulled up to the church just as Sunday school was over. Sunday school attendance hit a record low that day. All the bus children missed Sunday school, and the college girls' teacher missed his class as well!

That experience convinced me that I was not cut out to be a teacher. Right then and there, I determined never to teach again—especially young ladies!

Two weeks after I graduated from Wheaton, I caught a Grey Hound bus and headed east for an intensive study in French at Middlebury College in Vermont. I looked forward to this college stint because every aspect of college life was to be in French. I was to experience total immersion in a foreign tongue 24/7: lectures, note taking, exams, and all conversation. Any student who spoke English was dismissed from school.

The bus arrived at Albany, New York; from there I had to transfer to a bus for Vermont. As I waited in the depot, I held on my lap the box with my summer stuff. I was a college graduate who didn't own a suitcase! Tired from the long trip, I dozed off for a few minutes. When I woke up, my arms were in the same position as before I went to sleep, but the box between them was gone. In that little time while I slept, I was robbed!

In the box I had my Middlebury enrollment papers, college diploma, camera, and a few clothes. All I had now were the clothes on my back, bus tickets and check book, which I had put in my coat pocket. I went on to Middlebury; but when I arrived, it took a while for me to get admitted and settled in my dorm. To this day I have no diploma to show that I graduated from Wheaton College. *C'est la vie!*

But getting back to teaching those girls! After that bad experience, I did not teach any class whatsoever for the next six years. Then I became a pastor of a small church, and necessity prevailed. The one and only option was for me to "volunteer" to teach the young people's class. God used that experience to show me that I could teach after all. A year later, I began teaching Bible college students, including ladies; and I have been teaching them for over forty five years. I'm no longer afraid of their faces!

15

The Attack Cat

Upon finishing my summer term at Middlebury, I went home for a few days to relax. I loaded up my trunk with all of my earthly possessions. No more boxes for me! Then, as a diploma-less-French-speaking college graduate, I enrolled at Dallas Theological Seminary to work on a master in theology degree.

During my four seminary years, I made several trips from Dallas to Iowa. I took different routes, one of which took me through Tulsa, Oklahoma, where my sister Frances, her husband Bill, and their six children lived. On one occasion, I stopped in Tulsa to take some of my nephews and nieces along so they could visit their grandma in Iowa. A four-legged passenger joined us. Fran had asked me to take a kitten along and deliver it to a relative back home. I complied gladly.

On the way to Iowa, the children asked me to tell them some stories. These were made-up stories, not historical events. My tales began with a simple thought, which my imagination then turned into fantastic tangled-up yarns as we wound our way down the road. None of the yarns weaved their way into the printed page, and none were ever published; they never came back to haunt me.

The event I am describing right now, however, is not made up, nor are any of the other accounts in this crazy book. On this trip home, I had company with me: some nephews and nieces from grade-school age, up to preteen years.

And a cute half-grown kitten.
It sat calmly in the back by the rear window.
Until I started driving down the road.
At that moment, the kitten got scared.
It meowed, hissed, and yowled.
And it zoomed wildly from one place to another.
Around the back seat.
Down to the floor.
Under the seat.
Up to the top of the back seat.
And from there it took a giant leap—
Right onto my neck and shoulders.
It dug its claws into my back.
And hung on for dear life.
I yanked it off my back and tried to calm it down.
The children grabbed it's scruff.
And plopped it back by the rear window.
Here it lay calmly until—

A semi-truck with a worn-out muffler passed us on the road, and the kitten began its meowing, hissing, and yowling recital and acrobatic antics. It took a flying leap and landed on my back, dug in deeply, and hung on for dear life.

Every time something scared it, the cat performed its circus-like-acrobatic-solo routine and wrapped it up by landing firmly on my back. The crazy feline must have thought that I was its trapeze partner. Or maybe it thought that the children's cheers and shrieks were a call for an encore.

By the time we arrived in Iowa, my back felt like a sieve full of sharp, kitty-claw holes. Like the three little kittens of old, that naughty kitten had lost its mittens!

16

A Case of Mistaken Identity

A bleak room in a dorm for single students was my home for four years while I was a seminary student in Dallas. Though not homey, this dorm was practical since it was right on campus. Most married students lived in apartments or rented houses scattered about the city. Some of them lived in large old houses that were located on the seminary block. The school owned these houses and had remodeled them and converted them into multiple apartments. The school usually charged less rent than other apartment owners. Also, campus apartments were convenient and minimized the need for transportation.

Mr. Nuñez and his family lived in the downstairs apartment in one of those big old houses. He was an older, seminary upper-classman. Before coming to Dallas, he had taught for fifteen years at a Bible school in Guatemala. He had come to the states eight months ahead of his family and had lived in the dorm for single men. When his wife and four children joined him, the family moved into the largest apartment, known to the seminary family as the "White House on Apple Street."

I became acquainted with the Nuñez family the summer after my freshman year when I had surgery on my nose. After the procedure, I had to wear bandages across my nose and cheeks for several weeks. The only visible features on my face were my mouth and my eyes, which were awfully bloodshot—I was certainly not a pleasant sight to behold!

One Sunday night shortly after surgery, I walked to church. On my way back to the dorm, I came upon a couple of young pretty ladies who were obviously sisters. My blood-shot eyes stared into the big brown eyes of one of them. Gazing at my beat-up face, she asked me with a distinctive Spanish accent, "What in the world happened to you?"

Surprised at her frank demeanor, I replied, "I had surgery on my nose a few days ago."

She blurted out, "Oh, if I had known that, I would have visited you."

There I was, a shy Dutchman, visiting with two gregarious señoritas. From our brief exchange on the sidewalk, I learned that the name of the chatty one was Martha, that her sister was Sara, and that the Nuñez family lived in the "Big White House on Apple Street."

I thought about Martha all week and decided to risk it—I determined to ask her out. The following Sunday, I planned my church walk to coincide with the time when I had run into the sisters. It worked better than I had expected. Martha was alone! I invited her to go to church with me in two weeks.

She seemed happy to go. However, she had to check with her parents to make sure it was okay. She promised to let me know. Her father knew me from some classes I had with him; so he approved, with these stipulations: It was to be a walking date to church with a meal at a restaurant within walking distance, and I had to have his daughter home by 9:00 p.m.

Two weeks went by, and the Sunday of our church date arrived! After church, Martha and I walked to a nearby restaurant, where we enjoyed a simple meal and a delightful visit. Her outgoing personality and sense of humor motivated me to come out of my shell.

Besides that, although my eyes were still a little bloodshot, my face bandages were a thing of the past. I felt as free as a bird, and my hopes for the future soared high. In the meantime, nine o'clock was approaching, and I must get my "Cinderella" back home. Our time had certainly flown by too fast! When I returned to the dorm, I said to myself, "She is the one I am going to marry someday!" It was love at first sight for me.

Two weeks later, I met her at the same spot on the way home from the Wednesday night service. I asked her if she was free to go with me to church again on Sunday. She smiled and said, "Yes."

After we parted, I knew something was not quite right. I realized that this time Martha looked a little different. The more I thought about it, the more I was convinced. To no one in particular, I hollered, "That was not Martha! It must have been Sara!" My half-way-bloodshot eyes had deceived me! I felt like Jacob, the Israelite patriarch of the Old Testament.

I asked myself, "Now, what do I do?" Her sister was nice, but I was interested in Martha. A horrible thought crossed my mind, "Martha will never have anything to do with me again."

However, Sara had told Martha about what the shy Dutchman had done. They laughed good-heartedly about it. Then, they come to this conclusion: The whole thing had been a case of mistaken identity. A few days later, I saw Sara on campus and confessed to her that I had mistaken her identity; and she graciously cancelled the date. Two weeks went by before I built up enough courage to ask Martha out again. She accepted!

Ever since then, she has been my one and only love. The resident of the "Big White House on Apple Street" became the apple of my eye!

17

Wake Up! Sleepy, Sleepy Head!

The first wheels I ever bought, were attached to an old 1942 Chevy, the last of the cars made before World War II. I bought the Chevy with money I had saved from working at the hatchery. However, the purchase left me with little money for gas. This shortage of cash meant that I hardly ever drove my car. From sitting so long on the street, it soon became victim to the Second Law of Thermodynamics (SLTD).

When I went to Chicago to finish college, I boarded a train in Sioux City and traveled via rail to the Windy City. After college graduation and my short stint in Vermont, Greyhound Bus Lines did the honors of transporting me to Dallas where I attended seminary.

To fund my tuition, I landed a job in the U.S. Post Office. As a substitute, I worked anywhere from two to twelve hours, depending on how much mail came in. Initially, I caught cheap rides with other students; but if their shifts ended before mine, I had to walk back to the dorm. This could be at 10:00 p.m., 3 a.m., or 5 a.m.—unsafe times to walk through downtown Big D. Later, I bought an old 1953 Plymouth and drove myself.

Then, I caught a love bug. The old Plymouth had to go! Martha, the petite, brown-eyed lady had come into my life, and I laid eyes on a brand new, black VW bug—perfect for her size. So, I bought it. My VW had a 36-horse-power engine in the "trunk." The real trunk was in the front of the car. It was

Wake Up! Sleepy, Sleepy Head!

an efficient vehicle to drive, but it did not have much "get up and go."

My little black bug enabled me to make a number of trips back and forth from Dallas to Iowa. The trip took much longer back then; Interstate highways were a thing of the future in our area, and highways went through each town. Storekeepers profited from this, and so did the police coffers. Also, the stop signs along the way increased travel time, making it a two-day trip. An elderly Kansas couple, who took me under their wing, let me stay in their home overnight.

On one occasion, I got up earlier than the birds and left Orange City before sunrise. My plan was to make the trip in one long day. The journey went fine until about the middle of the afternoon when I began to get sleepy. It was siesta time! I pulled over by a small town park and slept in the car. To do this, was neither unusual nor dangerous in those days. Refreshed and rested, I went on my way.

I drove for an hour and did not realize how sleepy I was getting again. Since it was summer, I opened my window way down. Iowa-farm aroma always wakes up sleepy drivers. But Kansas air didn't! A rumbling noise woke me up! It was the sound of the car engine echoing off the concrete guard-railing of a long bridge.

Startled, I realized that I had drifted over into the left lane. I looked up and saw a metal giant at the end of the bridge. I was wide awake now! I steered a hard right just in time. Within a split second, that 18-wheeler rig barreled past me in the other lane. Because I had the window down, I heard the rumbling sound in time to move over to my lane. In His providence, God had delivered me from imminent death.

If that semi driver and I had met head on, my little black bug would have become burnt, metal pizza with Dutch bratwurst topping!

18

The Oklahoma Peanut Farm

As seminary students preparing for the ministry, we were eager to start putting into practice the training we had received so far. Several of us decided to pair up and drive to southeastern Oklahoma. Here we held church services for small groups in rural areas. We left Dallas on Sunday morning before sunrise and returned late in the evening.

The seminary sent us off with bag lunches: peanut butter and jelly sandwiches, an apple, plus a couple of cookies. We had to notify dining services on Saturday in time for them to have the lunches ready by Saturday evening. We picked them up Sunday morning before going out on our two-by-two-outreach ministries.

Invariably after the church service, one of the farm families invited us to their home for a delicious home-cooked meal. The invitation also included a place to rest for the afternoon. Their kind hospitality was truly refreshing. The family re-charged us for the evening service as well—they laid out tasty leftovers.

However, we did not always pair up with the same students. One Sunday I went with a student who had never ministered with me or in that area. I will call him Andrew. Our trip from Dallas was uneventful, and the Sunday school and morning service were well attended for that rural setting. After church, everyone scurried out of the building, and we were left standing alone by the front door. I was surprised that no one had invited us for lunch. That was truly unusual!

I spoke to Andrew about it, and he informed me that one of the farm families had indeed invited us to dinner, but he had turned them down.

I felt like asking him, "Why in the world did you decline?" But I didn't.

I thought about the wife who had cooked extra food for guests but was turned down. Images flashed through my mind of a table spread with delicious home cooked victuals. We had missed all that good food!

I pulled the P&B sandwich out of my bag and got ready to eat. I was about to pray and thank God for it, though it was difficult, when I noticed that Andrew did not have his lunch bag with him. I advised him to get it and join me, but he didn't move. The situation was worse than I had imagined. Andrew told me that he had failed to notify dining services. I shut my mouth and opened my heart, and I shared my meager lunch with him. Unlike the little boy's lunch with five loaves and two fishes, my lunch didn't multiply. Andrew ate half of it and left us both hungry.

Instead of a restful afternoon on a soft bed with a colorful quilt, we were stuck in the old country school house where the services were held. Moreover, there was no water to drink. As the afternoon wore on, our stomachs began to growl with hunger. Finally, we got so hungry that we decided to scrounge for food.

The field next to the school had been planted with peanuts that year, and the harvest had come and gone. But we looked carefully and found some occasional peanuts that got missed. The field was all sand, and we did not have a shovel or spade. Crawling on our knees and using our bare hands as tools, we dug in the sand and found a dry peanut here and there.

Not only were the peanuts raw, so were our fingers from all that digging. With the wind blowing down our necks, we spent over an hour in that Oklahoma field, doing what moles do naturally. And we found only a handful of raw peanuts. We were *plen'y* of hungry, but the peanuts were scanty! Indeed, Oklahoma was not doing fine on that windy autumn day!

Tired and half-starved, we led the evening service. Then, we started out on the long drive back to Dallas, which always seemed longer than the morning one. However, that particular night, the journey seemed even longer. I was famished and exhausted.

To this day, I cannot understand why Andrew did not accept the gracious hospitality of the farmer's wife. He must have had a good reason; I certainly don't hold a grudge against him. I have transferred my resentment to raw peanuts. They, along with peanut butter and jelly sandwiches have not made it on the list of "My Favorite Foods" ever since that day.

The moral of the story is this: When two seminary students drive a long way to preach at your church, make sure you invite both of them for lunch. One of them is bound to be hungry and will respond gladly and thankfully right on the spot to your, *"Répondez, s'il vous plaît."*

*They that sow in tears
Shall reap in Joy.*

—Psalm 126:5

19

Rats!

In the days when I was studying for my Th.M., seminary classes were open only to male students. During the school year, I lived in Stearns Hall, the dormitory for single men. In the summers when the dormitory closed down, single students who stayed in Dallas because of jobs had to find their own housing.

On the other hand, married students who lived in apartments leased them year around. Some couples liked to return to their home towns during the break or were involved in summer ministries away from Dallas. They sublet their apartments to single students who remained in Dallas.

One of the apartment buildings generally leased solely by married students was only about three blocks from the campus. It was convenient, and the rent was cheaper than other available housing. Each summer, at least one or two seminary couples were eager to sublet their apartment to needy single students. It happened that one time, two other students and I subleased one of those economical apartments for the summer.

The cut-rate rent turned out to be even cheaper for us because we split it three ways. As soon as our school year ended, we moved into our two-bedroom-summer housing. We worked hard that day, moving and getting settled. Each of my two buddies claimed a bedroom, and I was left with the fold-up bed in the living room. This was to be good training for the future.

Late that first night I heard rattling in the kitchen. I got up and discovered that the noise came from under the refrigerator. I thought maybe there was something wrong with the motor. My two buddies did not hear a thing. They had closed their bedroom doors and were already sawing wood!

Through the next few weeks, besides the rattling sound, I also heard chirping and squeaking noises. The kitchen was usually quiet in the day time; but soon after all three of us settled for the night, the fridge under-parts began their annoying concert.

We asked the tenants in the other apartments if they heard noises in their kitchens as well. They told us that they had the same problem. Then, to our horror, they revealed to us the cause of the noise: it was rats! Now we understood why the rent was so cheap!

We also learned about the root of the problem. The old apartment building had been built of hollow block tiles, but on the outside they looked like large bricks. Some of them were partly broken and rats had moved in! The landlord had tried several strategies to get rid of them; but when facing extermination, the rats darted back into their "block-tile fox holes."

It was absolutely unnerving to hear the noise under the refrigerator now that I knew its cause. But since none of us could afford a better place, we stuck it out and wished for summer's end. It was comforting to know that none of us had ever seen a rat in our pad.

Through the apartment grapevine, we heard this awful news: A rat chewed a hole through the ceiling of a couple's bedroom while they were sleeping. Then, the rat fell through the hole and landed right on the wife's face! When the disgusting news broke, we had only thirty days until the beginning of the fall semester.

It was too late to find an apartment for just one month's lease. We were trapped in a rat hole! The other two fellows had a great advantage: They could close their bedroom doors at night. My fold-up bed was in the living room, which connected to the kitchen via an open arch. Every night, I opened my fold-up bed carefully. Honestly, I was afraid that a big rat might have beaten me to bed. Lying there, trying to go to sleep, I had visions of rats scurrying into the living room and crawling over my bed. Weary from a hard day's work, I eventually fell asleep.

I worked in the post office on the evening shift; much of the night was over by the time I came home. Our rats were mostly nocturnal creatures and rested during the day when I slept. It may be that I was tired and slept so soundly, that I never heard them or felt them once I fell asleep. The thought of it still makes my skin crawl!

Then one day while my two buddies were at work, I went out shopping around noon. When I returned home and opened the door, I saw a big fat rodent right in the middle of the living room floor. I froze, and so did the rat. Standing just barely inside the room, I glanced down and noticed a pair of shoes lying near my feet. I reached down slowly, picked up a shoe, and threw it at the rat as hard as I could. Surprisingly I hit it bull's eye and killed it on the spot! I could not have done that again even if I tried.

Two weeks later, school started. I was never so happy to go back to Stearns Hall in all my life! My bleak dorm room with its concrete floor and walls, painted a dull gray-green, felt absolutely cozy.

I was home! And no rat could ever break into that concrete, prison-like cell!

20

Three + One + One Is a Crowd

It happened on one of those trips from Dallas to my home in Iowa, as I trudged along the state highways in my black VW. My little black beetle had served me well up to this point. Its ability to go 40 miles per gallon was easy on the pocket book.

One problem was that the state highways always went through every town, no matter how large or small it was. Sometimes the trek through town was a blessing, because semi-trucks had to slow down. Then, once they were back on the open highway, it was easier to pass them. It took the loaded semi-trucks longer than it did cars to build up speed again.

I had come upon three 18-wheeler rigs just as I was a mile from the next city. I followed the truckers' convoy as it rumbled through town. Then, the instant the fleet came to the city's edge, I had an opportunity to pass it and get on my way.

At this point, the truck drivers had left plenty of space between them, and I did not have to pass all three of them at once. I passed the truck making up the rear and got back in line between the middle truck and the rear truck. When the road was free of oncoming traffic again and no hills were in sight, I passed the middle truck. It took my VW a little longer to do this because the trucks were picking up speed.

As soon as the coast was clear again, I pulled out to pass the leader. Meanwhile, the trucks were going faster and faster. I started to pass the convoy leader and got halfway around it when that driver shifted into high gear. It was the open road and we were not yet quite up to the speed limit. I floored my VW, only to find that the foot feed was almost down already. It was impossible to go faster. This was all my VW's little, 36-horsepower engine could do.

The only option I had was to fall back behind the leading truck and get back in second place. When I tried to do that, I discovered that the middle-truck driver had closed the gap between him and the leader. This was illegal in Iowa back then. Suddenly, a fast moving oncoming car appeared in the distance.

Quickly, I glanced back to see if I could fall behind the middle semi, but the gap there was closed as well. It would take too much time to try to drop back behind both the middle rig and the one carrying the rear. The approaching car and my VW were headed for a crash.

I looked at the left lane ditch and thought about veering into it. Then, I recalled an article about a recent accident where the passing driver and the oncoming driver both took the ditch. And both met their death after colliding head on right in that ditch.

"Play it calm." I thought. "Let the oncoming car driver know what you're doing."

I snuggled up against the big semi like a little chick against its mother hen. The oncoming car driver got the point and went as far to his right edge of the highway as he could. Going 60 mph, in opposite directions, we met three wide on the highway—with just a few inches between the truck and me on my right side, and between the oncoming car and me on my left side.

Amazingly, we averted an accident and did so without even a scratch. My guardian angel must have taken the rest of the day off!

21

Drive, Baby, Drive!

To enable Martha's father to attend seminary, the family did without a lot of material things like a phone and a television; and they never owned a car while they lived in Dallas. Her father was in the Th.M. program at that time and was planning to continue with his doctoral studies soon afterwards. Because the family lived right on campus and public transportation was only a couple of blocks away, a car was not a necessary item.

Since the family had no car, Martha had never driven one. On a beautiful summer day, I offered to teach her how to drive. For our practice field, we used the seminary parking lot. It was almost empty because school was out. More importantly, it was next to the "Big White House on Apple Street," the Nuñez' family residence; so we didn't have to travel far.

For the Driver's Ed. practice vehicle, we used my precious, brand new VW. I instructed Martha how to start and steer the car; what the clutch was for; and how to go faster or slower, adjust the mirrors, signal, etc.

She was a quick learner, and we started off going around the parking lot slowly. She was a *fast* learner. The more we went around and around, the more she got used to driving, and the faster she went.

An anxious lump from my stomach was making its way up to my throat. Obviously, she had it all down. It was time to quit the driving lesson for the day. Instantly, I pointed to a parking spot right behind Martha's house and told her to park the car there.

The parking place was next to the back yard, which was surrounded by a white wooden, rickety, old fence. Martha drove down the driveway toward her house, then turned to the right, and headed straight into the parking space, with a confidence that made me a little nervous. She was not going fast, but she was not stopping either.

I cried out, "Stop! Stop!"

But she didn't stop. She ran right into the fence! Fortunately, because the wooden fence was rickety and old, the crash did not damage my precious, brand new VW at all. However, the little bug damaged the fence; one of its rickety, old sections collapsed.

To this day, I am convinced that I did a good job of teaching Martha how to drive but failed to tell her how to stop. Martha claims that she knew how to stop, but was acting silly and failed to stop quick enough. Either way, right then and there, Martha refused to take any more driving lessons that summer.

The upshot of the whole incident is that ten years went by before Martha got behind the wheel again!

A glad heart
Makes a cheerful countenance.

—Proverbs 15:13

22

Westward Ho!

In May 1963, Martha and I were engaged. What a joyous day that was! I knew all along that she was the one for me. When she said, "Yes!" it was a dream come-true! Her big brown eyes and pretty smile were to go with me, wherever the future took us. We set our wedding date for the next summer—after my seminary graduation. Also, this gave us plenty of time to plan the wedding.

The following December, Martha's older sister, Sara, got married in California. True to my ancient namesake, Ivanhoe, I became a knight in shining armor and offered to drive to L.A. the entire family: Martha, her parents, her eighty-eight-year-old grandmother, her younger sister Blanca; and her little brother Tony.

My selfless offer transformed me into Johnhoe, the knight in an old white coupé! All six of us crowded like scared turkeys in an old, white, repossessed car. This was the vehicle's background: Someone bought it in California then took it to Kansas. Eventually, he stopped making payments on it, and the California car dealer repossessed it. Through a middle man, the dealer made arrangements for me to drive the car back to L.A. This way we did not have to purchase plane tickets.

To cut expenses even further, we brought food along. The major expenses for the trip were gas (16¢ a gallon) and cheap lodging. As a result, this trip for seven people turned out to be

Westward Ho!

economical, and we were able to do some sightseeing on the way as well.

On the day of our departure a winter storm swept through Dallas, leaving its streets blanketed with several inches of snow—uncommon for Big D. The city was littered with accidents and stalled cars because most people in the south are not used to driving on snow. Shortly after we departed, we came upon a Baptist church bus that could not make it up a hill. Behind the bus was a van full of nuns, and we brought up the rear in the crowded, old white coupé.

Since I was a native Iowan, driving on snow-covered roads was no challenge. I, the Iowan Johnhoe, offered to drive the bus if others were willing to push. The only passenger in the Baptist church bus was the driver; so the nuns, decked out in their habits, piled out of their van and pushed—a picture perfect scene for sure! It took eight nuns pushing a Baptist bus to get one Baptist over the hill! Then, we went on our way.

We drove through west Texas, New Mexico, and Arizona. It was an exciting time for me since I had never been in those states. As a relief from the crowded conditions in the car, we picnicked at parks that were surrounded by beautiful scenery. After several days of driving and sightseeing, we came into California.

We had not driven very far into the Golden State, when a highway patrolman stopped us! The reason he gave me was that the drive-away-car had no back license plate. Here I was driving a car that did not belong to me with a whole bunch of Latinos—packed like sardines. I told the patrolman that it was not my car, and that I was just returning it to the dealer, who had reclaimed it from some defaulter.

The whole affair sounded suspicious to the officer; he asked me for proof. I showed him the paper work, and he leafed through it. Then he ordered me to open the trunk. I did, confident that he would find nothing but the baggage of a whole bunch of Latinos. He rummaged through the luggage; and "Lo and behold!" in a corner, under the luggage lay the old rusty license plate. When he saw it, he ordered me to put it on the car. I did, and he waved us on our way!

I was used to driving in Dallas, but Dallas seemed small in comparison to Los Angeles, whose landscape was sheer concrete covered with vehicles as far as the eye could see! We drove on mix-masters, on and off ramps, and multiple lanes. Cars passed us on the right side as well as the left.

In the midst of this confusion, we needed to locate Sara's apartment. I stopped at a gas station and gave the clerk the address. He was kind enough to look it up and said, "Keep going on this highway and take the left exit; it is the only left one. All the others are to the right." That was easy.

From there I could follow the map and find Sara's place. We went back on the multiple-lane highway, and I veered to the far left lane. I knew that if I missed that one left exit, we were bound to get lost for sure. I slowed down to 45 mph and drove and drove. The left hand exit was much farther than I thought!

A couple of more miles down the highway, a motor cycle came up quite fast behind us. I thought to myself, "You will have to slow down because I do not want to miss that left-hand exit. If I do I will be lost forever."

After about a quarter mile, the motorcyclist suddenly turned on a flashing red light. He was one of those trendy cops! Since the car now had a California plate, he figured I was a Californian, and he pulled me over. I explained that I was from out of state, but my explanation went into deaf ears. He issued me a ticket for going too slow. I got an "Anti-speeding ticket"!

Then, he ordered me to follow him to the police station. All of a sudden, another motor-cycle officer came out of nowhere and took up the rear to insure I did not get away!

Westward Ho!

Off we went—escorted like criminals, crowded in a mobile prison cell. Meanwhile, I kept thinking, "That left lane better not show up before we reach the police station. Otherwise, I'm going to be desperately lost again!" As our convoy trekked down the road—now on the far right lane—another car came flying by and cut in front of me, barely missing my front bumper and the motorcycle officer in front of me.

The policeman behind me quickly sped around me and went after the wild driver. That driver and I were escorted in a caravan to the police station. The other driver got a ticket for reckless driving and cutting in. My ticket for going too slow seemed insignificant to all of us crowded in the old white coupé!

When I paid the fine at the police station, I got a receipt and kept it as a novelty. After all, how many people get a ticket for going too slow? We resumed our trek and came to the left hand exit, which finally led us to Sara's apartment. The next day I turned in the wretched, old car to the dealership.

We rode with family members to the church for Sara's wedding; it went well, and so did the reception. All who were there enjoyed it immensely. It took place in another part of Los Angeles, and Martha's family was split up. We caught rides with different people who had attended the wedding ceremony, and who supposedly knew their way around the city.

Martha and I were assigned to a French family. They were not native Californians but had lived in Los Angeles for five years. We scooted into the back seat, happy that we did not have to find our way around Los Angeles this time. Our driver knew the way!

We sat back and relaxed as the Frenchman drove and drove and drove. We thought the reception must be a long ways away from the church. After an hour, signs blazing the words, "Long Beach," caught our attention. Our French driver diplomatically confessed that he was lost. Eventually, He did get us to the reception—two hours late. When we came in the house, we discovered that we were Johnny-come-latelies, and that everyone else had already left. We drove all the way from Texas to California and had missed Sara's wedding reception!

A year later, I received a letter from the state of California stating that I was subject to arrest at any time once I crossed back into the Golden State. The specified reason was that I had skipped out and not paid the fine for driving too slow.

However, I was not worried at all by their threat! Thankfully, being a sentimentalist, I had kept that ticket receipt. Thus, I informed the California highway patrol headquarters that I had paid the fine to officer so and so; and that I had a receipt with his signature on it. In my letter I enclosed a copy of the receipt.

Then I asked, "Where did that money go?" After a month, another letter arrived from the Golden State. It said "Your record is cleared."

Who pocketed the money? Was this how California refilled its coffers?

23

The 4th of July Switcheroo

On the 4th of July, 1964, three weeks before our wedding, Martha and I went on a picnic with her family and several family friends. Car-less people caught rides with those of us who had cars. Once again, a whole bunch of Latinos packed into whatever vehicle was available! A young man and his girlfriend jumped into the back seat of my black VW.

As we traveled on that beautiful summer morning, the couple focused their attention on one another. Every so often Martha and I interrupted their conversation by directing their attention to some interesting sights. But the scenery held no interest to them; obviously, they were more interested in each other!

We went to a roadside park by a small lake near Dallas. The weather was warm so the swimming was great; and the food, cooked on grills in the park, was delicious! After lunch, the young couple that rode with us wandered off by themselves, and we did not see them for the rest of the day. Martha and I had a nice time with her family and friends, talking and telling stories—funny ones, of course.

But the fun had to end! As the sunset drew near, we all decided it was time to go home. We packed our belongings and walked leisurely to our cars. When we reached my VW, we discovered that our passengers were missing! We looked all over for the couple while the other people crowded into their designated vehicles. Finally, we saw the couple walking towards us; but when they came up closer to us, it became apparent that the woman with the young man was not the one who had ridden in the car with us earlier.

Astounded, I asked him, "What happened to . . ."

Before her name and the question mark had emerged from my mouth, he opened his mouth, and nothing came out of it at first! Then, when his vocal chords functioned again, he awkwardly informed me that he and his former girl friend had an argument; so she had gone home with another family.

Sheepishly with a grin on his face, he asked if he and his new lady friend could ride back with us. What were we supposed to say, "No!"? The other cars were already crammed full. Naturally, I replied, "Alright." The young man and his new girl friend jumped into the back seat of my black VW.

As we traveled back to Dallas on that beautiful summer evening, the couple focused their attention on one another. Every so often Martha and I interrupted their conversation by directing their attention to some interesting sights. But the scenery held no interest to them. Obviously, they were more interested in each other!

A happy person Does not hear the clock strike.

—Author unknown

24

Wedding Bells (part one)

The day of our wedding rehearsal arrived. Martha and I had been engaged for a year. During all that time, we had planned our wedding carefully. We wanted to make sure that everything went well. You and I know that things can and do go wrong at weddings.

If time and space permitted, I could tell you about the couple whose pastor forgot to send in their marriage license for a whole year; the wedding where the soloist was accompanied by an old hound dog; the best man who accidentally dropped the wedding ring, which then rolled into the floor furnace; the pastor who gave the wrong name for the groom; and the groom who did not know that at the last minute the best man had stuck the words "Help me!" on the soles of his shoes—imagine what happened when the couple knelt with backs to the audience. (It looks like another book is in the works!)

Yes, unexpected things do happen at weddings; but unwelcome surprises were not going to happen at *our* wedding! Therefore, we carefully thought through every aspect of it. With Martha's input, I made lists of every detail. In the end, I even had a list to keep track of all the lists.

Let's backtrack a year from our wedding when I began making these lists. The first item on the master list was, "Wedding, Thursday evening, July 30." You may ask, "Why a Thursday, instead of the usual Friday or Saturday?" The answer is a practical one: Martha's parents wanted to attend their daughter's wedding.

Papá Toñito and Mamá Sarita were teachers in Guatemala. A Thursday wedding gave them and the few relatives who were coming by car enough time to arrive and return in a single week, without missing too many school days. The school year in Guatemala is different than ours. Their "summer" vacation is during our winter season and vise versa.

Soon after we were engaged, a dear couple who were close friends of Martha's family offered us their backyard for a garden reception. Though they were not relatives, we called them Uncle Jack and Aunt Ruth. They took us under their wings and helped us along the way. Uncle Jack and Aunt Ruth started to get their lawn ready with meticulous care and lovely landscaping. That gave them a year to prepare for our big day. Having accepted our friends' kind offer, we ran into the first hitch. Their house was miles away from Scofield Memorial Church, our home church.

Martha and I missed her sister's wedding reception because our chauffeur got lost in Los Angeles. We definitely did not want our guests to get lost in Dallas on their way to our reception! We had to take care of our first hitch ASAP. The next day, as we drove around Uncle Jack and Aunt Ruth's neighborhood, a beautiful Baptist church appeared right before our eyes!

It was a small brick building with stained glass windows and a tall, white steeple reaching up to heaven! Most importantly the church was only three blocks from Uncle Jack's house. The plan was to enable our guests to go from the wedding ceremony to the garden reception without getting lost. The following Sunday, we visited the church and made arrangements with the pastor to rent the church's sanctuary for our wedding. Then, we put a check by that item on the list.

Wedding Bells (part one)

Aunt Ruth helped Martha in many ways as the details of the wedding were set in order. We went over our lists regularly. One by one, we checked off matters as we took care of them, like contacting the maid of honor, the bridesmaids, the best man and groomsmen; the ordering of the wedding cake, flowers, candles; and a host of other items. The bridesmaids' dresses were the product of Aunt Ruth's skillful labor. She happened to be a seamstress.

About six months before the wedding date, I checked in with the pastor of the Baptist church to make sure the building was reserved for us on July 30. He assured me that all things were in order. For our peace of mind, Martha and I attended that church the Sunday before the wedding and checked again with the pastor. All was ready to go!

It was a busy week. People began to arrive from the south, north, and west. Martha's folks arrived on Tuesday. Their long trip by car from Guatemala had taken them all the way through Mexico and Texas up to Dallas. My mother and siblings drove down from northwest Iowa a couple of days before the wedding. Martha's sister from California as well as other out-of-state guests converged on Dallas.

Everybody had arrived by Wednesday evening, the time set for the rehearsal. Since the church was not our own church, its pastor was not going to perform our marriage ceremony. We had made arrangements for a retired missionary-pastor to officiate. He had known Martha and her family from the time she was a little girl. Before the preacher arrived, the men helped me set up for the rehearsal. We removed the platform furniture and replaced it with two candelabras.

Our careful planning began to pay off with the rehearsal—everything went smoothly, even the "rehearsal dinner." Actually, there was no rehearsal dinner on our list. We were poor and unable to have one. The officiating pastor and his wife graciously offered to have a small get-together at their home for the wedding party, and they treated us to coffee and home-made cake.

After the rehearsal, we checked the church again to make sure everything was ready for the wedding: The platform stood empty except for the two candelabras decked out with their tall, white candles ready to be lit on the next day. We spruced up the pews with big, puffy bows, and had the white carpet roller ready to be unfurled as the bridal party made its grand entrance. The only thing left was the flowers. Because they were cut fresh, the florist was delivering them the next day—on the wedding day.

We all could rest in peace, knowing that everything was ready. And we did. Martha and I were relieved that we had accomplished another one of the goals toward our wedding day. According to my plan, we would achieve the remaining matters without a hitch.

Undoubtedly, our wedding was destined to be the first one where everything went right!

As the bridegroom rejoices over the bride,
So shall your God rejoice over you (Jerusalem).

—Isaiah 62:5b

25

Wedding Bells (part two)

July 30, 1964, our wedding day, was a beautiful sunny day! One of our worries about having a garden reception was that it could be rained out. However, even if that happened, we had it covered. The pastor of the Baptist church had offered us the fellowship hall. But, no need for that—the sun came through for us!

Late that morning, I went to the church again. When I walked in the church, there they were in all their loveliness!—the fresh-cut flowers enhancing the simple beauty of the candelabras that stood tall behind them. Everything else was in its right place. Our plans were perfect.

I left to have lunch with Martha and her family. Afterwards, we hoped to rest a couple of hours; then the groomsmen and I were to meet at the church at 6:00 o'clock, allotting us an hour to change into our tuxedos.

Martha and the bridesmaids were getting ready at Aunt Ruth and Uncle Jack's place and planned to arrive at the church at 6:45. I was not to set eyes on Martha in her wedding dress until she came down the aisle. Traditionally, that was the moment when the groom saw his bride in all her glory for the first time.

At 6:00 o'clock sharp the groomsmen and I arrived at the church. We went to the main door, just as I had done earlier when I checked on the flowers. But this time, when I tried to swing the door open, it did not budge. It was locked!

I was surprised because back then many churches never locked their doors. Churches were considered sacred places—a safe haven from evil intruders. We tried the side doors. They were locked! So was the back door. Oh well, that was no big deal, really. All I had to do was call the pastor of the church to let us in.

We still had fifty minutes before the wedding was to start. I drove the three blocks to Uncle Jack's house to call the pastor and ask him to please let us in. There was no answer. The pastor was not home! And then it hit me. We had planned the church matter well. We even had the pastor's number with us in case we needed something. Unfortunately, our plans had one thing missing: We did not have a phone number for any other congregation member. We were locked out!

I went back to the church, and the groomsmen and I walked around the building a second time. Every so often I looked up. Suddenly, out of the clear-blue summer sky, a gleam of hope caught my attention. A little window sat open way up on the second floor! Next to the window was a one-story overhang roof above a side door. The overhang rested on a metal pole that was twelve feet high and two inches in diameter.

I grabbed the pole and pulled myself up hand over hand until I reached the edge of the roof. Then, I swung a leg over onto the roof and stood up. From there, I walked toward the little open window and crawled through it into darkness. It was a good thing I was slim—I was six feet tall and weighed 137 pounds!

Once inside, I saw that I was in a restroom. I rushed out and went downstairs, found my way into the sanctuary, and headed for that same side door under the small overhang. The door had a push bar on the inside; I opened it and let in the groomsmen.

Wedding Bells (part two)

Standing in the semi-dark auditorium, we noticed something shocking. Our flowers were gone and so were the white pew bows. The candelabras were gone. Everything related to the wedding was gone! The platform was set up for Sunday services—the pulpit was back and so were the chairs. And the wedding was supposed to start in forty minutes!

The groomsmen and I scattered and scurried around the church to see what we could find. The big main entry doors were locked with a large bolt.

One of the groomsmen exclaimed, "Let's get a hacksaw and saw through it."

I said, "No! We don't want to destroy any church property! Besides, it would take way too long, even if we could cut through it."

As we were carrying out the pulpit furniture, a groomsman rushed in and said, "We found the flowers and the candles in the trash room!" I shouted, "Hurry! Hurry! Bring them out!"

Thankfully, the flowers were still in pretty good shape. Someone else found the candelabra and the pew bows. Then, we encountered another problem—a serious one. It was July, an extremely hot time of the year. A week before, the scorching heat had shattered a window of my little black VW. The day of our wedding, the church was stuffy and incredibly hot. The air-conditioning had been turned off!

I asked a couple of groomsmen, "See if you can find a list of church members, or better yet, a deacon."

Thankfully, the church-office door was not locked. My "detective" buddies barged in and began to rummage through desk drawers and files, desperately trying to find somebody—anybody who could open the main entry door for us.

It was now 6:35 p.m. The groomsmen and I were still dressed in blue jeans. Since the day was drawing toward early evening, the temperature outside was beginning to cool down.

However, inside it was still extremely warm. Due to the heat, the former tall, white candles were warped and kept bending down.

At 6:45 p.m., one of the groomsmen cried out some good news! He had found a list of the deacons. I told him to call through the list until he found a deacon who was home and had a key. After a few calls, my buddy found one. The deacon said that the church was a ten-minute drive from his home and that he was leaving right away.

All this time, Martha and her bridesmaids had been having a great old time getting dressed for the grand event. As soon as we contacted the deacon, I called Uncle Jack to tell him the bad news and the good news. I trusted him to do the right thing with this vital information. He did not disappoint me. He told Aunt Ruth, who told Martha and the girls, who went into a giggling spree!

Our accomplished organist began to play delightful music as the first few guests arrived. The ushers let the guests in by way of the two side doors—one on each side of the platform. The guests probably thought it strange to be ushered into the sanctuary by way of the side doors, but they did not know anything else about what was going on. They may have thought that's how things were done in Guatemala!

My watch said 6:50 p.m. One of the groomsmen came to me and said, "You better get changed into your tux, the wedding starts in ten minutes!" About the same time, a runner for the bridal party got word to me that the bride and the bridesmaids had arrived and were outside the church, ready to march in. We sent word back to Martha to wait there because the deacon was unlocking the main entry doors as soon as he arrived.

At 7:10 p.m., the deacon arrived with a key and rushed confidently to the big main doors. He tried to turn the lock.

Wedding Bells (part two)

But, it did not turn! In his haste, he had grabbed the wrong key! Now, we had to wait at least twenty minutes—the time for him to make the round-trip home and back. Off he went to get the right key. Our accomplished organist continued to play and play and play delightful, and somewhat lively music to keep the guests alert for the bride's grand entrance.

I got word to Martha about the added delay and suggested that she come in by way of one of the side doors. But Martha refused to even hear of such a thing! The master "To Do Wedding List" had her coming into the church down the center aisle. Besides, she had dreamt about her grand entrance since she was a little girl. Walking through the side door to the tune of the wedding march was definitely not an option!

My brother-in-law, Bill, came up with a brilliant solution. During the rehearsal the night before, he noticed that on each side of the main entry there was a small room with a beautiful stained-glass window. From the inside, the window went nearly down to the floor, but from the outside, the window's bottom was about five feet off the ground. The window included a stationary center and two narrow side panels that could be opened from the inside.

Bill's strategy was to open one of the side panels, walk inconspicuously down the side aisle, run outside, and then shove Martha and her bridesmaids into the small room through the panel. No one would know how Martha and her cohort had entered the church!

Bride Squeezes Into Married Life

8—Section 1　　The Dallas Morning News　　Thursday, August 6, 1964

The doors wouldn't open, so the bride went in the window.

Wedding Bells (part two)

Having decided on his plan, Bill went to work immediately. In no time at all he was standing outside ready to shove the giggling girls through the window. He put Martha on his shoulder, but a problem arose. Martha was wearing a wedding gown with a hoop! Quickly, Aunt Ruth and the bridal party wrapped the wedding gown tightly around Martha, who then looked more like a mummy than a bride!

Then, Bill shoved her through the window panel into the little church room. He did the same one by one with the maid of honor and the bridesmaids—and even with Aunt Ruth. Our photographer was outside as the drama was unfolding, and he shot a number of pictures of the ladies going in through that narrow window panel. As Martha was being unwrapped, she turned around and saw Aunt Ruth who was standing wide-eyed, befuddled by the whole experience.

Martha's father had walked discreetly up the side aisle, and was waiting for Martha to emerge from the little room. As soon as the ladies' dresses and hair had been re-arranged, our courier brought me the long-awaited message that the wedding could now start!

It was 7:20 p.m. From that point on, everything went as planned, except for one crooked matter: one of the candles (straightened out earlier by a groomsman) was not able to withstand the hot auditorium and bent over. Blanca, Martha's younger sister, had to snuff it out to prevent it from falling off the candelabra and starting a fire.

As the officiating pastor proclaimed, "I now present to you Mr. and Mrs. John Hartog," we turned to face the audience. Then we saw the neatest picture, the deacon with a great big smile framed by the wide open front door! We smiled right back at him.

The garden reception under the stars was beautiful. Martha and I learned that no matter how much you plan and how hard you try, something will always go wrong at a wedding. It may start later than planned, as ours did. However, in spite of everything, our wedding started only twenty minutes late. Or it may take climbing a pole to open a locked church door. To this day, I don't know how I performed such an acrobatic feat. I'm convinced that I could never climb a pole like that again and will never have to!

My father-in-law was right. When he heard about what I had done to get into the church, he exclaimed, "You certainly must have wanted to marry Martha!"

All you need for happiness is
A good gun,
A good horse,
And a good wife.

—Daniel Boone

26

Wedded Bliss

We spent our first night of married life in a fancy hotel in downtown Dallas. Then, we drove to a lake in northeast Texas where we rented a cabin for a week. We took long walks together in the resort grounds and along the shore of the lake. One time, our walk took us through a bushy area by the lake. It was a hot day and I was wearing shorts. As we walked and talked and kicked the sand, I kept swatting bugs off my legs.

Suddenly, I felt something crawling on my knee. I looked down and was ready to swat it, when my eyes beheld a huge scorpion griping my knee with its claws. It was ready to strike me with its venomous stinger!

Instantly, I wacked it sideways with my hand, knocked it off, and sent it sailing to the ground. With my adrenaline still flowing, I used a big piece of drift wood to pulverize that wobbly critter and sent it off to the land of no return. Martha, of course, stood by shrieking the whole time, even after the scorpion was unrecognizable! Somehow, I escaped without a sting. The only injury was self-inflicted—a big red bruise on my knee from that fierce whack.

When our honeymoon was over, we returned to Dallas and headed home—a little white house that we rented from an elderly widower. Our first "home sweet home" was in an older part of Dallas on Llano Street and sat way back from the road.

After a few days in our "new home," some of the groomsmen came over, and the first thing they asked us was, "What did you think of your house when you came back from your honeymoon?"

I replied, "Oh! We liked it! It's a nice little house in our price range."

Then, with a puzzled look on their faces, they asked, "Did you notice anything unusual about it?"

We said, "No, nothing unusual. Why?"

They finally revealed the reason for their curiosity! They confessed that they had TP'd our house, the trees and the bushes, and had done a mighty good job! We were surprised to hear about it and told them that there had been no sign of any toilet paper when we drove up.

A few weeks later we met our neighbors, an elderly couple who had lived in their house for many years. Soon after the introductions, the husband declared with a firm countenance, "Some pranksters came just before you moved in and wrapped toilet paper all over your place. But we cleaned it all up for you! We didn't want our neighborhood looking junky!"

Thus we were introduced to our wedded bliss in the quaint neighborhood on Llano Street. The thrill of getting settled in our new house replaced the excitement of planning our wedding and solving the glitches. The pre-wedding plans and problems had found a place in the backburner!

However, soon after getting settled, we learned the "who," the "how," and the "why" the church door had been locked on our wedding day. The pastor called us to apologize and provided the following information: When the church custodian arrived at the church on Thursday afternoon and saw the rearranged and decorated auditorium, he immediately thought the wedding had taken place the night before. So he took down all the wedding decorations, set up the church for Sunday services, and locked the doors. Fortunately, he did not

Wedded Bliss

discard the decorations into the trash bin as he had done for another wedding. Because he got in trouble that first time, he decided to put our stuff in a closet. We thanked the pastor and let him know that we were not upset at all, and we truly were not.

About that time, our photographer came by with the proofs of our wedding pictures—about 150 of them, including some of Martha and her bridesmaids going through the window. Come to think of it, he also went through that window! He had a picture of Aunt Ruth fixing Martha's veil in that little crowded room.

As we were looking and laughing at those pictures, he said to me, "You might want to send one to your hometown newspaper in Iowa. They might publish it."

I eagerly replied, "Let's send it also to *The Dallas Morning News*!"

"Well," He said kindly, "a big-city newspaper like that will never print it, but your hometown's might."

Being an optimist, I decided right then and there to send it to *The Dallas Morning News* anyway. And I did! A few days later, Martha received a friendly call from a writer for the "Social Events" section of the Dallas paper. She came to our house, and Martha excitedly shared with her the wedding events.

The next day the picture of Martha going through the window and a brief article describing the event came out in *The Dallas Morning News*. This catchy caption appeared with the picture: "Bride squeezes into married life." As it often happens, the news writer did not report all the details correctly. For example, she had me climbing a drain pipe to the roof. She also said that Martha was locked out of the church because she was late. Otherwise, the rest of the story was accurate.

But that was not the end of the story! Others found it interesting and worthy of publication. The Associated Press

(AP) picked up the article, and it made national news. Several seminary professors were speaking around the country during the summer, and the picture in various newspapers caught their attention. Some of the Profs clipped and shared with us the newspaper articles from Oregon in the west to Massachusetts in the east, and places in between.

But the story still had more feet! By now, Sara, Martha's sister, was back in Los Angeles. One day, as she was watching the news, the picture of Martha going through the window appeared on the screen. Some friends from Central America saw the Spanish version on television as well. A missionary in France read the article in a French publication. Even a few years later, the story appeared in a book about planning weddings, which was published by Moody Press.

As the account left its "footprint" on the various printed pages, not everything was reported accurately. That is why it was important for everyone to hear it now from the horse's mouth!

Rejoice in the Lord always:
And again I say, Rejoice!

—Philippians 4:4

27

Brother, Do You Have Ten Bucks?

During my bachelor years as a seminary student, my little VW had transported me faithfully on all of my trips back and forth from Texas to Iowa. Gasoline was cheap, and the black bug gave me excellent mileage. With gas at 16¢ a gallon, a car that gave me 40 miles per gallon, and 15¢-hamburgers, I could drive all the way from Dallas to Orange City for $5.00—and still have some change left in my pocket.

A few months after Martha and I were married, my high school class held its tenth-year reunion. I told Martha about it, and she enthusiastically agreed to go with me. Since two of us were traveling, I decided to take along $20.00—$10.00 for each way.

The trip up to Iowa went like a breeze—fast and delightful! I was excited about showing off my new bride to my former classmates, and Martha was eager to learn all she could about them before we arrived. As we traveled the winding roads up to NW Iowa, our conversation included memories of my high school days and interesting tidbits about my classmates.

I had a good time telling her stories, funny ones, of course; and she listened and laughed. Before we knew it, we were entering Dutch country, and ten dollars had more than covered the trip for both of us. Besides attending the reunion activities, we were able to spend time with Mother. The Dutch mature woman and the Spanish young bride began to bond. After a few days we headed back to Texas with $10.00 in my billfold.

All went fine until we reached central Kansas, and our black bug began coughing up a black storm! It's a good thing that it happened near an interstate exit. I took the exit and pulled over on the side where we were protected from fast-moving traffic. Then, I got out and lifted up the hood located on the back of the VW. I saw BLACK! Oil was splattered all over the hood and the engine. Something was drastically wrong. I knew that forcing my little bug to crawl a few more miles was bound to impair it beyond repair. Our little engine could not go!

Cell phones were still a quarter of a century in the future. That fall day in 1964, we needed a phone urgently; we let our feet do their walking. After going a little ways, we saw a house across a field on the side of the road. We climbed the field fence and started walking briskly toward the house.

When we rang the door bell, the lady of the house greeted us graciously; and she let us use her telephone. VW dealerships were scarce, but we finally were able to contact one that was forty miles off to the west. The dealer promised to come and tow us in, as soon as he could find a wrecker. We were stranded in the car for about two and a half hours.

True to his word, the VW dealer sent a wrecker; but by then it was too late for anyone to work on the car—the dealership had closed for the day; so we had to stay overnight. Spending the night in a motel was out of the question; we did not have enough cash or any credit cards. In the recent past, I had applied for a couple of them, but was turned down because I had no credit record. I had always paid with cash.

We did what we had to do and slept cramped in the black sleeping bug, parked outside the car dealer's shop. It's a good thing Martha was tiny and I was skinny, although I was six feet tall and could not stretch out. The next day, a mechanic fixed our car, and the dealer accepted payment by check even

Brother, Do You Have Ten Bucks?

though we were out of state. We did have money in the bank, and I assured him that the check was good.

The day before, we had used part of our second $10.00 for gas from Iowa to Kansas, and some for meals along the way. We also bought a candy bar to munch while stranded at the dealership. It was now early afternoon, and we had an extra forty miles of driving to get back on the interstate. Since the day was now more than half over, there was no way we could make it to Dallas that night. This meant extra money for meals and a little extra for gas.

The VW got good mileage, but it also had a small gas tank that needed a drink a number of times along the way. To save what cash we had, each time we filled up I offered to pay for the gas with a check. But, no gas station was willing to accept out-of-town checks.

By the time we reached the middle of Oklahoma, darkness had overtaken us again. We spent a second night cramped in the black sleeping bug. Of course, we could not spend any money on food, and having enough money for gas was touch and go. Whatever money we had in our checking account was worthless.

It was now the third day since we had left Iowa. If only *one* gas station would take a check, we could make it. About 160 miles from Dallas, we needed gas again. My meager cash was down to 35¢. I stopped for gas and told the attendant about our car troubles along the way. Then I asked him if I might pay with a check.

He answered, "No, the owner will not take out-of-state checks."

Not surprised, I said to him, "Then, give me whatever 35¢ will buy, and we will go as far as we can. That is all we can do."

The two gallons were enough to feed our little bug for about 80 miles. I assured him that I had money in the bank and that my check was good. Then I briefly recounted our sob story, including the fact that we had not eaten for two days.

As he listened, his eyes glimmered with a spark of compassion. He then spoke these words that were truly music to our ears, "Make out a check to me personally for a dollar, and I will put in a dollar's worth of gas in your car. That should get you home. If your check bounces, I will take the loss myself."

Encouraged, I thanked him and assured him again that the check was good. Now, we were able to go on our way. When we arrived in Big D, we went to the bank, cashed a check, and headed for our favorite cafeteria. Their every-day, lunch special was "All you can eat for a dollar." Martha and I were famished! We loaded up our trays with so much food that the cafeteria made no profit on us that day.

The next week, I applied again for a credit card to ten companies—something I would never do today. One came through from Phillips 66. Then I re-applied to the other nine companies, and mentioned the Phillips 66 card. One after another, all the other nine companies came through as well! I tore up all of them, except two, which I pay on time and get cash back.

After all, I am Dutch!

28

Wendy, the Educated Dog

Martha tells people that one of the stipulations that a man had to meet to qualify as her husband was that he must love animals, especially dogs. Well, she married such a man! A month after we were married, we inherited a dog. She became ours on a windy day; so I named her Wendy (I fudged a little on the "i"). Wendy was a hybrid. Some people might say that she was a "mutt," but we never used that word in her presence. She was half collie and half German shepherd. Since we never met her father or her mother, we could not say for sure which parent she favored.

However, it was obvious that her German gene dominated and determined her appearance. Yes, she looked and behaved more like a German shepherd than a collie, except that the tips of her ears flopped just a tad like a collie's. One of her most outstanding traits was her loyalty, the other was her intelligence. It didn't take long for Martha to train Wendy, and for her to become accustomed to our every-day life.

I worked in the post office (P.O.) at night to provide for my lovely bride and to help pay off school bills. I was a "sub"; so I never knew how long I had to work. I could never say to Martha, "Good-by! See you at midnight!" or at any other particular time. The P.O. had to keep us two hours; but if the mail was heavy, they could keep us twelve. My shift started at 5 p.m.; thus I could be there until 7 p.m. or until 5 a.m. the next morning, or any time in between.

This is why we adopted Wendy. Though our trust for protection rested solely on God, it was nice for Martha not to be alone when I was at work, especially on long work nights. When Wendy joined our home, she became Martha's shadow and her fearless guard dog. A knock on the door triggered a loud, deep growl to emerge from her throat; and she bared her teeth—it was definitely not a smile! What made her "smile" was car rides.

Soon after we were married, I traded my 36 hp VW bug for one of those cars that Ford Motor Company released the year we were married: a 64 ½ Mustang. It was a burgundy beauty with a 289-cubic-inch V-8 engine (210 hp). Since gas was cheap, 16¢ a gallon or less if there was a "gas war," we could afford joy rides on Sunday afternoons. Wendy loved to go along. Whenever we asked her, "Do you want to go for a ride?" she bounded to the door and wagged her tail as if saying, "Come on! What's taking you so long?"

One day, as we rode merrily on a joy ride, we came upon a highway-patrol road block. We thought maybe it was to check drivers' licenses. A long line of cars stretched ahead of us, but eventually we came to the front of the line. With his hand, the officer gestured for me to roll down the window. And I did.

He then put his head through the open window and opened his mouth to say something. Instantly, Wendy interrupted him rudely. Her hair stood up on her back; she showed off her guard "anti-smile"; and then she let out a blood-curdling growl. With his mouth still open, the officer jumped back! He tried to say something, and what came out was, "Go on! Go on!" And I did. We didn't get to ask him why the road block was there. We just rode merrily on our Sunday afternoon drive.

Wendy was a well-trained housedog. A corner in our back yard became her "to-do business" spot. Often when she went on her "personal" trips, a homely Pekinese dog across the

Wendy, the Educated Dog

alley barked at her. It was obvious he was interested in her and wanted company. Finally, one day, Wendy gave in and walked up to the Peke. That's all it took! From that day on, Wendy and the Peke became doggy buddies.

For Wendy's sake, we did a little investigation and learned that her boy friend's name was Mr. Chan. Since he was fenced-in, he could not come out and play with Wendy; but they enjoyed rubbing noses through the fence. Actually, Wendy put her nose through the fence because Mr. Chan couldn't—he had a pug-nose. Whenever we were inside the house and called out, "Mr. Chan! Mr. Chan!" Wendy ran to the back door and barked and whined for him.

After her "personal" trips, Wendy scratched the back door or barked to let us know she was ready to come in. One night, she went out and did not come back. Martha and I went up and down the alley and through all the neighborhood front yards. We called for her, but Wendy did not come. We searched for several hours. Finally by midnight, I said, "Somebody must have taken her."

So, we gave up the search. I was sad and Martha was in tears; she was convinced that Wendy was lost forever. We decided to go to bed, but it was impossible to sleep. As I lay on bed, I pictured Wendy with her ears flying in the wind on our Sunday joy rides.

I sat up and shouted, "Let's drive around and look for Wendy!" We jumped into our Mustang and drove up and down the dark alleys. Several blocks away we saw a dog run across the alley ahead of us. I got out of the car and called Wendy's name. The dog did a quick turn around and bounded toward me. As soon as I opened the car door, she jumped into the car!

From then on, when Wendy wanted to go outside, we hooked her chain to one of the clothes lines in the back yard. Then, she was free to go back and forth but could not wander off. This tactic also worked whenever we had company who did not like animals, especially if they were afraid of dogs.

One day, we invited Uncle Jack and Aunt Ruth for dinner. Before they arrived, we hooked up Wendy, actually her chain, on the clothes line. After a nice long visit, Uncle Jack and Aunt Ruth got ready to go. Since it was now dark, we turned on the front yard light and walked with them to their car; and we visited as we walked. Uncle Jack opened the door for Aunt Ruth, and she got in the car, but she kept talking. Uncle Jack stood holding open the passenger door, and he waited patiently as the ladies talked.

The echo of our voices, in an otherwise silent night, was too much for Wendy. She broke the chain, ran around the house, and headed straight for the car. Coming all of a sudden out of the darkness, Wendy looked like a wolf, and it scared Uncle Jack out of his wits! He jumped into the car and landed right on Aunt Ruth's lap!

Wendy was a good watchdog and a good house dog. She was well trained and did not "paw" anything that was forbidden to her. Martha is neat and likes to have everything in its place. It was easy to train Wendy because some of the "off-paws" things were always in the same place.

The day that Martha's younger sister, Blanca, graduated from high school, we took her out for lunch. On the way to the restaurant, we stopped by the house to change. Blanca brought her diploma with her so we could see it. Of course, she didn't want to take it along to the restaurant. When we got ready to leave, she laid it on a lamp table by the door.

Meals are always fun when Martha and Blanca get together! Lunch was delightful, and everything went well until we came home. First of all, Wendy did not greet us at the door as she usually did. Then, as soon as we stepped in the house, we noticed that the diploma was gone. A quick search for it yielded nothing.

We were certain that wherever we found Wendy, the diploma would be lying next to her. Our fear was that the diploma might no longer be recognizable. Soon, we discovered evidence that confirmed our fears: little pieces of chewed up paper and a ribbon were scattered under the dining room table!

That day, Blanca graduated from high school, but Wendy got the diploma!

A mind that's filled with noble thoughts
A heart that's fixed on God . . .
This brings a happiness so sweet,
And springs up from within.

—Walter Isenhour

29

Mrs. Black

It was a pea-soup-like, foggy morning when I ran into Mrs. Black. Literally! Our little rented house on Llano Street in Dallas had a long gravel driveway. Because there was no turn-around pad by the garage door, we always had to back out of our driveway.

That particular foggy morning as I walked to the car, I could barely see the end of the road in front of our house. More cautious than usual, I backed out slowly trying to watch for cars coming from the right or the left. I stopped when I reached the end of the driveway and looked both ways. There were no lights visible through the fog on either side.

I backed out into the street ready to go on my way when I heard a loud, crunching sound. Immediately, I stopped to see what had happened. At first glance, I could see nothing. Then, as I drew closer, I spotted something: there camouflaged by the dense fog was a *gray* car! It was parked right across the street in front of our neighbors' house, and we had never met them.

In the year and a half that we had rented our little house, no one had ever parked a car there. Today of all days, someone had! My mustang didn't even have a scratch on the bumper, but the side of the gray car showed some major damage. I felt as if the heavy fog was pressing down on me. My mood, like my surroundings, became dreary!

Mrs. Black

I drove my car back slowly into our driveway, got out, walked across the street, and knocked on the door. No one was home. There were no witnesses. I attached a note to the door with my name, telephone number, and the fact that I was the one who had run into the gray car. Then, I went off to run my errands.

When I returned home, I went back to the house across the street and knocked on the door again. Someone opened the door and stood smiling at me. That's how I first met my neighbor, Mrs. Virginia Black, the owner of the gray car. I told her what had happened, and she thanked me for my honesty. She informed me that her car was brand new, and that she had just purchased it the day before!

I gave her my insurance information and we visited briefly. Through our conversation, I found out that her husband had passed away recently; that she had moved into that house soon after his death; and that a young adult daughter was living with her.

Mrs. Black asked about my family, and I told her about Martha, who was "sitting on the nest" awaiting the birth of our first baby; he was due in a few months. My neighbor brightened up and said that she wanted to meet my wife. Thrilled, I crossed the street, ran to our house, and asked Martha to come with me. She and Virginia hit it off right away. You could say that they were of a kindred spirit.

After visiting for a while, we learned that Virginia was a Christian who loved the Lord! Martha sensed that Virginia was lonely and was grieving deeply the death of her husband. She needed a friend. Virginia invited Martha to come over for coffee the next day.

It was nice for Martha to get off her cozy "nest" in our little white house and go across the street to visit Virginia. Because Mamá Sarita, Martha's mother, was living far away in Guatemala City, Martha looked up to Virginia as her mother-like mentor. Her wise counsel on child-birth was invaluable to Martha, especially since she was to be a first-time mommy.

Their regular chit-chats provided opportunity for the ladies to pray. Before long, Virginia shared with Martha a personal burden: the doctors had diagnosed her with breast cancer, and she had to undergo surgery within the next few weeks. We brought meals over and prayed faithfully for her and with her.

The surgery was successful. However, a few years after we moved away, we heard that Virginia's body had succumbed to the devastating effects of cancer again, and she passed away. In the meantime, Mrs. Black, a mature woman who was on the threshold of death, mentored a young mother who was about to bring forth new life.

On June 2, 1966, God blessed Martha and me with a sweet baby boy. He was due on June 3 and surprised us by arriving a day early! I, the head of the Hartog household, named him John Hartog III. Martha and I thanked God for our son and rejoiced greatly. Mrs. Black celebrated along with us! She continued to mentor Martha on baby-care and child-rearing, until we moved away later that summer. Consequently, the birth of John bonded the women even closer.

While we lived on Llano Street, God used Martha and me to encourage Mrs. Black; and in turn, she mentored Martha. One day, Virginia told Martha that the accident had been a God-send. We all realized that we never would have met and become good friends if it had not been for my hitting that gray car. Truly, God had worked out the circumstances.

That dreary, foggy day had turned into a ray of sunshine for Mrs. Black and for Martha, too!

30

A Hole in One

Soon after our second anniversary, we moved from Dallas, a bustling metropolis, to the sparsely populated section of the Texas panhandle. Texas is indeed a great place to call home. Because of its size, it offers much to see and enjoy. Before Alaska became a state of the Union, Texas touted its rank as the largest state.

In those days a Texan might say, "If you started driving across Texas from east to west at the crack of dawn and drove until dark, you would still be in Texas." Or a Texan might exclaim, "Texas covers more square miles of land than Ohio, Indiana, Illinois, Wisconsin, and Michigan combined!" Or again, "You could drop two whole *states*, into one Texas c*ounty*."[3]

Nevertheless, not everything in Texas is big. The town in the Texas panhandle that became our hometown was a little *tiny* town called Lipscomb. It was the county seat of Lipscomb County and featured a typical court house.

According to the U.S. census, this little *tiny* town had a population of seventy people. When my wife and I and our two-month old baby, John, moved into town, its population grew by four percent over night! Lipscomb became Texas' fastest growing town—for one day! How did our family end up in this rapidly growing town of seventy-three people?

---

[3] Rhode Island and Delaware into Brewster County, Texas.

The only church in Lipscomb needed a pastor. The church had been closed for several months. Then, one Sunday in the middle of July, the doors were open for a homecoming reunion. Although neither Martha nor I had ever darkened the doors of that church, I became the invited speaker for their special reunion.

Mr. Akers, the most faithful, active member and self-appointed "pulpit committee" of the temporarily "resurrected" congregation, had never set eyes on me; nor had he invited me personally to be the speaker. He had sent an urgent request for a speaker to Dallas Theological Seminary, and the lot fell on me!

Instead of our Sunday afternoon ride around Dallas, our joy ride began early Saturday morning. We traveled 400 miles; stopped in the home of complete strangers for the night; and the next day drove one mile up to a sign emblazoned with the words, "Welcome to Lipscomb." Then, we made our way through one of Lipscomb's two main "arteries"—both of them were dirt roads. At the blink of an eye, we reached our destination, Lipscomb Union Church.

Following the morning message, the temporarily "resurrected" congregation extended me a call to be their pastor. If I accepted their call, they could re-open the church and keep it going. They did not know anything about me, and I did not know anything about them. Befuddled, I replied that I had to think and pray about it. Martha and I needed wisdom and time.

In addition to the call, Mr. Akers, the self-appointed "church treasurer," disclosed to me the church's compensation package, which included no life or health insurance, no retirement, and no pastoral expenses; but it did contain a bi-monthly salary payment. It was meager because the "resurrected" congregation was *tiny*—about 20 people, including the children Consequently, I needed to find additional resources during the week to provide adequately for Martha and John.

Mr. Akers, self-appointed "school board member," told me that the school needed a bus driver. The job was mine if I took the pastorate. Also, the people decided to show us the parsonage, just in case we agreed to take the church. It was a modest-size house, but it needed new flooring throughout and painting inside and out, especially the kitchen cabinets. They were bright orange! But we just looked around, appeared interested, and said nothing.

Following the evening service, we traveled the long, 400 miles back to Dallas. I knew that a major turning point awaited us if I were to pastor the church. It meant leaving everything behind in Big D and starting life all over in a *tiny* town—a drastic change in my life and the life of our family, indeed!

After thinking and praying about it for a week, Martha and I were assured of God's will. I called Mr. Akers, the self-appointed "chairman" of the "pulpit committee," to tell him that I was happy to be the pastor. I also informed him that it would be a month before I could start. We needed this time to give a two-week notice at my P.O. job and to prepare for the move.

As soon as the one-month waiting period ended, Mr. Akers, the self-appointed "mover," arrived in Dallas, loaded our few belongings into a U-Haul truck, and drove off with them. Martha, John, Wendy, and I followed in our Mustang. When we arrived, the church people greeted us with a wonderful surprise: They had remodeled the old parsonage completely!

New carpet and linoleum covered the floors; the walls were clad in a fresh coat of paint; delicate sheer curtains bordered all the windows throughout the house, and the kitchen cabinets had been transformed from orange to white! Martha was thrilled! She likes bright colors, a reflection of her Spanish heritage; but we knew that orange cabinets in the kitchen were bound to send her bouncing off the walls! Once we were unloaded and settled, we began our brand new ministry in our new *tiny* hometown.

Because Lipscomb had only twelve to fifteen houses, it was impossible to have a typical church visitation program. In an hour or two, at the most, we could visit every home, which left none for the next week. Martha and I came up with a tailor-made-for-Lipscomb outreach program: We decided to spend one evening a week with each family.

This required that we call the people first, and ask them if we might visit. When we called, they all said, "Sure! Come on over!" In that *tiny* town, news traveled at a speed faster than lightning—as you will see later. All seventy inhabitants had heard about the new preacher with a pretty Latin wife and an adorable infant. Everyone wanted to meet us.

Some of the first people we visited were an un-churched couple with two children. The family lived two blocks from the parsonage. Our friendly neighbors invited us over for dinner and table games. Pleasant talk around the table enabled all of us to become acquainted a little bit.

The husband was obviously a cowboy—His carriage and dress gave it away; he worked as a ranch hand. The wife was a small woman with a bubbly personality like Martha's. They connected immediately and made plans to go cattle counting the next day—which is another story! That night, as usual, we made sure that our conversation included the gospel.

After the meal, the husband brought out a bag full of marbles and a board for playing a game they called "Wahoo." (It also goes by the name, "Aggravation"). It was evident that the board was hand crafted. Sometime after we had received the dinner invitation, our cowboy neighbor had turned an old board into a Wahoo board by drilling each hole needed for the marbles.

The object of the game was to get our marbles "Home." It took some time for the first player to go all the way around and reach "Home" with his first marble. I happened to be that player.

I was eager to plunk my marble into its home base when we all shouted, "Oh! No!" The hand-crafted game board had no "Home" center hole!

Confidently, our host said, "No problem. Let's go outside. I'll take care of it."

I pictured him crafting the center hole with an electric drill. However, when we went outside, he set the board against the base of a large tree, cocked his head, and stared at it.

I thought, "Now what?"

He shouted, "Wait here a minute! I'll be right back!" And he dashed into the house. Shortly, he came out with a loaded gun! He looked straight at me and commanded, "You stand over there!" With gun in hand, he pointed to the spot where I was to stand.

I felt like singing "Lord, I'm coming home!"

Next, he pointed his gun, pulled the trigger, and shouted, "Bull's eye!"

He had shot a hole right in the middle of the Wahoo board! Grinning widely, he turned to me and said, "Let's go in."

We went in and finished the game. I let him win!

31

Locked Jaw

Typical Sunday crises started the first day of our ministry at the church in Lipscomb. We drove up to the parsonage late that first Saturday and were tired from the 400-mile trip. We had planned the move well, just as well as we had planned our wedding.[4] We loaded our belongings in the truck, except for what we called "essentials" which we crammed into the trunk of our Mustang. This stuff included baby items, linens, and enough food for the first two days at our new home.

When we arrived, the men from the church rushed right to the truck, unloaded our belongings, and dumped them on the living room floor. Martha and I had labeled every box carefully. We thought that sorting through the boxes and hauling them to the right rooms would be a breeze. As planned, Monday was to be sorting and unpacking day.

After the men left, we stood in the middle of a sea of boxes, looked at one another with weary eyes, and said, "Let's go to bed!" In that moment it hit me! Buried in that jumbled sea of boxes was a "treasure chest"; in it were my sermon notes for the next day.

It had taken me eight hours to prepare each sermon. Unlike a few preachers who can get up behind the pulpit and jabber, (what they call "preaching") for an hour without notes, I needed my notes. While Martha put the baby to bed

---
[4] See "Wedding Bells (part one)," story #24.

and unpacked the few boxes that had traveled with us, I went "deep-sea diving."

Tired but full of energy, I plunged into the cluttered boxes in our living room! In no time at all, I had sorted all the boxes into different piles according to their labels. Most importantly, I had found the "treasure chest" containing my sermons. We went to bed later than planned—exhausted but relieved. We slept like *our* baby!

Later it happened again! Another Sunday crisis! That particular Sunday morning, after we had been living in Lipscomb several months, I woke up early with the birds. Our baby was still sleeping and so was Martha. I got up quietly and went to the kitchen to study. As I reached for my Bible and notes, I yawned a big, gratifying yawn that involved opening my mouth extra wide and free! But wait, something was wrong. When I tried to shut my big mouth to a normal position, it did not move—much less snap back in place.

I tried and tried and tried, but my mouth would not go shut! Then I grasped my chin with both hands and pushed on it with all my might. But my mouth stood widely open as if still in the midst of a yawn. I tried the two-hands-pushing-on-the-chin tactic several times, but all to no avail. The fear of cracking my jaw gripped me. I changed tactics.

I tried the wiggle-my-mouth-from-side-to-side approach. No go! I was getting anxious! With my mouth wide open, I could not eat. I could not drink. I could hardly swallow. However, breathing was no problem; I could turn my head from side to side.

Even so, there I was, with my big mouth set on the gawking position forever! Oh! Yes! And since I could not close my mouth, I also could not talk. Only a loud, guttural, moaning sound came out of my throat. To me it sounded something like, "*Unh. Unh. Unh.*" At that moment, I remembered that it was Sunday morning—I was supposed to preach in a couple of hours!

Martha was still sleeping, and I did not want to scare her. But I was at my wits end. I went to the bedroom and gently shook her to wake her up. She opened her sleepy eyes and looked right into my wide open mouth and asked, "What's the matter?"

All I could do was to point to my mouth with my forefinger. More concerned, she asked again, "What's the matter? Tell me!"

I wished I could have told her, but I couldn't. I replied to her plea with that guttural, loud moaning sound, "*Unh. Unh. Unh.*"

From a peaceful sleep, Martha woke up to a "day mare" that scared her half to death! Now she was also at her wits end. She sat up quickly and stared at me. Then, unexpectedly without a word, she raised her hands up to my face and whacked both sides of my jaw at once. Everything happened so quickly. I never knew what hit me! But, lo and behold! My jaw bones had popped right back into place!

Since then, sometimes when I yawn a little bit too widely, my jaw still gets stuck. However, instead of pushing up from the bottom of my chin or getting all worked up, I simply put my palms on my cheeks right next to the lower part of my ears and I push. It takes care of the problem every time!

No way would I ever think of "*Unh-ing*" Martha for help again and waking her up suddenly. My bones are too brittle to withstand her harsh physical therapy.

Nonetheless, that infamous Sunday morning, Martha's whack did the trick!

32

The Original "On-Line" Phone System

The *tiny* town of Lipscomb boasted in its standing as the county seat of Lipscomb County and as the location of the Lipscomb Telephone Company (LTC) head-quarters. The other public company in Lipscomb was the general store, which had only one employee: the store's owner. Of course, the government-controlled entities—the post office and county courthouse—also provided work for a few other townspeople.

A totally independent telephone company, the LTC served the citizens of Lipscomb and the surrounding area. The "surrounding area" meant that the telephone lines went out at least twenty miles in each direction, to reach the handful of ranchers who lived throughout that region. One woman was the sole switchboard operator at the central LTC. To correspond to the *tiny* town, we'll call her Minnie—not her real name, of course.

Minnie linked a web of customers by manually plugging and unplugging their telephone connections. Those wires almost became overheated when the latest town gossip made its way from customer to customer. Minnie's was a key position. Any distraction could result in her linking the wrong wires, thus triggering interesting conversations.

Sometimes people ended up talking to someone they had not intended to contact, and the person on the other end of the line learned much that was none of his or her business! Other times, when a distressed resident called a friend for encouragement, the LTC became a "Crisis Hotline"—a sizzling one indeed! Several customers jumped into the counseling session and offered advice simultaneously.

The telephones were the antique-style ones, which had disappeared long ago from most American homes. What we called telephones in Lipscomb were wooden boxes with an attached mouth piece and a listening device on a cord. The telephone also had two bells and a crank. The crank was for calling the operator, and the bells rang to alert customers that their phone had an incoming call on the way. Each LTC customer (there were about fifteen of us) had a separate ring: two longs and a short, three shorts, a short-long-long, etc.

The problem was that every ring rang in everyone's home; so if you were used to answering your phone whenever it rang; you answered your phone whenever it rang. Very simple! But not for brand new Lipscomb residents like us!

The first time our phone rang, we automatically picked it up and answered it, "Hello! This is the parsonage." Immediately, Minnie's voice boomed back, "Hang up! This is not your ring!"

In time, we became accustomed to our ring and to Minnie's booming voice. Moreover, all of us knew everyone else's ring! This knowledge, as you can imagine, made it interesting to live in such a *tiny* town.

Many LTC customers considered the parsonage ring the "community ring." When our ring came through the wires, receivers went up instantly throughout the LTC web. People wanted to know who was calling the pastor, and they thought it was their right to stay on the line to hear the preacher's discourse.

Their curiosity, however, interfered with the volume and sound quality of the conversation. When too many LTC customers picked up their phones to listen, I said firmly, "This is Pastor Hartog. All you, listeners, please hang up! So I can

Lipscomb Telephone System

hear my caller!" At that point I heard the "click, click, click, click" as receivers were hung up.

The "on line" telephone system had this great advantage: Gossiping was non-existent in the church. You never saw people whispering to one another and saying, "Did you hear what the preacher told so and so?" Or, "Did you hear what so and so told the preacher?" Everyone knew it already!

The happiest people
Are often those who enjoy
The simple things in life.

—Author unknown

33

The Musical Boy

Singing is not my cup of tea! In reality, I have no musical ability whatsoever, but the rest of my family does. Both John and Paul have a nice singing voice and play musical instruments; and as young boys, they learned how to lead singing, under Martha's direction. Our sons' musical talents, which they certainly did not inherit from me, have afforded them several ministry opportunities since they were in grade school.

Martha's musical talent is minimal, but even in that area, she strives to fulfill God's intended purpose for her as my wife. Her desire to be my loyal helpmeet was strikingly evident on the account about my locked jaw. This reminds me of another incident when I was the pastor in *tiny* Lipscomb. Since the town was *tiny*, the church membership followed suit.

Of the few members, only one little old lady saint played the piano. In the past, she must have struck the piano keys with fast-flowing fingers. Now, she strained to keep up with the song leader—our one and only one. He led the congregation at his own pace, completely disregarding the piano player and also the congregation if they could not keep up with him.

Often he ended up singing impromptu solos. A few others thought that they could sing and provided special music. Martha sang solos, especially at funerals when some people were inattentive. One time she even led the congregational singing. She did it as a "help-meet-have-to duty," not as a "gladly-to-do-it duty."

That Wednesday night, it was slim pickings in the congregation. Besides Martha, John, and me, the only other faithful attendee was our sweet, elderly piano player. John was about eight months old and should have been in the nursery. But that would have left the piano player and me alone in the auditorium; so, Martha decided to move the playpen by the piano.

I don't have a single musical bone in my body but enjoy "singing" the good old hymns. However, leading the singing that night was beyond my pay-rate. All it took was a look from me, and Martha grasped her new help-meet function. The roles that night were these: Martha led the singing; I was the congregation and the preacher both; the elderly lady played the piano; and John, at first, quietly observed from his playpen.

After my opening prayer, Martha stood up with hymnal in hand, announced the hymn number, looked toward the piano player, and waited till she struck the first note. Martha did her best to lead the congregation (me) in singing. It was not easy. By now, John was babbling away in his playpen; I was singing joyfully off key; and the older lady was playing *s—l—o—w—l—y*. As usual, it took a while to get through the song, especially since we sang all four stanzas.

In the meantime, things had become livelier in the play pen. Somewhere between the third and the fourth stanzas, our little son had stopped babbling. Now, he was dancing up and down to the tune of the piano, giggling merrily and showing off his toothless smile.[5]

Music was definitely in his blood! To this day, he still loves music!

---

[5] John's first tooth finally came in when he was nine months old!

34

Murphy's Law on Wheels

Along with a *small* church in a little *tiny* town came a *tiny* salary. Housing was no problem since we lived in the parsonage, but I still had to take care of normal living expenses. Thus, I took the bus-driver job extended to me. At first glance, driving a nice bus full of lazy kids up and down the four blocks of *tiny* Lipscomb might appear like a cushy job. And certainly, since the route was so short, I could spend most of the day at home. But that was not the case!

My route started at seven in the morning, and I returned home about five in the evening. In the middle of the winter, I left home in the dark and came back in the dark. I did drive up and down the four blocks of *tiny* Lipscomb and picked up junior high and high school kids. But after that, I zigzagged back and forth across the southern part of the county, and kids from the ranches boarded the bus.

Then, with a rickety, old bus loaded with sleepy kids, I headed straight to Canadian, where the school was located. Most of the ride was nice and quiet; but as the bus approached closer to Canadian, the kids began to stir. Upon our arrival, the halls of learning welcomed a noisy brood that was fully awake and ready for . . . learning, of course! Canadian is a Texas town located thirty miles from Lipscomb. But, by the time I had picked up all the kids from the area ranches, the route distance had increased to forty miles. This added mileage created a problem: The school district did not budget gas money for me to drive back home during the day. Martha did not know how to drive; but, even if she had known how, we could not have afforded the extra gas expense either.

We agreed on this practical, economic plan: Martha packed me a lunch, and I stayed in town. During the week, the rickety old bus became my office. I furnished it with mobile bookcases (cardboard boxes) for my commentaries and a lap desk (a board) for my portable, manual typewriter.

This arrangement had two benefits: One, it provided a secluded office with no "Pastor's Office" sign, no secretary, and no telephone. It was truly every pastor's dream come true! I was able to prepare sermons without any interruptions and get far ahead—something that has not happened for the rest of my life. Two, it enhanced our family life. When I came home, the whole evening was ours to spend as we wished.

In the fall, the bus was comfortable during the day; but as the year wore on and the days got colder, so did the temperature in my "office," which had no adjustable thermostat. Instead, I adjusted the position of the bus several times during the day. I parked it at an angle that caught the sun's rays for solar heat. The old, yellow bus turned into a solar house on wheels. During the coldest part of winter, I worked in the semi-abandoned train depot—No one left or arrived while I was there.

Because my "office" did not have all necessary facilities, I visited the public library when nature called. The library trips benefitted Martha who loves to read. She counted on me to check out books for her and return them on time. Thus, Martha had a personal "library mobile." For variety, I also visited the museum whenever its doors were open. Eventually, I was asked to serve as an "amateur curator" on a limited, voluntary basis. You do what you have to with whatever it is and wherever it happens to be!

That year was the driest on record for Lipscomb. All the moisture (rain, snow, and sleet) added up to less than an inch. We experienced numerous thunder storms through the fall and winter months, but hardly any rain fell—only a few drops. In the evening, thick-dark clouds traveled across the sky, and we could hear the thunder roll throughout the night. But when morning came, the parched ground was still as dry as a bone.

"Dry thunder storms"—that's what the native residents called them. Newly-arrived residents like us considered them a freak of nature. Also, for the first time, we saw tumbleweeds driven by the strong winds. Because weather conditions were so dry, the winds also blew the clay dust off the roadways and exposed the rocks, some as big as oranges and even grapefruits.

The rocky roads took their toll on the school bus. Things began to go wrong and went wrong at bizarre times. The old bus reminded me of Murphy's Law, which states, "Anything that can go wrong will go wrong and at the worst possible moment."

On several occasions, when I took the bus to the garage for a tune-up, the mechanics discovered that only one or two bolts were left supporting the engine. The fierce bouncing on the roads dislodged the engine's nuts and bolts. Then, the bouncing of the kids, as we rode on the rocky roads, jiggled loose some of the seats.

Early on, I reached up to adjust the rearview mirror, and it came unglued. In addition, the back door nearly flew open—permanently; the windshield wipers got tired and quit, not from being "rain wipers" but "dust wipers"; the hub caps popped off one by one; the stop sign attached to the bus disappeared into the dust. Even things that were not connected to the bus were affected. At the end of one of the routes as I swept the bus, the broom head stayed under a seat, and I was left standing "at attention" grasping only the broom handle!

One day the kids shouted, "Hey! There goes one of the wheels!"

I thought they were joking. Nevertheless, I still glanced quickly at the outside rear view mirror—just in case. Reflected on it was one of the rear duels rolling down the hill behind the bus. Later in the year, the outside rear view mirror decided to take a hike on a fast-moving truck as it passed us.

Sometimes the engine sputtered and suddenly quit. As a stubborn Dutchman, I kept trying to start it until it kicked in. On one of our home-ward treks, we stopped at a convenience gas station between Canadian and Lipscomb. Actually, this was the only store of any kind in the forty-mile stretch of our route. The kids bought their goodies and returned to the bus, but it refused to start again. Sometimes a good push will start up a car that refuses to go. With that in mind, I asked the kids to get behind the bus and push with all their might.

They did, and the bus began chugging along; but it died again as soon as I stepped on the brakes to let the kids on board. They all got out again and pushed—not as vigorously as the first time. But the tired, old bus started once more. This time I did not stop it, but kept driving it slowly to give the kids a chance to hop on. The kids, running after the bus, made the scene of Pied Piper of Hamelin and the children come alive!

After a few minutes, I thought the engine might not die; so I drove s—l—o—w—l—y. Then, as fast as they could, one by one the kids hopped on the bus. It chugged along as if nothing had happened. However, weeks later something happened that forced us to leave the old yellow clunker stranded on the roadside.

We were on our home-ward trip, when a big bang boomed and shook the bus! Quickly, I stepped on the brakes and discovered that one of the back duals had blown out. I relied on my math: 6 tires - 1 tire = 5 tires. We could make it home! But, two miles down the road, another big bang boomed, and the old bus stopped abruptly! The single tire had blown to smithereens!

Stranded as we were, with no way to contact anyone and no houses nearby, our hope was for someone to come by soon. In time, a Lipscomb couple driving back from a shopping spree in Canadian stopped and crammed their car full of kids. As they were driving off into the sunset, I hollered, "Please send someone out to deal with the blown-out tires!"

Now and then, cars headed for Lipscomb stopped; all the kids and I eventually got rides home. I then called the school board chairman and told him, "The bus . . . ." He cut in and said, "I've heard all about it. Two of the guys, (meaning board members) will take care of it." Naturally, the news had reached just about every LTC customer including Mr. Akers, the "self-appointed bus repairman."

I jumped into our Mustang and followed the two board members. When we came upon the bus, it was on jacks and both back tires were gone, wheels and all!

I exclaimed, "Look! Someone stole our wheels!" They responded, "That had to be Akers!"

They knew him well. They reckoned he had taken it upon himself to purchase tires and was headed for Amarillo, Texas, which was 115 miles away.

They shouted, "He must be stopped!"

Board members qualified for a discount, but Mr. Akers did not. He was unbelievably kind and always wanted to help, but sometimes his good heart carried him away. Wasting no time, the men jumped into their car and sped away, burning rubber. They intercepted the "Good Samaritan" just before he reached the auto supply store. The next morning, my yellow rickety "buddy" was parked on the parsonage driveway, and it was sporting two brand new tires.

That fall, my mother and Dad Jacobs (my step-father) drove down from Iowa to visit us. The next morning after their arrival, Dad Jacobs asked if he might ride the bus on the return trip to the parsonage. I replied, "Of course." That afternoon, Mother, Martha, and John dropped off Dad Jacobs in Canadian, and he rode the home-ward bus.

I was used to the rocky roads that weaved in and out of the ranches, but Dad Jacobs was not. Sometimes the roads, which were more like paths, took sudden sharp turns, either to the left or to the right. Just before we approached the top of a hill, it was difficult to tell what direction the road was going to turn.

I knew the route by heart and the course each road took. But poor Dad Jacobs did not know what to expect next. He sat at the edge of his seat with his head stretched out, trying to see which way the rickety, old bus was going to go. He must have felt like he was in a wild roller coaster ride—sideways! That's how he appeared when I looked at him on the rear-view mirror.

When we dropped off the last child and stopped in front of the parsonage, Dad Jacobs staggered into the house and went straight to bed—not even mentioning supper. He did not get up until the next morning after I had already left on my daily roller coaster ride!

35

Our Fair Lady

A car radio! That's what I needed for the bus! Forty miles was a long way to ride twice a day to and from school. The afternoon route seemed to be twice as long as the morning one. The reasons were obvious: The kids were tired from all the "learning" they had done during the day; they were growing like weeds so they were famished; and a few of them were just plain ornery and liked to pick on each other. I thought that a radio tuned to nice, pleasant music would promote an orderly atmosphere, especially on the home-ward ride.

The school board definitely did not grant me the funds for a radio. Therefore, I called a Hartog-home—business meeting. After supper that night, when all of us, (Martha, John, and I) were gathered together, I brought up the recommendation to purchase a car radio for the bus. Martha seconded it and voted, "Yes"; and John, sitting on his high chair, smiled in agreement.

The next morning after dropping off the kids, I walked to the only automotive store in Canadian, and bought my car radio. Then I had it attached to the dash and wired it to the electrical system of the bus.

That first afternoon when the kids boarded the bus, they were greeted by pleasant music. I made it clear that only my fingers were to touch the radio: the tuning button and the volume button. The children settled on their seats, listened to the radio, and talked about their day. It seemed that my plan, as usual, was going to work like a charm. And it did—most of the time.

Of course, the kids were still tired, hungry, and a few were even ornery. Consequently, one Thursday afternoon on the home-ward ride, some of the older boys took rubber bands and shot paper wads at some of the younger kids.

Friday, the next day, when I delivered a child to his home on the range, something unusual happened. This child's father, who happened to be a school board member, got on the bus and sternly scolded all the kids for misbehaving on the bus the day before.

That following Saturday, late in the morning while we were still in bed playing with John, a hard knock on the door startled us and ended our fun. I got up, put on some jeans, and went to the door. Standing on the porch was a woman who was obviously angry.

I stepped outside and left the door ajar. Instantly, she read me the riot act, at least that's what her angry countenance showed me. From her loud, angry, rapid outburst, I gleaned the following information: She was the mother of one of the school children. She was upset that her son had been lectured by the board member.

I just stood there and listened and tried to decode the loud, angry words flowing rapidly from her mouth. She went on for quite a while, almost foaming at the mouth. Since the door was partly open, the woman's voice carried clearly into the house, and her words offended Martha to the point of tears. I kept my cool, and let the woman talk until she ran out of steam. Throughout her rampage, I did not say a word.

As more and more minutes passed, her volume and speed decreased. Then, she stopped yelling so loudly, and her voice became softer and softer; and her speech became slower and slower. Finally, she stopped talking altogether. She reminded me of someone turning down gradually the volume button of a loud radio until it's completely off! We stood face to face for a moment and looked at each other in silence.

Then I broke the silence and said, "Your son was not involved in the paper wad shooting." She did not know what to say. She turned around and left.

A few days later, there was a knock at the door again. I opened the door. Standing on the porch was that same woman. She guardedly asked me, "Do you like fresh milk?"

Pleasantly surprised, I replied, "Yes, we sure do."

With a smile on her face, she handed me a gallon jug and said, "This is for you." From that point on, as long as we lived in Lipscomb, she supplied us with free, fresh milk!

Being a school bus driver, as well as a pastor, provided me experiences that I could not have had any other way. As a bus driver, I became acquainted with all the kids in our small town and surrounding ranches. We started a youth training hour on Sunday evenings, and I was drafted as the teacher. Our youth group of three, when we started our ministry, grew to thirteen; among them were the milk-lady's kids. God used my ministry with the young people to show me that I could teach.[6] Knowing that I could do so changed my life.

Shortly before we left Lipscomb and moved on to another ministry, all thirteen youth honored us with a special get-together. It included softball, a treasure hunt, hot dogs, and home-made ice cream made from fresh cream—provided by . . . Our Fair Lady, of course!

---

[6] See I'll Never Teach Again!" story #14.

36

Rattlesnakes!

What do you do for family recreation in a little *tiny* town called Lipscomb? What is something that is exhilarating for the entire family, including the babies? You go rattle snake hunting—that's what you do!

We became acquainted with this family sport, the first time we went to the only general store. We went there to chew the fat with the town folks. This was another family pastime in Lipscomb. Now, don't get the idea that we went to the store, bought us a slab of bacon, and began chewing it for fun! As you know, "Chew the fat" means that the folks gathered to chat and repeat the latest gossip we all had heard already on our LTC contraptions.

We arrived ready to "chew the fat" when a gruesome sight just outside the store startled us. On a rickety rack, of all things, were dangling half a dozen rattle snakes! Their limp bodies sagged toward the ground, and the tails of a couple of them still rattled, though slowly. Up to that point, the only time we had set our eyes on rattle snakes was at the zoo and in the World Book Encyclopedia!

Martha, with John in her arms, was ready to do an about-face, jump in the car, and drive right back to Dallas! Remember, she didn't know how to drive. Any time Martha sees a snake, she behaves irrationally. This time she was dreadfully rattled.

I grabbed her by the arm and asked one of the gawkers, "What's going on?"

Oh!" he said as he pointed to an older lady and a mother with two children standing by the loaded rack, "Them women just got back from rattlesnake hunt'n."

By now, more people had arrived to witness the latest hunt. The women talked excitedly about their kill, as if they had just shot a twelve-point buck. Martha was more concerned about the few tails rattling softly and kept pointing to them. I finally asked that friendly gawker if some of those snakes were still alive.

"Oh, no!" he responded, "Them's just the rattlers' nerves still at work." Martha breathed a sigh of relief, and we stepped a step closer to the rack.

This was our introduction to rattlesnake hunting, Lipscomb's exhilarating recreational activity for families. For fun, but mostly out of necessity, this sporting event occurred periodically. When it did, the hunters used buckets to transport the snakes to the store then plopped them on the rack to dry. At first, it was a little unnerving to walk past buckets half-full of curled up rattle snakes, or to catch sight of a rack decked out with big, fat ones with tails still rattling. But after a while, we got used to the whole scenario.

One day, Martha, John, and I received an invitation to participate as a family in Lipscomb's exhilarating sport. The grandmother and the young mother with the two young children, who turned out to be our neighbors down the road, were planning their latest hunt—out of necessity, of course.

Rattlesnake hunting protects livestock. The snakes set up housekeeping in prairie dog dens scattered throughout the ranches. The roaming livestock then become easy target for the venomous bites. Cows and horses usually survive, unless they get a nose bite. This causes swelling of the face and nostrils that result in death due to suffocation.

The women, whose husbands happened to be ranch hands, volunteered to spearhead the latest hunt. On the appointed day for the "big hunt," we rode in the back of a pickup to a near-by ranch inhabited by a prestigious prairie dog colony. In no time whatsoever, the ladies were taking aim at the prairie dog holes. The women were good! Instinctively, they knew which ones to hit, and invariably they killed their targets.

Martha and I did not have guns or shoot any rattlers. We just gawked wide-eyed. When we saw a viper, we pointed at it and hollered, "There's one!' and covered our ears. Our main fear was that a big, fat snake might slither out of a prairie dog hole under the pickup, slide into it, and sneak up beside us!

Though an interesting experience, rattle snake hunting did not become our favorite family pastime. However, soon after our "big hunt," I learned that the largest rattle snake ever killed in Lipscomb was the one shot right on the parsonage lawn.

Since I didn't own a rifle and could not go hunting on our yard, I mowed down the grass, in reality the weeds. Nothing that could be called grass grew in that dry and parched land—not even artificial turf! At any rate, I sheared the weeds so short that even a centipede would not have been able to crawl unseen across our yard—much less a rattle snake!

Are you looking for something exhilarating to do with your family? Take a vacation to Lipscomb, Texas, and go on a rattlesnake hunting expedition. You'll never be the same again!

37

Testing Time

"We need a teacher-librarian!" This was the plea that came to us in Lipscomb from a small Bible school in Montana. The school year and my bus-driving job were about to end. Martha and I thought that the church needed a fully supported missionary pastor—no bus-driving job for him! We shared our thoughts with the church people. They agreed, but they also let us know that they were going to miss us.

I began to explore the needs of the Bible school and also of the church. For some reason, I called the Bible school president first. Lo! And behold! In the past, he had been president of a mission that served only rural churches. This valuable information enabled the church to contact that particular mission.

In the meantime, Martha and I prayed about the teacher-librarian position. Only a few years earlier, the plea for a teacher would have landed on deaf ears![7] Now, my ears were open to the plea, and so was my heart. God used the experiences in Lipscomb to change my perspective: (1) teaching the young people in the church and (2) interacting with them in the school bus.

The librarian position had a drawback, however. I had no training or experience. The only library skill I had was checking out books and returning them on time—most of the

---

[7] See "I'll Never Teach Again!" story #14 for the reason.

time. To become a librarian, I had to hit the books again! At supper that night, Martha and I had an informal Hartog-home-business meeting.

We discussed two items: moving and going back to school. John sat on his highchair, turning his head from left to right, depending on which one of us was talking. Then, we reached a decision: "Yes" for both items. Montana Institute of the Bible was going to get its librarian-teacher.

We planned the steps for the transition and started packing. Our plans went well as expected, with a few glitches, of course. Here are some highlights of the first step, "Starting Library Training":

(1) We packed most of our belongings, U-hauled them to Kansas, and dumped them in a friend's garage. They had to sit there until we picked them up at the end of that summer and U-hauled them to Montana.

(2) We crammed the rest of our belongings in the Mustang. Then Martha, John, and I headed for Dallas, where a seminary couple had sublet us their *tiny* apartment for the summer. This explains why most of our belongings ended up in Kansas.

(3) I enrolled at East Texas State University in Commerce, Texas, to pursue their graduate degree in library science. That's why we couldn't move to Montana directly from Lipscomb.

(4) Martha got a summer job in Dallas, where her parents were living; Papá Toñito was working on his doctorate at Dallas Seminary. John and Mamá Sarita got along splendidly! She talked to him in Spanish and he babbled back. They both giggled. She became his babysitter—an important determining factor for living in Dallas instead of Commerce.

Every week day that summer, I drove the 60 miles from Dallas to Commerce. While I was in classes, my 1964½ burgundy Mustang baked in the sun all morning. A sweltering car awaited me at one o'clock every afternoon. The steering wheel was so hot, that I could not hold onto it for more than a few seconds. You may wonder why I didn't turn on the air conditioner. The reason is simple: That was an extra perk when we purchased the car, and we could not afford it.

Testing day arrived at the end of the summer session. It was also a rainy day with a plus and a minus: The rain cooled down the hot temperatures, but it also made the roads slippery. I was driving east to Commerce at about 55 mph. Suddenly, the back end of the car swung around! I was still going east, but the front of the car was facing west. My car had hydroplaned!

Within a split second, the Mustang went into a spin on the highway and went around and around and around. Then, it slipped off the road and kept going around and around. In a flash, it slid into the ditch! A sea of green whirled around the windows. I was certain the car was going to roll over, but the slippery grass prevented this disaster. The car stopped abruptly at the bottom of the ditch and splashed into a foot of water.

A man in a pickup, who had been driving behind me, saw it all happen. The kind, burly Texan stopped on the side of the road directly above me and hollered with a deep drawl, "Are ya'll right?" He stepped closer and said, "Dudden look like ya'll r'hurt."

Then, he informed me that it would take a tow truck to pull my car out and told me to jump into his pickup. Somewhat disoriented, I jumped in beside him and hitched a ride the ten miles to Commerce. A crucial step for advancing library training awaited me. I dealt with that first. I took my exam.

Afterwards, the whole highway episode started to sink in, and my hands began to shake unexpectedly. For just a moment, I thought about what had happened and what could have happened. However, I was still alive! It was time to call the towing company.

Before long, a tow truck pulled up at the building where I was waiting and took me the ten miles back to the car. Then, the tow truck driver went to work. As I stood at the edge of the road watching the rescue, my delicate, slick pony-car held on tightly for dear life onto the powerfully-built towing hook. My Mustang looked beautiful rising from the watery ditch.

In spite of what happened that rainy day, with God's help I passed the test with flying colors. And so did my Mustang—with not one scratch on its lovely burgundy coat!

*True happiness may be
Sought, thought, or caught
But never bought.*

—Author unknown

38

Penny Pinching

It was the worst of all times; it was the best of all times; it was the time I was teaching at the Bible school in Montana. Since the school was small and did not have a lot of financial backing, our salaries were low. Nevertheless, Martha and I were able to pay our bills.

On the one hand, we had no car payments, and we only needed money to put in the offering plate; pay rent and utilities; buy food for the table, gas for the car and lawn mower, and clothes and shoes, especially for John. He was the only one who was growing like a weed. On the other hand, we had no savings on which to fall back. Our bank account stood at zero! But as long as our bi-monthly pay check cleared the bank, we thought no more about finances.

Then things changed! In the middle of the school year, the administration announced that there was no money to pay salaries for that two-week period. No one, from the president on down, got paid. We determined that we could survive for a few weeks until the crisis was over. But as it turned out, it was not a two-week problem. We went for five months without any pay checks.

We had to tighten our belts. That meant only hand-me-downs for "new clothes," and participating only in recreational activities that were free. Thankfully, the house we were renting belonged to the Bible school; it could not evict us for not paying the rent. We did not qualify for unemployment checks because we were not unemployed. We worked every day. We just did not get paid.[8]

For food, we had a few groceries on hand, and these took us through the first few weeks. The situation stretched to five months, but the Lord provided in unbelievably wonderful ways. On a farm near Billings lived a generous chicken farmer who raised layers—skinny white Leghorn chickens—whatever they eat turns into eggs. After about two years, the chickens get lazy, or tired, or just plain forget how, and stop laying eggs. They turn into fat white chickens.

These chickens become (1) Campbell's chicken soup; (2) chicken-flavored cat chow; (3) chicken-flavored dog kibbles; or (4) chicken-a-la-one-thousand-delectable-ways in the kitchens of Bible college teachers, after they pay a fee of 25¢ per chicken to the generous chicken farmer for cleaning them.

Whenever I came home from work, I did not ask my industrious, creative wife, "Honey, what are we having for supper?" but "Honey, what did you do with the chicken today?" Oh, yes, since the birds were old, their meat was tough. Therefore, either Martha cooked it all day, or we had to chew it all night!

Our small life insurance policy came in handy, too. We borrowed what we could from it. With that money we paid for gas to go to work and for food staples, besides chicken. One day, a brand new grocery store was having a "Grand Opening Day." They invited the public to their celebration. Besides the usual sales for such an event, they were also giving away two sacks full of groceries to a fortunate patron.

Of course, we responded gladly and thankfully to their *"Répondez, s'il vous plaît"* and went shopping on that "Grand Opening Day." Upon entering the store, every person received a ticket, each with a different number. When I heard the first

---

[8] During the summer, the Bible school caught up on all our back pay.

numbers blaring through the intercom, I instantly looked at my ticket. Unfortunately, I missed being the winner by just one number. It was so close, and yet so far!

I walked several aisles until I found Martha. She had not even bothered to take the ticket out of her pocket to look at her numbers. When I told her about my ticket, she took hers out and looked at it. The big smile on her face told me she had the winning ticket. We went home with two big bags full of groceries and two hearts full of gratitude.

We did not have much money to spend for those five months; but they were still the best of times. Because we all were in the same boat, the financial troubles bonded the Bible college family in a special way. For entertainment we played ping pong and table games at each other's houses and munched each other's home-made snacks!

Not one faculty member or staff member left the school during those five months. The close fellowship we had carried us through. It was the best of times!

Happiness is a cup of hot chocolate
By a warm fireplace on a snowy winter evening.

—John Hartog II

39

One in a Hole

Teaching Bible to college students was a blessing! Nevertheless, setting up the library became my main objective at the Bible college in Montana. After achieving my goal, Martha, John, and I moved back to Iowa. Here we bought our first house for $9,000. That's what a 600-square-foot house sitting on a double lot cost in Polk City, Iowa, our new hometown. I had accepted the position of teacher/librarian at Faith Baptist Bible College (FBBC) in Ankeny, Iowa.

In addition to the living room, that *little bitty* house had two bedrooms, one bath, a "linen closet" for the water heater; a floor furnace under a four-foot long "central hallway," and a kitchen-dinette area with hookups for the washer and dryer. By the time we moved our stove, fridge, table with fold-down leaves,[9] the youth chair,[10] and washer and dryer into the kitchen-dinette area, we had plenty of room to stand—as long as John was in the high chair!

The selling point of the home was its 750-square-foot detached double garage. We joked that as our family grew, we could turn it into a master suite and let the kids have the house. Its faulty feature that poor folk like us ignored was: it had no basement—only a creepy, crawl space, and it was barely deep

---

[9] We left the leaves on the folded down position to provide much needed room.
[10] This was a high chair minus the tray—the thrifty Dutch way to turn a high chair into a youth chair.

One in a Hole

enough for the floor furnace that was located under the four-foot long "central hallway." From the front side, all the houses in our neighborhood looked similar, except for the house number and paint job. But looks are deceiving!

To the south of us lived a young couple, a little older than Martha (I'm nine years older than she is), and they were also more uppity-up than us. They had built an addition to their 600-square-foot house; this doubled its size. They also had a boat parked by their double garage. Before long, we became neighborly with them. From John, my neighbor's real name, we learned that some of the houses now had basements. Using hand power and shovels, the owners had dug out the four-foot deep crawl spaces and had turned them into eight-foot basements.

As I heard this, I could feel my biceps expanding and my grip tighten around a shovel; and then I imagined myself standing alone in a 600-square-foot basement under our house! I decided to make that vision become a reality. After all, if some of the neighbors had dug out their crawl spaces to make basements, I could dig out our crawl space as well! Besides, we did not have the money to hire it out.

The only way to get into the crawl space was through one little basement window—about two feet wide and about eighteen inches high. I concluded, "If Martha, wearing a hoop under her wedding dress, was able to crawl through a narrow, church window on our wedding day,[11] I could crawl through that basement window today!"

One afternoon in early fall, I opened "my" window, *crawled* through it with a shovel in hand, and *crawled* around to survey the land. I couldn't stand up because it was only four feet deep. They don't call it a crawl space for nothing! Then I

---

[11] See "Wedding Bells (part two)," story #25.

dug in, shoveled the first shovel full of dirt, and threw it out that window.

Before long, I was one in a hole! I had a hole that was wide enough and deep enough for me to stand up in. Standing straight and pleased with my dig so far, I spanned the vastness of my "archeological dig"[12] and gazed up to the window. Instantly, a sun ray lit up my brain! It dawned on me that if I dug much deeper, I would not be able to reach the window. Scared out of my wits, I crawled out, ran to the garage, grabbed a small step ladder, shoved it through the window, and exclaimed, "There—that takes care of that!"

Outside, there was now a small pile of dirt. I shoveled it into my wheelbarrow and spread it out over the garden. Each evening after I got home from school, I dug out a little more. All this digging was good exercise after teaching all day. However, the more I dug out, the farther I got away from the window, and the farther I had to walk back with the shovel full of dirt. It was a slow process. Just like this story!

Moreover the days were getting shorter, and darkness arrived earlier, especially in my dig. I hooked up an extension cord for a light; then I could work longer. Crawling in and out of that little window was a pain on my back. Besides, I had to figure out some way to get into the basement after it was all done. Martha refused to crawl through a window ever again!

Bingo! An idea came to light, "I'm going to add a room unto the kitchen, just like the neighbors did!" Right then and there, I turned into a "self-appointed architect." In my head, which had plenty of room, I designed the whole addition: a dining room with a stairway room on the side.

Now, things were going to move faster. At least that's what I thought. Anyway, on the outside of the house, I dug a three-foot-square hole that I planned to enlarge for a future

---

[12] An appropriate name as you will see in the next story.

One in a Hole

basement stairway. Then with a sledge hammer, I pummeled the concrete blocks for the basement doorway. Getting a pain on my back every time I entered my dig was a thing of the past! Also, no more walking back and forth with a puny shovel! I plunked my wheelbarrow down the three-foot-square hole and introduced it to the dig.

If you think that all this talk about digging dirt is getting old, just think about what it was like for me. World Series to the rescue—it was that time of the year! I brought a TV down into my dig and watched the games while I dug out dirt.

All that digging created a big problem: Dirt! Lots of dirt and its disposal. We had spent $600 to put up a four-foot-high chain-link fence around our back yard. If I continued spreading the dirt back there, the fence was destined to become a one-foot-high chain-link fence. Martha rejected such a thought. They say, "Living with a Dutchman builds character." Martha is proof of that.

Somewhere nearby there had to be a big cavity that needed to be filled! We took a Sunday joy ride through town. Sure enough, right in the center of town, we stumbled onto an empty lot with a large ravine running across it. The owners said that my dirt was welcome on their property. Today, the ravine is filled; a gas station sits on that lot. But back to my story. All I needed now was a *BIG* old pickup to haul the dirt there.

About that time, a young man, who lived down the road, drove by in his *little* Model T pickup to check out my dig. Just what I needed! Seeing my plight, he kindly let me use his pickup to haul away the dirt.

That Model T wanted to make sure everyone knew we were coming with a load. Every now and then, it backfired with a loud "Bang! Bang!" that sounded like gunfire. One day I was driving down the road right by the town saloon, when the Model T decided to "Bang! Bang!" Almost immediately, the sheriff and several other men came flying out of the saloon. I felt like I was back in the Old West!

Fall gave way to winter. With the first hard frost, my dig come to a halt on Christmas Eve. I let my shovel hibernate through the winter. Also, I laid ply-wood boards over the "basement entrance" hole to prevent our water pipes from freezing. Nevertheless, on an extremely cold night, they still froze. I needed a blow torch anyway. I bought one and took care of that minor problem before any of the pipes broke. I also covered them with a thick blanket of insulation that kept them warm, even through bitter cold days.

A blast of wind must have moved one of the plywood pieces a little bit, just enough for stray cats to crawl in and set up housekeeping in my half-dug-out basement. I felt sorry for the critters and let them stay. We minded our own business, and so did they—quietly.

That changed drastically an early morning, just as spring was peeking around the corner. An earsplitting "yowling!" woke us up abruptly from a peaceful sleep. We put up with the "yowling" alarm clock for a few days, but it became louder and more frequent.

Then, one early Saturday morning, the high-pitched "yowling!" continued non-stop. We awakened downright perturbed and sat up quickly! Looking at one another's rumpled hair, we "yowled" at each other, "Yenough is yenough!"

I jumped out of bed, grabbed an old pair of shoes, went outside, pulled back the plywood, dashed into the hole, and flung an old shoe at the wall above a couple of yellow-eyed yowling cats.

Then it happened. What seemed like hundreds of yowling, petrified cats appeared out of nowhere in mass confusion! I stood flabbergasted, no longer one in a hole, as all the cats (twenty-four of them) made a beeline past me for the one and only exit!

I nailed the plywood over the entrance hole to ensure that the "*catas non gratas*" did not return and set up housekeeping under our house again. The plywood remained untouched, and my dig was put on hold until warmer days arrived.

*Happiness consists in being happy
With what we have got
And with what we haven't got.*

—Charles H. Spurgeon

40

Hold Your Tongue!

Our home had been bark-less for a couple of years. Wendy, our first dog,[13] learned to climb the barbed wire fence at the parsonage backyard in Lipscomb, Texas. On one of her escapades, she tore up her leg on a barb, resulting in an acute infection. Wendy passed on peacefully in the vet's office. It was time to get another dog! Martha and I liked Saint Bernards and miniature Dachshunds. Since our house in Polk City was so *little*, we opted for the *BIG* dog—a Saint Bernard.

About that time, we read an article that featured a purebred Saint Bernard dam that had whipped—oops! She had whelped fourteen puppies—all in one litter. The breeders had kept the picks of the litter, two female pups that were now a year old and thus housebroken.

We called the owners of that remarkable dam, and they said we could come to their house and see her. John was about two and a half years old and was looking forward to visiting the *BIG* dogs. We had advised him to be a good little guest: don't touch anything and stay close to us.

We arrived at the breeder's house, and three beautiful massive Saint Bernards met us at the door. John stayed close and did not touch! One of the pups was energetic with tan markings. The other pup was passive with dark mahogany

---

[13] See "Wendy, the Educated Dog," story #28.

markings. They say that opposites attract. John was energetic and blond. He liked the passive, dark pup. We did too!

However, getting this pup required time and thought. Wendy was a mutt that had cost us $10. This pup was a purebred that cost $150, fifteen times more than our mutt. After one week and several Hartog-home-supper-business meetings, we voted unanimously in favor of the pup. We devised a business plan with her as our partner. We would purchase her, breed her once, and sell all her pups to help cover her incurred expenses. In addition, although she was show quality, she was to be our family pet—nothing more.

It is my sole privilege as the head of the Hartog household to name our children and pets, except the chickens. Martha helps me name them. She gives them silly Spanish names, like "*Chiquita, Bonita, Chulita.*" Such a name was certainly an insult for a purebred Saint Bernard! Even before the new dog joined our household, I asserted my privilege and named her Juliana Bernardina Von Bora.

Her first name evidenced my Dutch heritage; Juliana was a former Queen of the Netherlands; Bernardina verified her breed; she was a Saint *Bernard*. Von Bora confirmed my eccentricity. This was the maiden name of Martin Luther's wife Katie. Of course, there's absolutely no connection there, except that the pup reminded me of Martin Luther's pictures, which I had seen in my church history books.

"Juliana Bernardina Von Bora," her registered name, was fitting for a beautiful, one-hundred-and-fifteen-pound purebred like her. However, "Juliana Bernardina Von Bora" was a mouthful to say, and soon our *gentle*, massive dog went simply by "Julie."

We picked up Julie in our Mustang. The breeders helped us shove her into the car, and stretched her body between the bucket seats. Her rump landed on the back seat, and her nose almost touched the gear shift. Then she moved and tried to take over the whole back seat. John kept telling her, "Move over Julie." Since she did not budge, she became his "dog seat."

When we arrived home, she took one look at our *tiny* house, and she refused to get out of the car. For one whole hour I shoved, heaved, and pulled one hundred and fifteen pounds of dead weight to no avail. Then a strong push finally thrust her out of the car, and she landed on the grass just outside the car door.

I tried to lift her up and move her, but each time I advanced only about five or six inches. When Martha came out to observe my slow progress, I asked her to bring a piece of meat as a treat to coax Julie. This helped, but it took another two hours of my coaxing and her crawling to reach the inside of our doorway. Here she flopped and slept through the night.

The next morning, she responded to her little master's touch. She got up and followed John and me to the back door; we walked outside with her so she could do her business. Having done that, she followed us back into the house on her own. Julie was home!

A small space next to the kitchen doorway was barely big enough to fit her water and food dishes. Every time she drank, she left a trail of slobber across the kitchen floor. Her back was even with the top of our table, and her tail, which seemed to wag constantly, knocked over end-table lamps and a few knick knacks.

At bedtime she squeezed tightly under our bed; only her rump and constant, wagging tail stuck out. There she slept and snored and shook us through the night. To protect our skimpy belongings, we gave her pig-leather "chew bones." But in a few bites, she had chewed them all gone, leaving "¡*Absolutamente nada!*"

It was time for Julie to move outside! We had put up a four-foot-high chain-link fence around our *BIG* back yard, which spanned the entire extra lot behind our *little* house. Julie could romp around and wag her big, bushy tail without bumping off things. Julie became an outside dog, but she remained closely attached to us.

She continued her daily, two-mile walks with Martha and John. The quaint trio triggered smiles on the faces of onlookers. John and Julie became close playmates; so I built them a playhouse—a roomy dog house—and put it in the fenced yard. We often found our dog and her boy cuddled in their "playhouse."

To help Julie pass the time, even though she had plenty of distractions, I went to a meat locker and bought a cow leg bone stripped of its meat. Julie loved to chew on those big bones, and she never buried them. She just left them lying on the grass. Our liquid propane (LP) tank was also located in the fenced yard. One day when the LP tank driver arrived to fill up our tank, I walked with him to the gate. Then, he saw Julie. Our big dog scared the burly driver half to death!

Like Julie when she first arrived at our house, the man refused to budge! Unlike her, he did not flop, but he stood firm and exclaimed, "No way am I going into that yard with *that* dog!"

Smiling I replied, "She's as gentle as a little lamb!"

Then he pointed to the big bare bone and mockingly exclaimed, "Sure! Is that what happened to the last guy that went in?"

He handed me the end of the gas hose over the fence and shaking nervously yelled, "Here! Hook it up yourself!" He directed me how to do it; then he opened the truck valve so that the gas could flow.

Julie had a rumbling bark that could be heard all over our neighborhood. Shortly after we brought Julie home, new neighbors moved into the house next door. Julie was not used to them; and when they came outside, she barked and barked at them. I decided to put an end to all that barking.

Soon after moving in, the neighbor lady came out to shake some rugs, and Julie's bark thundered through the air. I went outside and shouted, "Julie! Be quiet!"

The lady brought her rug-shaking to an abrupt stop and ran into her house. The next couple of days Julie did not bark much, nor did we see hide or hair of the new neighbors.

A few days later, Martha baked a pie and took it next door as a "welcome to the neighborhood" gift. After introducing herself and John, Martha asked the lady, "And what is your name?"

"Julie," she replied.

Martha smiled nervously and said her good-byes speedily. When I came home, Martha told me about her visit and encouraged me to go next door and get acquainted with the neighbors. I went and was met by a husband, a wife, and a little girl. After introducing myself and telling them about *our* Julie, we all laughed! They realized it was *our* Julie that I had told to be quiet.

The little neighbor girl and John played together often. As a result, he came up with a great solution to the name dilemma. His buddy was "Julie Dog" and the mommy of the neighbor girl was "Julie Lady."

We still had to call down "Julie Dog" when she barked; but from then on, before we shouted, "Julie, be quiet!" we glanced to our neighbors' house to make sure that "Julie Lady" was not shaking some rugs.

41

The "Archeologist"

Flowers were in full bloom, and the trees sported shiny, fresh new leaves. April showers had brought May flowers, and graduation had brought the school year to an end. I had taken time out from the half-dug-out basement during the winter. It was time to wake up my shovel and start digging again. Back to work!

As I dug my way farther from the window, I saw something half-buried in the dirt: a wheel and a bicycle-like handle. Instead of digging to the contraption, I crawled closer to it and discovered my first "archeological find" in my dig. It was a hand-powered cultivator from the 1940s! I dragged it outside through the basement window. It was a tight fit.

Once outside, I pushed the cultivator a few times, and it worked like a charm; it was just a little rusty. In time, I gave it a new coat of red paint and got the wheels moving faster with a quick WD40 oil spray. The "archeological find" got a new lease on life. Forty-five years later, I'm still using it in my garden!

No sooner had I returned to my dig, than it had to be put on hold again. As a college teacher I had summers off, but as a student I had summer school. I must hit the books again and resume my library degree. The plan had been to finish it in four summer sessions. I had two done and two to go. This time, we went the practical route. Martha and John stayed in

Polk city, with Julie as their guard dog; and I drove down with Mamá Sarita to Texas.

Now you're wondering, "How did Martha's mother end up in the car going to Texas?" The explanation is simple: She came up from Dallas to inspect our "new house." At least that's what I thought. In reality, however, she came to inspect the "hole" under our new house. When she saw it, she put the crazy idea in Martha's mind that the house was going to cave in!

Before Martha's mother and I left for Texas as we were outside saying our good-byes, she gave Martha a final order. Pointing to the hole and then to me, she told Martha—in Spanish, of course, "Hire someone to shove the dirt back into that hole while he's gone this summer!" And off we went! All summer I hoped that Martha would disobey her mother, this one time.

When summer school was over, I made a beeline to Polk City, hoping to find everything like I had left it. And everything was fine—the hole was still there! I resumed my digging and kept at it until school beckoned again. The plan was to start the addition in the fall and complete it by the end of that year.

Like the excavation of the basement, the addition had to become a reality through the labor of my own hands and on a frugal budget. Financial know-how is an inborn Dutch trait, but my building know-how was zilch. The death of my dad, when I was six years old, had robbed me of some practical knowledge that fathers used to pass down to their sons, like mechanics and construction know-how.

As usual, my venture had taken some planning. This time instead of lists, it was a hand-drawn "blueprint" of the addition. I knew that I was bound to run into glitches, since my construction know-how was zilch. However, I was eager and willing to learn how to build. I put my tired, old shovel to

The "Archeologist"

work on my second dig—the crawl space under the soon-to-be addition. I only excavated a crawl space to save time and money; a basement required twice as many concrete blocks. That's most likely why the original builder went the crawl-space route as well.

With the crawl space dug out, I asked more questions. Since I didn't have the know-how, I had to learn the hows. So I learned how to put in a foundation and how to lay concrete blocks. Our 600-square foot house was about to increase by thirty-three and one-third per cent. The ten-by-twenty-foot addition that I had designed looked good on paper, but now I needed help putting the wooden expansion on concrete blocks.

Thus, I lined up some work for my hammer and saw. It was time to ask another question: "How do I frame walls?" My "How-to-Build Handbook" became Dr. Art Walton, a faculty member at the Bible college. Often when I asked him building questions at school, he answered them with pencil-lined drawings. He got tired of this. With his hammer and saw in hand, he showed up at my building site. I became his apprentice.

He worked with me on the floor joists and the plywood sub-floor. Next, it was time to frame up the walls! I had no idea how the penciled walls on my "blueprint" were to turn into real wooden walls, but Art showed me how. We constructed each wall by laying it out on the floor according to my design, including the windows and the door frames.

It was exciting to see the walls go up in our *tiny* "hut." My learning curve was on full speed, but I still had a lot more to go. After the walls were up, Art asked me to get him a small stub of about eight inches. I took an eight-foot stud, cut an eight-inch stub from it, and handed it to him.

Instead of saying, "Thank you," he hollered, "Don't ruin a full stud! Find the smallest piece that is big enough and cut what you need from it."

Point well taken! Being a good Dutchman, I learned that lesson well. Art then passed on to me his passion: He taught me how to roof. Nailing the shingles on that roof was elating. It is a job that I enjoy to this day.

From that exhilarating roof-top experience I had to go back down to my gloomy crawl space and dig. By now I was tired of trade school. I knew nothing about dry walling and mudding; the whole process was clear as mud. Besides that, our budget was reaching zero. The completion of the addition must come to a speedy conclusion. I covered the walls with light colored paneling and the floors with inexpensive carpet tiles. The addition was finished!

Martha was thrilled. She and John could jump and run in a fourth of the house without worrying that it was going to cave in. The addition became our family room. Martha and John dragged stuff into it from the rest of our house. They moved the dining room furniture and youth chair from the kitchen; the TV from the living room; and the toy chest and little rocker from John's bedroom. It was the shortest-distance move we have ever made. Our addition was completely furnished, and we didn't have to go into debt!

In the meantime, I went back to my first dig. In time, as I dug dirt from the edges to the center of the crawl space, I ran into *the* supporting post. Since the house was so *little*, one wooden supporting post was plenty. The remaining weight of the house rested on the outside walls. Yet, I couldn't just knock out the old post. It was too risky.

With that in mind, I put up two new adjustable steel support posts, one on each side of the old wooden one. Now the old, tired post could retire from its job. That old post was

The "Archeologist"

6" x 6" and rested on a concrete block; excavating completely around it exposed the second "archeological" find of my dig.

My new "archeological" discovery was a gigantic 4' x 4' x 4' block of worthless concrete! After removing the old-tired center post, I tried to demolish the worthless monstrosity with a sledge hammer, but all that pummeling did not cause even a dent.

I did not want to have the huge concrete block as part of my basement décor, but ten men could not have lifted it and carried it outside. I decided to bury it. Right beside it, I began a second-level dig—a deep 5' square grave. I was almost done digging the enormous grave, when Martha made her appearance—her first one since the onset of my dig.

She has an aversion to basements, and she thought I was crazy for excavating one. Moreover, convinced by her mother, Martha worried constantly that the house was going to collapse any minute. She certainly didn't want to be under the house when this happened!

That day, she only stood at the doorway and surveyed the dig. She looked at the hole, and with a stunned look, she asked me, "Are you crazy? Whom are you planning to bury there? Me?"

Guess who's crazy? I didn't answer her. I simply pointed to my worthless "archeological find."

I always wondered why physics was required in my high school academy. That day I found out why: because some day I might have to figure out how to *lift* and *dump* into a hole an old concrete block that weighed tons more than I did.

I put my almost long-forgotten physics to work. I rested the middle of a long metal pole on a pile of concrete blocks. Then I wedged one end of the pole into the sand under the edge of the gigantic block on the side away from the hole. Next, I pushed down with all my might on the other end of the pole that was sticking up in the air like a titter-totter, and immediately the back of the block raised up and tilted toward the hole—just enough so that the huge old, concrete block tipped over, and fell into its grave.

This is all to say, "I did it!"

If you think the whole procedure sounds confusing, you should have been there when I was trying to figure out what end was what, and what end to push so I that didn't tumble into the hole and end up scrunched up in that 5' x 5' grave. Back in those days, I was 6' tall! (I've shrunk since then.)

Using the principle of leverage, I had sent the worthless "archeological find" to its final resting place—under the basement floor. No one, except Martha and I, and now *you*, know where that is and will always be!

Make a joyful shout unto the Lord, all ye lands.
Serve the LORD with gladness:
Come before His presence with singing!

—Psalm 100:1-2

42

"Those Amateurs!"

The crawl space was now a basement space! I hauled the last pickup load to the ravine and flung the last shovel full of dirt with great delight. My dirt barely made a dent on that spacious cavity; filling it required that all my neighbors with crawl spaces follow suit.

I returned the Model T to my benevolent neighbor, walked back home, and went directly into my 600-square-foot cave—not through a *little* window, but through a *BIG* doorway. A sense of satisfaction surged deeply within me as I surveyed the land. This time I walked, not crawled; and I stood straight and pleased without a shovel in hand.

Next on the plan, was the basement floor—the future headstone for the humongous, concrete cube, already buried 5' below. I prepared the ground for its concrete cover. To ensure that our house did not become a status symbol with an indoor swimming pool, I laid out a drainage system: (1) I put drain tiles around the perimeter inside the new foundation and several laterals going out from the center of the basement. (2) I dropped a sump pump in a corner pit to catch the water from the tile and laterals. (3) I covered the drainage system with pea gravel.

The basement was ready for its concrete floor. Well, not quite yet. I wanted the floor to slope to the sump pump pit. Using 2 x 4s, I laid forms around the outer edges and slanted them toward the pit. Now it was ready! Let the ready-mix concrete trucks roar!

Oh, one minor glitch. I needed help! Once the concrete trucks began to arrive, it would have been impossible to keep up with them all by myself. Accordingly, I set up a "recruiting office" at the college. Only one brave man volunteered. He was the head of the maintenance department; we referred to him affectionately as "Uncle Herb."

Now we were ready! On the appointed day, I arranged for the ready-mix trucks to come. Uncle Herb and I were dressed in tattered, old clothes and high rubber boots; we were equipped with shovels, hoes, and a wheel barrow. Our plan was to start at the far-off corner of the sump pump pit, then work toward the *little* window where the "hole-project" began.

And then it arrived! The first ready-mix truck roared up and parked behind the house, stretched out its long spout, and shoved its tip through the *little* window. In concert with its revolving drum, concrete began to flow down the basement into a wheelbarrow.

Uncle Herb and I walked back and forth with our wheelbarrows, and we shoveled concrete to the rhythm of the revolving drum. Pushing the wheelbarrows, which were loaded with the heavy slushy concrete, was grueling because of the soft clay on the ground. But we carried on.

On one of my trips toward the window, I heard a voice resound through the basement, "Do you need help?" Without looking back, I replied, "We can use all the *volunteer* help we can find!" On my trip back with a loaded wheelbarrow, I looked toward the entrance and saw a burly man and a grade-school-age boy. By their looks I could tell they were father and son. Both of them were complete strangers to me.

Not taking the time for introductions, the big guy grabbed a shovel and started moving concrete. Instead of shoveling to the rhythm of the revolving drum as Uncle Herb and were doing, the stranger set his own pace—fast and furious. Working in a frenzy, he tore out one of my 2 x 4 markers, and then another.

I yelled, "Don't . . . !"

But before the words, "move those," came out of my mouth, the speedy worker walked up to the window and hollered to the truck driver, "Add three percent more water!"

Hearing his commanding voice, convinced me, "This stranger knows more about this than I do." I let him demolish all of my 2 x 4 lay-out. It was obvious that the forms were needless. He was able to slope the floor by sight. With his muscular build, determination, and speed we completed the concrete work much earlier than expected.

After the third and last truck left, he asked if I had any trowels handy. I had planned well, and had bought several. I handed him a trowel, and immediately he went to work. As he troweled the concrete, he looked like a whirlwind rotating on the basement floor. Uncle Herb and I got out of his way and watched him in amazement.

Then I turned to the boy, who was sitting on the stairs and did not seem fazed by the commotion. "What does your father do for a living?" I asked him.

The boy replied, "He is a concrete contractor." What a blessing! The concrete truck parked at our house must have caught the burly man's attention.

When he was done troweling, he looked down at Uncle Herb and me and gave us this order: "Keep an eye on it! When it gets hard enough, you can trowel it again, to give it a smooth finish. I will be back later about five o'clock."

Uncle Herb and I waited until four o'clock. We thought that the concrete looked hard enough to trowel again; so we decided to go to the far corner and trowel our way back to the stairs. When we arrived to the corner and turned around, we were shocked by what we saw! Our foot prints had left their mark on the semi-hardened concrete.

I said, "We better back out of here and cover our tracks!" We did not rotate like whirlwinds but strained rigorously all the way back to the stairs, troweling concrete that was setting up more and more.

Just as we reached the stairs, we looked up and saw the burly man standing at the entrance. This time he did not holler, "Do you need help?" Instead he looked at the floor with a scowl on his face and bellowed, "Those amateurs!"

He picked up a trowel and rotating on the floor like a whirlwind, he troweled the whole floor again. Then he turned to us, with a resigned look on his face, and exclaimed kindly, "That's the best I can do after you left tracks in it!"

I replied, "Thank you so much! It looks great!" Uncle Herb nodded his head in agreement.

Our "amateur eyes," could not detect any of our tracks anymore. However, whenever we mopped the basement floor, shallow pools in the shape of footprints appeared on the concrete—a reminder that we were certainly amateurs after all!

43

Family Expansion!

Some things happen according to plan, others happen as surprises! The business plan we had devised with our Saint Bernard, Julie, as our partner developed feet the moment we bought her. She began incurring additional expenses when we put up the chain link fence. It was time to put our business partner to work.

We were at the pet store looking at puppies, when Martha's gaze landed on a *Dog World Magazine.* Featured on its cover was the most beautiful, mahogany-marked, massive Saint Bernard! It was a pedigreed stud whose breeder lived in Independence, Iowa. The business plan developed running feet. As soon as we returned home, we contacted the breeder. He informed us that he must examine Julie to make sure that she was worthy of his stud.

Exam day *of* Julie arrived. We bathed and brushed her, cleaned her ears, brushed her teeth, trimmed her nails, and squeezed her sweet muzzle. She truly looked smashing—better-looking than that stuck-up stud on *Dog World Magazine!* It was her job to convince the breeder of that. And she did! We agreed on the pick of the litter as stud fee. He hauled Julie off to Independence, where she remained for a week.

Nine weeks later, Julie surprised us with six beautiful puppies: A, B, C, D, E, and F (practical names as she whelped them). Okay. I named them, Annie, Bruno, Cathy, Dirk, Elsie, and Fanny. About ten weeks later, Cathy, the pick of the litter, went to the breeder; and he sold her for $300. The rest of the puppies found loving, responsible homes with no problem at all; but we cried every time one left our home. Julie had done her part as our business partner. In fact, she had paid more than her incurring expenses.

The biggest surprise that year was not planned! All those puppies woke up the motherly instinct in Martha. Surprise! Surprise! She became pregnant with our second child. I won't bore you with the details but will fast forward to a month before her due date. It was now the middle of January—the bitterest time of winter. As usual, we planned well ahead.

John was getting a roommate. We set up the port-a-crib against a wall in his bedroom—opposite to the wall where his youth bed sat.[14] Martha went into nesting mode. She dusted, vacuumed, and mopped every corner in the house—as if it needed it. As when she was pregnant with John, Martha's intuitive "ultrasound" became active.[15] She sensed that she was going to have a boy again. It's a good thing she had kept all the baby items from John. She washed and ironed everything—as if it needed it. The make-shift "nursery" was ready!

I also got into the action and performed the manly duties. I took care of the transportation matters. The Mustang underwent a partial transformation: a tune-up and a thorough clean-up—it needed them. I drove the Mustang to Sears where a mechanic replaced two old—bald tires with two brand new ones—it needed them. The car was ready.

One Sunday evening, two and a half weeks before Martha's due date, we came home and had our regular after-church light snack. Martha devoured almost a whole loaf of bread in the form of cinnamon toast. Pregnant women crave the weirdest

---

[14] We had transformed John's big crib into a youth bed by keeping one side railing on the down position.
[15] Seventeen years later, in 1987, 3D ultrasound was developed by Olaf von Ramm and Stephen Smith at Duke University.

things! That night, it was as if cinnamon toast was Martha's last fling!

We went to bed after our "light snack." No sooner had we started snoozing, than the pressure from all that heavy, soggy cinnamon toast caused a deluge. Martha's water broke! Instantly in the darkness, she reached for the phone and called Dr. Mintzer. He instructed us to drive to Iowa Lutheran Hospital right away! No problem, we were ready!

I got out of bed and flipped the light switch. We were still in the dark. I fumbled my way throughout the house; it's a good thing it was *little*. I discovered that the kitchen and living room had electricity; the bedrooms and bathroom did not. A fuse had blown.

Still in darkness, Martha phoned Mrs. Drake, a kind church lady who had offered to help with John. In no time at all, Mrs. Drake arrived to pick up John. He was sleeping soundly—as usual; and he kept sleeping, even when I picked him up and put him in Mrs. Drake's car. He woke up the next morning in an Iowa farm house that was familiar to him.

As I walked through our house, my ears picked up the roaring sound of the hard-working floor furnaces. It was a bitter, cold January night; the actual temperature outside was -29°. The furnaces roared constantly trying to warm up our *little* house, which unfortunately had hollow walls—they had no insulation whatsoever in them.[16] "¡*Absolutamente nada!*"

---

[16] We had discovered this when we built the addition.

My 64½ Mustang, Martha and Our Sons

Family Expansion!

When I went outside to warm up the car, instantly I saw, of all things, one of the brand new tires was as flat as a pancake! I needed help! I thought it was too late to wake up anyone, except Art Walton. The Waltons also lived in Polk City, just a few miles away from us; and we had become close buddies.

Art often had said, "If you ever need help, just give me a call." Art and his wife, Ginny, had adopted a boy and a girl. When Martha got pregnant, Art and Ginny rejoiced with us; and they were eager to hear Martha's updates as her pregnancy progressed. That night, I called Art with the latest update. He said he was coming right away. Martha remained calm. We bundled her with a blanket to protect her from the bitter cold; then we shoved her into Art's car and headed for the hospital. Keep in mind that Art had never rushed to a hospital a woman who was about to have a baby.

My buddy drove fast and safely to Lutheran Hospital. He found a parking place close by the emergency entrance, and the three of us rushed into the emergency room (Art and I helped Martha along).

The three of us sat down and answered preliminary questions. The three of us, Art, a nurse, and I, walked briskly to the maternity ward (The nurse was pushing Martha in a wheel chair).

Right before we came to a lounge, the nurse turned around and looked at both of us (Art and me) and asked, "Is this your first child?"

Before I could say a word, Art spoke up, and pointing to me, said, "It's his second, and my first!"

The nurse gazed at him in astonishment. Martha almost jumped out of the wheelchair and pointed to me but said nothing. Surprisingly, she couldn't talk! The nurse, however, got the point.

This time, looking only at Art, the nurse said, "Sorry, sir, this lounge is only for the fathers awaiting babies. You will have to leave." Poor Art left. He would await my call. The nurse told me to sit in the lounge and then wheeled Martha to . . . I have no idea where!

In those days, a husband was not allowed to go beyond the small lounge. He was required to stay there biting his nails until the doctor came in and said, "Congratulations! You have a boy!" (or "You have a girl!" or "You have twins!" or whatever he had fathered). Then, a nurse led the nervous, confounded father to the room where, sure enough, the wife sat on a bed holding a baby!

After I waited almost twelve hours in the lounge, Dr. Mintzer finally came in and said, "Congratulations! You have a boy!"

Immediately I called Art and Ginny and gave them the *LATEST* update: "We had a boy!"

Martha's intuitive "ultrasound" had been right again. I, the head of the household, named our new arrival Paul Anthony Hartog.

Happiness is not perfected
Until it is shared.

—Author unknown

44

Lions and Tigers and Bears

Lone Star State! Ready or not, here we come! The seminary in Dallas called me to serve as assistant librarian, and I accepted the offer. We moved back to Texas around the time when some safaris "moved" from the African savannah to savannah-like prairies in America. Lion Country Safari landed in Grand Prairie, Texas, a suburb of Dallas.

A safari park is a large zoo where the animals roam free, and the ones in cages are the visitors. They drive in their "mobile cages" (cars) on paved roadways that snake through the safari zoo. Visitors must obey three basic rules, which are posted visibly throughout the park: (1) Drive slowly and carefully. (2) Don't stop too close to animals. (3) Keep doors and windows closed at all times!

When we heard about the fascinating safari near Dallas, we decided to explore it. The five members of our distinguished expedition were these: Martha and I, John (he had just turned five), Paul (a-year-and-a-half-old toddler still in diapers), and Michelle (Martha's two-year-old niece, also still in diapers). We planned and packed for the adventure.

Martha put water, lemonade, and snacks in a cooler and stuffed it with ice. She also packed a change of clothes for the children and extra diapers[17] for Michelle and Paul. Martha

---

[17] These were cloth diapers. Though disposable diapers had made their grand appearance, we could not afford them!

always packed extra when we were gone from home more than two hours. In an empty plastic bread bag, she stuffed half a dozen wet washcloths to keep little hands and faces spick-and-span. Most importantly, I had taken care of my manly duty. I had a custom-air-conditioner installed in our Mustang. Come what may, we were ready!

We crammed into our Mustang and took off, happy, clean, and cool. When we arrived, we joined a caravan of mobile cages full of gawkers like us. We drove slowly and carefully to avoid stopping too close to the animals. And, yes, our cage doors and windows remained shut the whole time. We all *"oooo-d,"* and *"aaah-d"* as zebras and antelopes galloped, ostriches strutted, and rhinos lumbered past our cage. Giraffes reached up high for their leafy munchies.

Next, our caravan arrived to the sector where the primates performed their antics. From our cage, we gaped at the apes jumping up and down, with out-stretched arms—opening their mouths in a wide grin, as if mockingly shouting, "We are free! We are free!"

Suddenly, a handful of monkeys decided to go for a ride on our Mustang. They pressed their faces on our windows and ogled at their *little* gawkers squealing with glee. That's why rule #3, "Keep windows and doors closed," was a good rule indeed. Also, that's why our well-thought-out plan began to fall apart as usual,

The outside temperatures were rising higher and higher; but inside we were still happy, clean, and cool, munching on our snacks. The new air conditioner was circulating its cool breeze properly, but we ran into a glitch: We could not stop and gawk too long! We had to keep moving, to get the air flowing through the radiator, to prevent our air-tight cage from overheating.

Our convoy arrived to the highly advertised selling sector that drew all the trekkers to the safari: the *BIG* cats—the lions.

Lions and Tigers and Bears

They roamed freely around the caged "hunters" who were in front of us. They were shooting their cameras and forgot to keep moving. We came to a complete stop, setting off a domino effect reaction that caused our well-thought-out plan to fall apart.

Our car began to heat up, which forced me to turn off the engine; which caused the air conditioner to stop working; which then stopped the cool breeze from blowing through the air vents. The inside temperatures began to race with the outside temperatures and won!

The children, especially Paul, became a great concern. It was time to go on survival mode! No need for the packed extra clothes! We stripped the children down to their undies. Their bodies were sweaty and red. Martha wrapped ice in the wet washcloths and used them as ice packs on the children's faces, arms, chests and legs. The children were clean and cool, but not happy!

Martha reached into the cooler, grabbed two hands-full of ice, handed the frozen cubes to the children, and instructed them to rub them on each other. Their squealing and shivering noises filled the hot air in our Mustang. The children were clean, cool, and happy again. Every so often, the engine cooled down a little, and I ran it to have air conditioning for a few minutes, but not for long.

We could not risk opening the windows, not even a *little* bit, to let in a breeze because the lions were meandering too close—right by our doors.

Caged in our Mustang, we wished it could gallop away swiftly. Instead it took one more hour to reach the last gate where we said our happy good-byes to the lions. The entire journey through the zoo safari took us two hours, one of those in a sweltering pen. It was not global warming. On the contrary, it was localized car heating—something that we hope not to experience ever again. For sure, we will not go through another Lion Country Safari in Grand Prairie, Texas![18]

With great expectation, Martha and I look forward to that new earth with vast savannahs and splendid "Lion Country Safaris," where wolves will live in peace with lambs, and leopards will lie down to rest with goats; calves, *magnificent lions* and bulls will eat together, and a little child like John or Michelle or Paul will lead them![19]

> *Happiness is contagious—*
> *Be a carrier.*
>
> —Author unknown

---

[18] The Lion Country Safari in Grand Prairie, Texas, opened in 1971 but closed in 1992. Of the six Lion Country Safaris that opened in the early seventies, only the original one in Florida exists today.

[19] See Isaiah 11:6-7.

45

Apartment Living (part one)

Hundreds of lamps had burned the midnight oil in "Old Relic"—what Martha and I called the now dismantled campus building; it had housed seminary students and their families for many years. Martha, John, Paul, and I,[20] along with several other families, were the last to call the Old Relic, "home sweet home."

Our family was the only non-student family in Old Relic. The seminary made an exception for two obvious reasons: One, the building had a few vacancies. Two, the seminary was about to speed up the effects of the Second Law of Thermodynamics on poor Old Relic.

Soon after we moved in, rumors started circulating that, in the near future, Old Relic was going to be demolished from under our feet. The blueprints for the latest campus lay-out proved it! However, the small tenant community of Old Relic ignored all the rumors and the blueprints, and we carried on as usual. Some tenants were newly weds; others were couples who had been married longer and were multiplying and filling the earth—particularly Old Relic.

In stark contrast to the old decrepit building, stood its pristine next-door neighbor, the seminary library, which was the most recently built seminary structure and was to

---

[20] Sadly, moving into seminary housing meant leaving Julie in Iowa. A nice church family welcomed her into their farm home.

be the trend-setter. Our family lived in an apartment on the side facing the library, about fifty feet away, not far enough to justify a home phone. We saved money on phone bills! Moreover, I could sleep in later, walk home for lunch, and come home earlier than if we had lived in the suburbs, like most of the faculty and staff did. No fighting Dallas rush hour traffic for me!

Living in Old Relic had its advantages. One was completing my masters in library science without having to leave my family for the summer. The greatest blessing was the bond that tied Old Relic neighbors as we awaited imminent eviction.

Our upstairs neighbors were Mr. and Mrs. Karamish[21] who were from India. When Mrs. Karamish cooked, curry scent spread its invisible but strong tentacles throughout our building and into the nearby library. For Mr. Karamish, the scent became his dinner bell. Whenever he was studying in the library, and the curry-scent bell rang quietly, he packed up his books and rushed home to enjoy whatever Indian delicacy his wife had concocted.

Downstairs next door neighbors in Old Relic shared "front" and "back" entries. Two refrigerators were jammed in each front entry. Instead of visiting at the well, like in Bible times, the ladies visited at the front-entry refrigerators and often discussed the menu for the day. The stairs going to the second floor were in the back entries.

If we had to hide something from our neighbors, we snuck it in through the back entry. Living in a close-knit community at Old Relic required wisdom to know where, when, and how to do what you needed to do, in order not to be too chummy and not be too aloof.

---

[21] Not their real last name.

Apartment Living (part one)

Our next door neighbors were a recently-married, young couple, Don and Donna.[22] As it was the case with several, newly-wed couples, Don and Donna's honeymoon had been their trip to Dallas. Since we shared entries, we became good, front-entry friends, but hardly ever saw each other at the back entry. It was a well-balanced relationship. Through our front-entry visits, Don and I discovered that both of us liked plants.

One evening, I went out to get a glass of milk from our fridge, and I bumped into Don as he was getting a snack. He told me about his failed attempts to grow a plum tree from seed. As I listened to his sob story and asked questions, his answers told me that he had done every thing right.

He had planted the seeds in rich-soil pots; he had put them in a sunny south window (a tricky thing in an Old Relic apartment); and he had watered the soil faithfully; but none of the seeds had sprouted.

I took a drink from my glass half-full of milk and asked him, "Where do the seeds come from." He replied, "From a can of plums." I just about chocked! And between coughs, I exclaimed, "No wonder! (Cough . . . Cough . . .) Those seeds have been cooked!"

With an of-course-I-should-have-known-that look on his face, he said, "Oh!" Later, as we became more front-entry friendly, I learned that his college degree was in botany. That explained the of-course-I-should-have-known-that look on his face!

The front entries promoted friendships, but they also created predicaments. One Saturday morning, Martha and the boys went across the driveway to visit a Costa Rican family. I slept late because I had worked into the night. When I got up, I set out my "Breakfast of Champions." Still in my pajamas and tussled hair, I stepped quickly into the front entry to grab

---

[22] Not their real names either.

some milk. Instantly, the door closed behind me, and I heard the lock click. My first reaction was to hide, but where?

Our apartment faced the side of the library that was all windows. Sitting at their carrels[23] in their glass "houses," the students could look right into my front entry. The moment I barely stepped past the fridge, they would see me, the Assistant Librarian, in my pj's! I pushed the fridge a little bit away from the wall—the space was barely big enough for me to squeeze into it.

I was a front-entry prisoner until Martha and the boys returned at noon. She saw me squatted in a corner in all my morning glory and hollered, "What in the world are you doing out here still in your pajamas!" She darted back into the kitchen without hearing my reply.

Our one-bedroom apartment was spacious because it was at the back end of Old Relic. The kitchen was small, but not crowded since the fridge was in the front entry. The bathroom served as a laundry room with no dryer.[24] The huge dining room was also the boys' bedroom and playroom. For my office, I claimed the walk-in closet. The narrow, comfy-sized living room remained just that. Martha and I settled in the one and only bedroom furnished with a double bed and dresser.

Since John and Paul were small, our apartment was *plen'y* big for our family. Then, we joined the ranks of couples who were filling Old Relic and the earth. Our family grew!

---

[23] Not choir member chairs, but single-seat cubby-stations for students.
[24] We stored our dryer in our back-entry closet under the stairs going up. Clothes lines were our dryer. Martha washed and hung out diapers daily.

46

Apartment Living (part two)

Yes! Our family grew—temporarily. A year after we became residents of Old Relic, Michelle, Martha's niece came to live with us for about eight months. Soon after that, Sam and Damaris, a Cuban couple, asked Martha to baby sit for their daughter, Monica. During the week, she spent the afternoons and evenings in our apartment. Sam enrolled in seminary, and Damaris, a registered nurse, worked at Baylor Hospital.

At that time, John was five years old; Michelle, almost two; Monica, about twenty-two months; and Paul, eighteen months. Consequently, Martha took care of three children who were two years and under and also a five-year old. Our one-bedroom apartment was no longer roomy! Michelle moved into my little office, where we crammed a youth bed and a small dresser. I moved my office to an upstairs carrel in the library.

We went shopping for fun—for other people, that is. Strolling through the isles, we sounded like a walking charismatic service, with a small congregation speaking in English, Spanish, and baby talk in both languages! By the end of the school year, we had lost two members of our congregation: Michelle went back home in March, and Monica went on a summer vacation with her family.

News that eviction was just around the corner traveled fast throughout Old Relic. The seminary was starting its campus expansion soon after graduation. The first phase of the grand plan was the demolition of Old Relic. The news was bad news and good news. The bad news was that our family had to find temporary housing for three weeks; so I could fulfill my seminary contract. We had already planned on moving to Indiana at the end of the summer.

The good news was that the boys were about to experience something wonderfully creative, which they had never experienced before and have not experienced since then. Up to that point, we had instructed the boys with this firm command: "Don't color on the walls!"

When the demolition news reached us, our severe instructions changed drastically. We presented the boys with brand new crayons, brushes, and water colors, and instructed them, "Here! Color the walls all you want!"

Our apartment walls became gigantic easels for our ecstatic, budding artists. For a month before eviction day, while a crew worked outside removing the brick veneer from Old Relic, inside our young Michelangelos created their frescoes on their spacious walls.

Then, a second crew recycled the old bricks by chipping off all the mortar from them. The mortar-less bricks brought a good price from builders who re-used them on new houses. Unfortunately we could not preserve the art work of our precious children.

It was time to move—to three different places, within a few weeks, in two different vehicles; and Martha did not know how to drive! Most of our stuff was going back to Montana. Our bodies and a few belongings were landing for a two-week Dallas-lay-over in a *tiny* cottage close by. From there, our bodies and the few belongings were scheduled to travel and land in Indiana on a nine-month, "resident-student visa." These moves took a lot of planning!

While I worked in the library, Martha took care of the complicated matters. She weeded and sorted our household belongings. Then, she sorted the leftovers and packed them

Apartment Living (part two)

according to their destination. I took care of the manly matters: the transportation vehicles.

To haul most of our belongings to Billings, Montana, I purchased a big old Budweiser Beer truck (empty, of course) for $75. When Martha saw the truck, she was indignant! She couldn't stand the idea of her two little boys and their mother advertising Budweiser Beer all the way from Dallas to Billings!

The vision of my wife, my two innocent boys, and then me driving a beer truck had crossed my mind, but the price of the truck wiped out that vision instantly. Martha calmed down when I told her that my plan was for the truck to get a new paint job. I didn't tell her who, how, or when.

I parked the truck in an inconspicuous corner on the seminary campus; ran into the maintenance shop; asked Mr. Montoya, the boss, if he had any left-over paint that he could spare; and he directed me to a tall shelf in the back. A palette of colors in the shades of a rainbow stood before me. I thanked Mr. Montoya and borrowed a five-gallon bucket. Into it I poured the paint from all the cans, and mixed it feverishly, as Mr. Montoya watched in amazement.

After my rigorous stirring, the paint turned into a drab grayish green, similar to the color on the walls at Stearns Hall.[25] That's why schools never throw away anything. It might come in handy some time. It always does! This time, old paint was to grant dignity to an old beer truck. However, my plans began to fall apart. The more I painted the truck, the better acquainted we—the beer truck and I—became; and the less I trusted it to haul our belongings all the way to Montana. Instead, a U-Haul must take up that privilege.

Still, I finished covering the truck with its new coat and drove it to a Chevy dealer. Ignorant of the truck's dubious

---

[25] See "Rats!" story #19.

background, he offered me $175 for it. While haggling with the salesman, a pre-owned pickup with a topper caught my eye; and I made a deal. I traded the green truck and my burgundy Mustang for that red Chevy pickup—a transaction I regret to this day. The pickup had a topper but not an extended cab; since the boys were little, all four of us fit nicely in the front.

We U-Hauled our belongings to Billings, and we dumped them in the basement of the Forsbergs, a dear elderly couple. We promised to return in nine months. The Forsbergs waved good-by with a worried look on their faces, wondering if we would keep our promise.

The next day, we boarded a half-empty Greyhound bus back to Dallas. To stretch out our legs a bit, we asked the bus driver to drop us off in Denver, Colorado. Here we visited Aunt Dora and Uncle Ed for two days. After a little sightseeing, we headed down to Dallas in a jam-packed Greyhound bus. From the Dallas Greyhound station, we took a city bus back to Old Relic. Its "D-Day"[26] was scheduled for next day.

We loaded the pickup with our few personal belongings and packed my books in a small home-made trailer. We drove a couple of miles to the *tiny* cottage located in the back yard of Pappy and Abuelita Lincoln, another dear elderly couple. Once upon a time, the *tiny* cottage had been an unattached double garage. It was renovated into a furnished, one-bedroom bungalow with a three-quarter bath, a living room, and a small kitchen. Instead of housing ordinary paraphernalia, the garage became a cozy haven for seminary couples. Sam, Damaris, and Monica, our Cuban friends, lived in this cottage during the school year; and they were letting us sublet it for three weeks.

While we were setting up our temporary *mini* home, massive Old Relic was about to go down permanently. Our

---

[26] Demolition Day

Apartment Living (part two)

seminary library work almost came to a stand-still when the demolition began. Every staff member rushed to the windows to watch in amazement the annihilation of Old Relic—the library's next-door neighbor. The contractors brought in a wrecking crew with a crane that had an enormous steel ball on a chain. The crane raised up the ball and then let it drop on Old Relic, over and over until all its walls came tumbling down!

Old Relic had disappeared forever from the Dallas Seminary campus, but not from our memories.

*Domestic happiness depends on
One's ability to forgive as God forgave us.*

—John Hartog II

47

A Christmas to Remember

Our social status went up when we moved to Indiana. From a downstairs, one-bedroom unfurnished apartment in Dallas,[27] we moved to Winona Lake into an upstairs, one-bedroom furnished apartment with two walk-in closets. We were there for one purpose: to complete the one-year-residence requirement for my doctoral program in theology.

But, the moment we arrived in our old pickup, with a home-made trailer full of books, my family's social status tumbled down the outside stairs that led to our high-rise pad. I was simply a poor seminary student!

A narrow front room welcomed us, furnished with a fold-down table, folding chairs, couch, desk, and fold-down double bed. To the right was the walk-in closet-kitchen with only standing room for the cook. The front room opened to a hallway that led into *the* bedroom with twin beds, a dresser and a walk-in closet. At the end of the hallway was the bathroom.

Immediately, the boys staked out the hallway as their "playroom." Each one claimed a twin bed in *the* bedroom, and all four of us shared the dresser and the second walk-in closet. The front room was the living room, dining room, office, and our bedroom. Every night, Martha and I moved the furniture to make room for our fold-down bed. A stubborn cranny—not

---

[27] The 3-week stint in the tiny, furnished cottage doesn't count!

a granny—ran across the mattress resulting from its folded-up position all day long.

We unloaded the pickup and found a place for everything since we had only what we needed for nine months.[28] Our plans were to live on a measly budget. Martha calls it *"eating frijoles y tortillas."* Besides taking a full load of graduate classes, I had to work to support my family.

The seminary had no grants or scholarships for doctoral students; but seminaries and libraries go together; so do librarians and libraries, especially libraries that need cataloging librarians. Bull's eye! I had a job! The seminary hired me for thirty hours a week and allowed me access to the library 24/7. It was a blessing indeed.

Martha, my loyal help-meet, also pitched in. She took care of our sons and the apartment; she also typed all my papers, babysat a neighbor's two-year-old boy two afternoons a week, and cleaned a neighbor's house once a week for $5. She and I hoped to hold up my diploma and yell, "Debt free!" Thus, we cut down our expenses like never before.

We put the pickup on a diet; we fed it only one tank of gas a month, because it worked only on the Sabbath and rested for six days. We let our feet do what God meant them to do: walk!

I walked to the seminary and back home twice a day.[29] John also walked to school and back home. Because we didn't want John walking alone, Martha and Paul walked to and from school twice a day. The whole family walked together to church; and for recreation, we explored the town and the lake

---

[28] The seminary allowed me to park the trailer full of books in an inconspicuous spot.

[29] I went home for supper and family time then returned to the library to work or study.

where John and Paul fed the ducks. We had no phone and no phone book. We let our feet do the walking![30]

After all that walking, Martha was ready for a ride! She refused to wash our laundry in the lake, and we could not hunt the ducks for food. Therefore, on Saturday, our pickup went to work. We rode a few miles away to Warsaw, the nearest town with a Laundromat and grocery store. We bought no pre-packaged food and no junk food. Our next stop was the day-old bread store where bread cost ten cents a loaf. From there we went to an egg farm and bought cracked eggs for twenty-five cents a dozen. We ate them and lived to tell about it! When we came home, the old pickup went back to rest for a week.

We did not have to walk into a clothing store. Before we left Dallas, Martha had shopped at the Sears Roebucks catalog for the boy's clothes, especially for John's first-grade wardrobe. Besides a few new clothes, Paul also had his brother's hand-me-downs. Due to all the walking, Martha and I did not gain weight and outgrow our old clothes!

The semester was soon drawing to a close. Thanksgiving had set the holiday season in motion, and Christmas was just around the corner. A young couple invited us for Thanksgiving dinner at their loft apartment. Martha brought her home-made dinner rolls and pumpkin pie. We gave thanks to our God for faithfully providing our daily needs.

Two weeks later, half of my doctoral residence year was behind us, and we were just one dollar over our budget! We had little money in the budget for Christmas. Moreover, our Christmas decorations were stored in Montana. We had none—"¡*Absolutamente nada!*" Nevertheless, that did not hold us back from celebrating Christmas. Every penny we had saved from Martha's earnings that semester was a penny saved for our Christmas fund.

---

[30] My work phone number went to relatives for emergency use only.

With those savings on hand, we took the boys Christmas shopping. First, we visited a Christmas tree farm. We looked at the beautiful trees and watched people picking just the right tree. Then, I noticed a pile of freshly trimmed branches.

I asked the owner, "May I have a few of those branches?"

In the spirit of Christmas, He replied, "Certainly, take all you want." And we each grabbed a handful.

Next, we went to the store and bought a few inexpensive presents, a spool of string and some construction paper in assorted colors. When we got home, I made a small tree by tying small evergreen branches to a bigger branch. The typewriter retired for a few days, and the tree took its place on the desk. Martha, John, and Paul made chains and small, multi-colored-cut-out figures from construction paper.

From the cracked eggs we selected half a dozen barely-visible-hair-line-cracked ones, blew out their "innards" through a pin-hole, and the boys painted them to resemble fragile "Christmas balls." The tree wore a pretty necklace made of popcorn "beads."

For the top of the tree, I made a big cardboard star, which Martha covered with aluminum foil. Just as long ago a star had directed the wise men to the Savior, our shining star directed our attention to our Savior. The only thing missing was the lights. But our tree did not need them. As we admired our gracefully decked-out tree, our eyes lit up with delight!

On Christmas Eve, we celebrated Jesus' birthday as we always do. To reflect on His birth, I read Luke 2, and we responded to Luke's tender description of our Savior's lowly birth by singing "Away in a Manger." Along with the boys, Martha and I pantomimed the melodious Christmas carol. I sang off key; John and Paul sang the melody; and Martha sang the harmony.

Our gifts to one another, in remembrance of God's greatest Gift, were few and small—most of them were homemade. Our special treat that night was hot chocolate and sugar cookies, which John and Paul had decorated.

Away from the usual glamour and glitter, our simple celebration in our humble abode, helped us focus on what Christmas is all about: It is remembering our glorious Savior's humble birth.

That Christmas in Winona Lake was one of the nicest Christmases we have ever celebrated. One we will always remember!

And the angel said unto the shepherds:
"Fear not, for, behold, I bring you good tidings of
great joy, which shall be to all people.
For unto you is born this day in the city of David
A Savior, which is Christ the Lord."

—Luke 2:10-11

48

The Black Out

Because of the self-imposed limits to our driving during my year of residence, we were unable to go home for the holidays or attend any out-of-town family activities. All this was about to change at the onset of the second semester.

One January morning while I was working in the library, my mother called to tell me the heartbreaking news. My five-year-old niece, Donna, had lost her fight with leukemia. Because we did not have a phone, I had to wait until supper to tell Martha about it. Disregarding our skimpy budget completely, we determined to drive straight through to Iowa for the funeral.

Since we had no money for motels, we returned to Winona Lake right after the funeral and drove all night. It was a long and tiring ride. I had to go to work the next morning, with only a few hours of sleep and overwhelmed by sadness at the loss of a little niece.

It was a beautiful morning! The sun was shining brightly through the windows, which spanned almost the entire south wall of the library. As the morning wore on, my work station became warmer and warmer. I got up and went out for fresh air, but a coworker stopped me. He talked a long time. Not wanting to be rude, I stayed there to listen.

All of a sudden, I felt lightheaded and fell backwards hitting my head on the concrete floor. I blacked out and have no recollection of what happened during the following two days. As I lay unconscious on the floor, my coworker realized right away that this was an emergency. He called the hospital in Warsaw, the town next door, and requested an ambulance. He also called one of our neighbors to notify Martha.

This neighbor, the mother of the little boy whom Martha babysat, came over to our apartment with the shocking news. Martha didn't know how to drive; so the lady waited a few minutes while Martha and Paul got ready; then she drove them to the hospital.

Martha had no idea what lay ahead in Warsaw. Her immediate response was to pray and ask God for peace and strength. God answered her prayer.

The doctor's report at the Warsaw hospital was discouraging. He told Martha that I was in a coma; X-rays revealed a fracture across the back of my skull; and I needed special care as quickly as possible. This meant that an ambulance had to transport me forty miles away to a larger hospital in Fort Wayne.

Our kind neighbor took Paul home with her, and Martha accompanied me in the ambulance to Fort Wayne. When the first responders wheeled me through the big hospital doors into the emergency room, I woke up briefly but immediately went back into the coma.

The neurosurgeon placed me in ICU and gave no hope to Martha about my survival. I was thirty-six years old, the same age that my father was when he passed away due to blood poisoning.[31]

Visiting ICU patients is limited—only a few minutes every hour, but Martha came and stayed all day. While in ICU, I underwent several tests.

During one of those tests, I remember shouting, "Get that log off from under my neck!"

---

[31] See "That House on Second Street," story #2.

The Black Out

Two days after I came out of the coma, Martha told me that the "log" was actually a rolled up towel, which a nurse had put under my neck during the test. I remained in ICU about a week; then was moved to general hospital care and remained there two more weeks. Nevertheless, the time went by fast since Martha was allowed to be in my room all day long. The doctor had expected me to be hospitalized a minimum of six weeks, but many people prayed. God graciously enabled me to leave after three weeks.

When Martha accompanied me in the ambulance to Fort Wayne, she had no idea how she was getting back home, or if she would find the boys there, or who might have taken care of them during the day. She had been in the Ft. Wayne hospital from mid-morning till about ten at night, and was allowed to see me only for ten-minute segments every hour. She used waiting time and the hospital pay phone to call my mother. She then passed the news around to the rest of the family.

While Martha waited in the ICU lounge, Wayne Knight, one of my seminary classmates, showed up. He drove Martha back to our apartment where she found the boys fast asleep. The next day, and every day of my hospital stay, Wayne put our old pickup to work. Its routine of six days of rest and one day of work on the Sabbath was over!

Since Martha did not know how to drive, Wayne drove her to the hospital early in the morning and returned to pick her up every night shortly after ten o'clock. During the day, several ladies took turns taking care of our boys. They were always tucked in bed when Martha arrived home from the hospital. This way, my dear family was able to have breakfast together before they went their separate ways.

After my release from the hospital, the doctors put me on restrictive activity. I could not work at all for a month, then only ten hours a week through the end of the semester. This meant that I could not earn enough money to support the family, but our hope was in God to see us through. He had supplied our daily needs during the first semester; we were confident He was going to provide for the second semester as well.

Our budget, like our social status, went tumbling down our outside stairs. Instead, our loving-kind God provided abundantly through His kind-loving people. The church had a food shower for us, and the walk-in closet off *the* bedroom became a pantry. It was as full as Grandma's pantry after canning season.

The people also gave us frozen meat and other frozen food. They did not know that our fridge freezer held only two ice trays one on top of the other. The church then let us store our food in their freezer. Before the accident, all we had was hamburger and chicken. Now we had roasts in the freezer.

One day, we were able to share a pot-roast meal with a family of four, who visited us all the way from El Salvador! They were "ambassadors" from Martha's parents and were especially representing her mother. Mamá Sarita had sent the Salvadorians to check up on us. All eight of us crowded in our little apartment and enjoyed God's rich blessings. John, Paul, and I sat and ate as Martha and her friends jabbered in Spanish.

A couple of galvanized milk "offering cans" labeled, "For the Hartog Family," showed up in strategic locations on the college and seminary campus. Moreover, at one of the basketball games, the college students passed around a blanket and yelled, "For the Hartogs!" The fans threw coins and bills into it.

After I came home from the hospital, my eyes were unable to focus well enough to read. My kind seminary professors allowed Martha to read aloud to me the required text-books and collateral reading for all the courses. One was a thick volume entitled, *Strong's Theology.* The outcome of reading the fine-print on that book was that Martha found another love—theology! Her help in a difficult time was a great encouragement, and I was able to pass all the classes with high scores.

Without God's provision, it would have been impossible to survive. Also, He graciously overruled the unwise decision we made not to have health insurance during that school year. The medical expenses we incurred because of my accident were the highest we had ever had. Again, God provided through His people's generous-monetary gifts and worker's compensation. By the end of that summer, all of our medical bills were paid.

Physically, it took me more than a year to get my strength back. The lasting effects of the head injury were only to my sense of taste, smell, and hearing. They all are diminished to some degree. Thankfully, the focusing ability of my eyes returned after a few weeks.

That year of residence taught us many lessons. The first semester we learned to be content with what little we had, to be careful with the money we earned, and to be thankful for God's daily provision.

The second semester we also learned anew that God is sovereign and greater than all man-contrived plans; that we have no guarantee that we will live to see another day, so we should make every day count for God; and that He uses His children to provide for His suffering people. We also should help those in need.

God had allowed this trial in our lives to teach us to trust Him. Trusting God through inconveniences and small ordeals had prepared us to trust Him through a big trial. Trusting God through this big trial has enabled us to trust Him through even greater suffering. We thank God for providing abundantly above what we could have imagined—not only the material needs, but most importantly granting us greater faith to trust Him.

That year of residence at Grace Theological Seminary involved more than just a theological education. We also had the opportunity to put that education into practice. Because of it, we can say with all confidence: Our loving-kind God is truly worthy of our trust!

> *Happy is he*
> *That hath the God of Jacob for his help,*
> *Whose hope is in the LORD his God.*
>
> —Psalm 146:5

49

Horse Mountain

Our nine-month, "resident-student visa" expired! It was time to trek northwest to Billings and move to our new home—in a roundabout way. We drove east to Fort Wayne for a last checkup with the neurosurgeon. He put me on anti-seizure medication because of the head injury I had sustained. We went back west to Winona Lake, oblivious of how the medicine was going to affect me on our roundabout trip to Montana.

We loaded up our few belongings in our pickup; found our long-lost, home-made trailer full of books; hooked it up to our old, red pickup; and traveled west to northwest Iowa to my mother's house in Orange City. After visiting Mother and other relatives for a few days, we resumed our journey.

Four happy campers, without a care in the world, looked forward to a smooth ride in our pickup pulling a trailer full of books. Our family was excited about leaving our cramped quarters in Winona Lake and moving to Big Sky Country. Once settled, we hoped to take a vacation—something we had not done in years. We dreamed and talked about going to Yellowstone National Park. In the meantime, our focus was to reach Billings, Montana as fast as we could.

Then it happened. I was driving merrily down the highway. And suddenly, I saw two cars coming at me. I was not sure which one was the real one. I turned to Martha, and she assured me that it was only one car. Sure enough, it was no more than one!

For a split second, I had seen double. It was truly unnerving! I figured the vision problem was merely fatigue; we took more breaks than usual and traveled more leisurely. Because my double vision reared its ugly head every so often, we got our longed-for vacation sooner than we had planned. Our journey turned into a "moving vacation."

We took a few minor sight-seeing detours. In South Dakota we marveled at the Corn Palace structure; visited four stone-faced presidents at Mt. Rushmore; had a good time daydreaming through the surreal Bad Lands; and gazed at Crazy Horse eager to be completed so he could gallop into the clouds. Then tired but unwavering, we stood up to Devil's Tower in Wyoming. John and Paul romped around the gigantic tower; Martha and I walked behind them and rested every now and then on a park bench.

Soon after we left Devil's Tower, Paul noticed that his black and white Teddy bear was missing. It was special because Martha had sewn "button-earrings" on its ears. Our mental backtrack led us to the Holiday Inn in Rapid City. Paul had obviously left it there, and it was too far to turn around. We promised to buy him a nicer one in Billings. Paul was sad but satisfied.

As we continued our scenic trek through Wyoming, we came upon a sign that said, "You are now entering the open range." I reminded the boys that in Iowa, all the farmers had fences to keep their cows, horses, and pigs from wandering away. But fenceless "open range" was a feature in some western states, like Wyoming. Our pickup, pulling the trailer full of books, took us on a roller coaster ride as it "chugged" slowly up the foothills and "rolled" faster and faster down the steep decline on the other side of the hills.

Horse Mountain

All went well until we came over a hilltop and saw a herd of forty to fifty wild horses galloping toward us from the right. I tried to slow down the best I could, but I knew it was a hopeless situation. If I stepped on the breaks too quickly and too firmly, the trailer was bound to jackknife and we would roll over. But if I kept going too fast down the incline, we were certain to plow into the whole herd of horses.

As we came unto the herd, my eyes saw triple, not double! The herd was split into three groups: Some had crossed the road, some were on the road, and others were ready to trot unto the road. A slaughtering house was about to open for business on the open range!

I shot up a prayer and shouted to Martha and the boys, "Quick! Bend over and put your head on your lap!" I hoped to protect them and prevent them from seeing the impending horrible accident.

In answer to my prayer, the horses on the road galloped into the left ditch, and the ones to the right stopped suddenly and stayed in the right ditch. We drove straight through the middle of the herd, missing horses by no more than a foot on either side. After our near collision with the wild-galloping targets, they raced off in a cloud of dust over the open range.

With our hearts racing but thankful, we headed northwest to Billings, Montana. We had escaped the looming carnage without a scratch!

50

Ditch all Your Belongings

We were heading deliberately northwest to reunite with our belongings in Billings. Our plan was to say, "Hi!" to them; then drive another 120 miles northwest to Lewistown, Montana; from there veer twelve miles northeast to the Judith Mountains; and then meander about four miles through the lovely Maiden Valley, until we reached our final destination. Martha, my directionally impaired wife, needed to know all this!

The Bible college where I was going to teach was moving that summer! It had bought an abandoned Air Force radar base in Maiden Valley. Lewistown, the nearest town, is at the exact center of the state. The Lewistown newspaper once claimed that the kitchen sink drain in a certain Lewistown residence was the precise center of Montana!

When something is a lot of trouble or bother, the Dutch say, it is *"drucht."* Moving to a new house is a lot of *drucht*. Moving a college to a new campus is a lot of *drucht*—multiplied ten times over! It involves relocating all the office, dormitory, and classroom furnishings; all the library books, all the maintenance equipment, and all the household belongings of the faculty and staff.

Nevertheless, this move was *not* as *druchty*[32] for our family. We were arriving in Billings, with all our earthly

---

[32] There's no such Dutch word. Martha made it up and uses it frequently.

Ditch all Your Belongings

possessions already packed in three places: our pickup, our small trailer, and the Forsberg's basement.

When we arrived in Billings, the Forsbergs were jubilant to see us! We had kept our promise to return. We were packed and all set to move, but no one else was ready. The school let us crash for about a month in campus student housing—a two-bedroom furnished trailer home near the Forsbergs. We unloaded the bare necessities from our pickup, unhooked the trailer full of books, and settled down to "student life" for part of the summer.

Four events happened while we waited to move. First, as soon as I could, I went to a neurosurgeon in Billings. He cut my medicine in half and told me that the med's double-vision effect would lessen in time.[33]

Second, we went to visit our friends, Corky and Leola. They had a tree house twelve feet up. Paul, who was three and a half years old, climbed it with John and our friends' children. When they climbed down, Paul didn't see them. He tried to go down the ladder the way he had gone up—head first; and he tumbled down from the top. He fractured his elbow on a rock.

Paul ended up in the Billings hospital for almost three days. He underwent emergency surgery. To make matters worse (from Paul's point of view), he missed his black and white Teddy bear. To cheer him, I rushed to Sears and bought him a Winnie the Poo Bear. Paul was still sad and not satisfied.

Third, some of the school family went on a tour of our new campus. When we arrived at the lovely Judith Mountains and drove through Maiden Valley, Martha and I were awed at the exquisite valley that was going to be the location of our next "home sweet home."

---

[33] Eventually the double vision disappeared and so did the medicine.

The Air Force had built the usual buildings to operate a radar base. It also included twenty-seven three-bedroom houses with attached garages. The chain-link fenced yards stretched up to Bureau of Land Management timber. The school assigned and rented these houses to administrators, faculty, staff, and to a few student families. We thought we were in paradise, not only because of our beautiful house, but more than that, the scenery all around us was breath-taking.

We returned to Billings eager to move. But not yet! We must participate in the fourth event—my brother's wedding. We got in our pickup and headed east to northwest Iowa to my mother's house. On the way, we stopped at the Holiday Inn in Rapid City.

I went inside and asked them if, by any far-fetched chance, they had found a black and white Teddy bear with "button earrings." The manager stared at me as if I were crazy, led me to a door, opened it, and a big closet full of stuffed animals and blankets stood before me. I found Paul's bear right away. Paul was thrilled!

We stayed at Mother's overnight then drove straight south to northwest Arkansas for my brother's wedding in Gentry. My vision problem did lessen, but all that driving aggravated it. My brother's wedding turned out be a "double" wedding.

Two Pauls promised to love and provide for two Velmas. And two Velmas promised to love and obey two Pauls. After the wedding, we headed straight north to northwest Iowa, rested a day at my mother's house, and then headed northwest to Billings, Montana.

Our roundabout meandering before moving was over! When we returned from the wedding, we joined the excitement and commotion taking place at the old college campus in Billings. Martha and the boys helped the Forsbergs pack their belongings. I walked to the school buildings and packed

Ditch all Your Belongings

the library books and furnishings. Loading day arrived, and everyone helped.

Crammed-full cars, pickups, trailers, and a few U-Haul trucks formed our moving caravan that traveled northwest on US Highway 87. Our pickup, pulling the trailer full of books, took its place behind a U-Haul carrying the president's possessions. That U-Haul broke down somewhere by the half way point. The radiator fan came off and came right up partly through the hood.

We all pulled over to the side of the road. Highway 87 was not particularly busy that day, but those who drove by stared in amazement at our caravan. They were wondering what such a long line of vehicles was doing on the side of the road in the middle of nowhere!

The cities and towns in Montana are few, and the distance between them is long; and not too many of these towns have U-Haul drop-offs or pick-ups. The only towns between Billings and Lewistown are Roundup and Grass Range, and we had no cell phones or short-wave radios to call for help.

One of the college-staff fellows drove to Roundup and called U-Haul to send out a new truck. In the meantime, we began unloading the disabled truck; took out every item; and put it in the ditch along the side of the road. Surrounded by all the paraphernalia on the ground, the old truck with its hood up looked as if it had spewed out all of its entrails!

By the time the new U-Haul arrived, daylight was about to say good-night; we began to load the truck quickly. We had packed the old truck carefully, but not this new one. With so many people shoving everything into the truck in such a hurry, it was difficult to keep track of what stuff was going where. We wanted to get on the road and get going before dark. Ultimately, everything fitted on the truck again, but not in the same order. That was not surprising. Moving casualties resulted from this fiasco. Someone loaded a heavy item on top of a beautiful, round oak table—splitting in half its center pedestal. Thankfully, a woodworker who was able to repair it lived in Lewistown.

We arrived in Maiden Valley late and tired, but happy to be home. We slept on the floor in our own house and left the unpacking for the next day. And the next day did come. When the majestic morning sun finally appeared over the mountain peak, the whole valley glowed. The pine trees sent forth their delightful scent, and the quacking aspen clapped their leaves.

And we rejoiced! The scenery was gorgeous. It might have been a lot of *drucht* to move, but moving to Maiden Valley was more than worth it all!

*All happiness is a perfume
Which you can't pour on someone
Without getting some on yourself.*

—Ralph Waldo Emerson

51

Just off the Road a Piece

Big Sky Country, one of Montana's nicknames, fits it to a tee. In land area, Montana ranks as the fourth largest state in the U.S.A. after Alaska, Texas, and California. However, in population, Montana is forty-fifth. When we were there in the seventies, its population was about 700,000 (4 people per square mile). California, a little bit larger in size, had a population of about 20,000,000 (136 people per square mile). In contrast to California's heavily populated areas with 1970's smoggy skies, Montana's skies were and are clear and their color is truly a beautiful sky blue. Yes! Montana is Big Sky Country!

Because of its large land area and small population, Montana's highways are not heavily traveled. Montana had no-speed-limit daytime driving, until the Federal Government imposed 55-mph-speed limits to save oil. Resenting this kind of federal intrusion and not needing the revenue, the Treasure State[34] set up a $5 citation as a speeding fine for "misuse of a natural resource."

The speeding penalty had to be paid on the spot, and it did not affect a driver's record. Travelers, who had to get somewhere fast, stuffed their pockets with $5 bills. At night the speed limit was 55 mph, enforced by a speeding ticket that did affect a driver's record.

---

[34] Treasure State is another nickname for Montana.

Montana's residents also are used to traveling farther to carry on typical activities like shopping or going to the doctor. We had not lived in Montana long when we became personally involved with its traveling culture. A church, 200 miles away from Lewistown, asked me to preach at their Sunday services. As a native Iowan, I figured that a round trip distance was like driving from the Missouri border to the Minnesota border and back—400 miles!

Martha and the boys went with me. We never knew what awaited us on these Sunday trips, but we all enjoyed the fun, fellowship, and food with Montanans. One Sunday for lunch, our cheerful hostess flipped a huge, juicy, sizzling steak on each of our plates. With a twinkle in her eye, she hollered, "Eat it up!"

John and Paul looked absolutely astonished; their eyes were almost as big as the steaks! Of course, the boys couldn't "eat it up!" even if they had only a little of everything else on the table. We took a "doggie bag" home and had enough steak for another meal. No question about it, ranch meals in Montana were marvelously delicious and plentiful.

That particular Sunday, as we eagerly anticipated our church ministry 200 miles away, we got up with the song birds and headed to our destination in plenty of time for the morning service. We were spending the day with our "mystery" host and returning home after the evening service. It was about a three-and-a-half-hour drive each way, and we planned to be back home by 11:00 that night.

We had a blessed day as usual. On the way home, we drove by a pickup that was stopped by the road side. It appeared that a young family was inside the cab. Martha and I looked at each other; without saying a word, we agreed to stop. Being a Good Samaritan is an important aspect of Montana traveling culture. In view of that, I turned around on the spot and parked behind the family in need.[35] The young father said he had car trouble and asked if we would take him and his family home.

I asked him, "How far is it?"

He said calmly, "Oh! It's just off the road a piece."

Taking him literally, I replied, "Sure I'll take you."

His wife, their two children, Martha, and our two boys, crawled into our pickup box and crunched down under the topper. When I glanced inside to make sure everyone was settled, both mothers sat with their arms around their children, who looked like little chicks hovering under their mother's wings in a cozy chicken coop. Nobody complained. The husband climbed into the cab with me, and we headed to their house *down the road a bit.*

I turned to the father and said, "Just guide me there."

After about a mile, we turned right unto a black-top road that eventually became a rough gravel road. Anxious about the up and down jarring effect on the crowded-box travelers, I asked the man, "How much farther is it?"

He sat up and replied casually, "Oh, just a bit!" Then he yawned and stretched and reclined on his seat.

After about forty five minutes, the road became a dirt trail. Before I turned and asked, "How much farther?" the father exclaimed, "We are almost there!"

Suddenly, a house loomed in the darkness. We had finally arrived to their house *down the road a bit.* When the ladies and children got out of their "cozy chicken coop," they were a little rattled but much relieved. We said our good-bys, and John and Paul jumped back in the cab with us. We slept the rest of the way home—except for me, of course.

The *"off the road a piece"* to their house ended up being over forty miles *one way*! We had driven about *eighty miles*

---

[35] Back then, it was safe to stop and offer help, especially since the towns are so far away from each other.

out of the way before getting back to the spot on the highway where we had picked them up. Instead of returning by 11:00 o'clock that night as we had planned; we got home about 1:00 o'clock the next morning.

A few days later, when I told a seasoned Montanan about our "off-the-road-a-piece" experience, he replied jovially, "Oh! Forty miles off the road is not much in Montana—be glad it wasn't farther!"

*The really happy man is one
Who can enjoy the scenery on a detour.*

—Author unknown

52

I Beg You, Have Mercy on Me!

Ten years! That's how long it took Martha to learn how to drive. After the minor crash on her first driving lesson,[36] Martha refused to drive. However, she claims that, even if she had gotten behind the wheel, she only would have driven around and around the seminary parking lot because of three reasons: first, accident # 1; second, accident #2; third, accident #3. We were involved in three accidents in rush hour traffic in Dallas, and none of them was my fault (really!). We were rear-ended twice and sideswiped another time.

Stubbornness, a Dutch trait, happens to be also a Spanish trait. When a Spanish woman marries a Dutchman, over time she becomes double-stubborn. This is what happened with Martha. She flatly refused to drive, even when I was seeing double!

Then, she changed her mind about driving—we moved to Big Sky Country! To Martha, the sparsely-traveled highways of Montana seemed like a gigantic seminary parking lot. Although she dislikes shopping, she liked to go to Lewistown just so that she could turn around and drive right back home. The view of the Judith Mountains from Lewistown to Maiden Valley was breath-taking. Thus, Martha wanted to drive to town by herself whenever it suited her fancy.

---

[36] See "Drive, Baby, Drive!" story #21.

However, gas prices had gone up, the pickup was a gas guzzler, and Martha refused to drive it. Soon after our 480-mile Sunday round-trip in the pickup, we went on a 240-mile round-trip down to Billings. There, we dumped the well-driven pickup on a Chevy dealer, and he dumped on us a lime-colored, sub-compact, hatchback Vega that functioned well for the first twelve thousand miles; then it metamorphosed into a lemon, lime-colored Vega.[37] For now, the conditions for Martha to learn how to drive were perfect: a Martha-sized car on sparsely-traveled spacious highways.

We went to the driver's license station in town for a learner's permit and a driver's license book. As soon as we were out of town, Martha decided to get behind the wheel, and I got in the passenger seat. Up to then, I thought seeing double while driving our pickup was unnerving. Being in the passenger seat as Martha's driver's education trainer was double-unnerving! You need to know that Martha pushes buttons and pulls levers and then asks, "What's this for?"

When we got home, she hit the driver's license book and studied it from cover to cover. She almost memorized it! In the meantime, Martha took advantage of every opportunity to drive. She braved driving around Lewistown, and she liked to take side roads.

Driving in spacious, seldom-driven highways, where day-light speed limits are not enforced, resulted in Martha's adopting two bad-driving habits: She acquired a lead foot, and she doesn't like driving behind any vehicle. When she comes upon another car, she says, "Get out of my way," even if the driver in front of her can't hear her. Also, she's constantly trying to figure out ways to pass vehicles that are in front of her.

---

[37] The Vega's problems tarnished both its own as well as General Motors' reputation. Production ended with the 1977 model year.

I Beg You, Have Mercy on Me!

Martha was ready to take her driver's test, except for one minor hitch. She did not know how to parallel park. The few times she had tried it, either she had driven over the curb and had started mowing the grass with her spinning back tire, or she had nearly locked bumpers with the car in front of her and behind her.

After a few more tries, she said, "Oh! Forget it!" I replied, "You won't pass the driver's test!" I tried to talk her into waiting until she had learned how to parallel park. However, being a Spanish/Dutch woman, she refused to learn how.

Driving exam day arrived! She passed the written tests with flying colors. Then, she got behind the wheel, and a patrolman slid into the passenger side. Brave soul! He had Martha go through the typical rigmarole for a driver's test.

Then, just as the patrolman was about to ask her to parallel park, Martha turned to him and begged him, "Please don't make me parallel park. I have never paralleled parked in my whole life and never will." The patrolman raised his eyebrows and gave Martha an "Are you crazy?" look.

But she went on, "I promise that when I come to town, I will always park at the grocery store parking lot and walk to wherever I need to go."

Craziness like stubbornness is contagious. The crazy patrolman replied, "Ok. Just pull into that parking lot across the road."

Martha "passed" the driver's test and got her license without parallel parking. To this day, she has never parallel parked. It's a good thing that the patrolman didn't ask her to back up. To this day, she can't do that very well either!

53

Where Has All My Honey Gone?

"Bees!" may be a terrified shriek from a person encountering a swarm of honey bees, or it may be a cheer of delight from someone encountering a swarm of honey bees, bagging it, and taking it home. My friend, Willie,[38] was the latter kind of person. He launched me into apiculture (beekeeping).

Bees have always intrigued me because they play a crucial role in one of my hobbies: growing fruit trees. Honey bees pollinate the blossoms, thus increasing my fruit yield. Also, they live up to their name; they produce delicious honey.

Willie lived in the city and owned a small homestead, where he kept a menagerie of creatures great and small. He had chickens, rabbits, goats, quail, pigeons, cats, a dog, a crow, and one time he even had a mink. His wife was more than satisfied with all the creatures, but Willie was not. He wanted honey bees.

Solid gold was a thing of the past in the Treasure State, and liquid gold had come on the scene. Willie heard that Californians were moving to Montana and were setting out apiaries on the clover-covered fields.[39] Willie wanted a taste of that liquid gold, so he set up an apiary (a bee yard). A visit to Willie included a tour of his homestead and the latest news

---
[38] Not his real name.
[39] Montana ranks in the top ten states for honey production in the U. S.

about his critters. After he went into bee-keeping, his apiary became the highlight of that tour whenever I visited Willie.

Willie was a kind, gentle individual who was always ready to lend a helping hand to anyone in need. On one of my visits I told him that some day I hoped to get bees to pollinate the few fruit trees I had planted in my back yard and to produce enough honey for our family. I certainly did not have the desire or time to go into apiculture full time.

Willie said, "I can get you set up with a bee hive of your own."

He sent me home with a catalog of apiculture supplies, and thus began my entry into bee keeping. I did not have money to buy a hive; so I measured one of Willie's hives, bought some cheap lumber from the lumber yard, and built a home-made hive.

True to his word, Willie ordered a package of bees, a queen, and several honeycomb frames. These are imprinted with little hexagons that the bees fill out in time. When the bees arrived, Willie brought them over to our house.

Since it was early spring, he suggested that we work in the attached garage, out of the cold and the wind. My wife stayed in the house. Better to be safe than sorry! I stood in the garage doorway that led to the great outdoors and observed from a distance, ready for a quick retreat.

Willie was calm and unafraid. He did not even wear beekeeper's gloves or a veil. When he opened the package and was about to shake the bees into the hive, I got ready to head for the hills; but curiosity motivated me to stay put. He dumped the clump of several thousand bees into the open hive, and they fell neatly into it and settled in. Willie made it seem so easy. Then, he put the lid on the hive, taped over the little bee entrance, and carried the hive outside to the farthest corner of our back yard. That's where Martha wanted it. Because of Willie, I was now an amateur apiculturist.

For a "Welcome-Hive Gift" Willie gave me one partly filled honey-comb frame to feed the bees until they found nectar, which was plentiful in our area. The fields and ditches on Maiden Valley were covered with clover. Also, across our back fence, lay the BLM forest area.[40] This was truly a banquet hall for bees. It had an abundance of pollen for their little tarsal claws and delicious nectar for their proboscis (their God-given straw for drinking nectar).

Spring arrived in all its glory. The quaking aspens welcomed it with open branches, all decked out in shiny leaves; and the pine trees released an extra dose of their delightful aroma. My bees got off to a wonderfully terrific start. The workers were busy from dawn to dusk. The colony prospered. The number of bees multiplied rapidly. They fed their queen plenty of royal jelly, and she thanked them by laying between 1,500 and 2,000 eggs a day.

At the peak of the egg-laying season, late spring through summer, an exceptional, well-fed queen may lay 3,000 eggs in one day—more than her own body weight. A queen may live between three and four years. In her lifetime, she may lay about half a million eggs.

After a while, I lost my fear of the bees—I had to! And I checked on them regularly. In the middle of the summer, I gave Willie the latest progress report on my bee hive. He was curious and decided to check it out personally. When he saw it, he was flabbergasted at how fast the bees had multiplied, and at how much honey they had produced already.

Before Willie left, I mentioned that the family and I were going on vacation for the next two weeks. Then, I asked him to "bee-sit" for me. Knowing Willie, I was sure he was happy to help out any time. He promised to stop by and check on the hive at least once.

---

[40] The government Bureau of Land Management.

When we returned from vacation, I ran out to our back yard to look at the hive. The bees were busy as usual, but things did not look quite right. The number of bees had gone down drastically. The first notion that came to my mind was, "Oh! No! A swarm!" I thought that maybe the queen had swarmed with half of the bees and had started a new colony in the middle of the forest.

When I told Willie that some of my bees had swarmed, he did not seem too alarmed. I asked him if the remaining number of bees was adequate to make enough honey to get the hive through the winter. Willie rocked his head sideways, back and forth, suggesting that he was not sure. He must have ended up with a sore neck! My bees did make enough honey to take them through the winter, but not enough for me to extract for ourselves.

Several months later, Willie explained to me what had happened when I was gone. About the same time that he had helped me get started with bee keeping, he had helped another of his friends get started as well. The other friend's bees did not do too well. Willie lent him a hand by capturing about half of my bees and transporting them to that friend's hives. In turn, those hives got a big boost!

He confessed, "You had so many bees, and the other bee keeper was in need. So I gave him some of yours to help him out."

That was Willie, always ready to help a person in need!

54

Baby Sitter?

Maiden Valley was beautiful, but not the best place for teenagers wanting to earn a little spending cash. BLM land and a couple of privately owned ranches surrounded our college campus. The college students took whatever jobs were available in the area. Maiden, the nearest town, was two miles away and was a ghost town—no jobs there! The next town was sixteen miles from our campus—Lewistown, the regional shopping center for the heart of Montana had a population of about 7,000 people. It might as well have been a ghost town when it came to jobs for teens. Only a few fast-food places were located there.

Maiden Valley was beautiful, but not the best place for married couples wanting to go out on dates. Most of our social life revolved around the college; and everywhere we went, our boys went with us. Our family activities included wading in the cold mountain streams; exploring the ghost town of Maiden and the old gold mine there; picking berries in the spring, summer, and fall; picnicking and hiking on the BLM land; watching all the wild life around us; diamond hunting up the Judith Mountains; and biking down the mountain to the highway, hoping for someone to stop and give us a ride back up the mountain road.

As a family, we certainly enjoyed these activities. Nevertheless, because Lewistown was small, it offered hardly any date options for Martha and me. Then, about a month after we moved to Maiden Valley, we heard about the artist series in Lewistown, which were promoted by the Central Montana Community Concert Association (CMCCA).

When we were in Central Montana in the early seventies, the association sponsored four different cultural events a year, and tickets were only $5.00 a piece for the college family. These concerts were a win, win situation! Martha and I could have our date night, and a teenager could earn some spending cash.

As soon as school started, the news spread on campus that the quartet, Los Romeros, was coming to town. CMCCA was sponsoring these Spanish classical guitarists known as "The Royal Family of the Guitar." Martha had grown up with classical guitar music and was excited to go hear Celedonio, Celin, Pepe, and Angel. I had never heard classical guitar music, but Martha convinced me that it was fantastic! Elatedly, I asked my wife out for a date.

Now all we needed was a babysitter. Then, I realized that there was only one teenager old enough to babysit our boys. John was seven and Paul was three and a half years old. The fortunate young man was David,[41] a fourteen year-old whose parents also worked for the college. Before anybody else could grab him, I hired David to babysit our sons.

We were all set for our first concert date in Lewistown! The boys were thrilled, and they planned fun games for the evening. They were not getting a boring teenage girl for a babysitter, but a cool teenage boy! Our directions for David were simple: He was to set out supper for the boys, read to them before bedtime, and send them to bed by nine o'clock.

We were confident that supper was not going to be a problem. When babysitters came over, we always had pizza and also pop, which was a special treat in our house. Going to

---

[41] Not his real name.

bed might be a little more difficult, but we had told the boys they must obey David, go to bed, and go to sleep.

We enjoyed our evening out. Martha was right. Classical guitar music was great! We returned about ten thirty and knocked on the door expecting David to open it and let us in; but he did not come to the door. We knocked harder a second time; still no response.

The lights were on in the living room; we stepped to the picture window and peeked in. Through the sheer curtains we saw David fast asleep on the couch! Then, we knocked on the window, but he did not budge one bit. We thought about going to the neighbors and using their phone to call our house, but the houses around us were dark; everyone seemed to be in bed.[42]

Martha said, "Let's try waking up the boys." I went around to the back of the house and knocked on their bedroom window. John and Paul looked stunned when they saw us standing under their window—they looked hilarious! Undoubtedly, they thought the same about us! I asked them to open the front door and make a racket. They obeyed. They flung the door wide open and welcomed us boisterously. Still, David did not wake up.

We whispered and decided to let David sleep a bit longer. We sat at the dining room table, and our quiet tone turned into laughter as we all talked about our evening. After a little while, we moved to the living room, but David continued to sleep. I did not want to scare him awake. I took his arm and shook him gently. Finally, David woke up from his deep sleep. He was startled when he saw the Dutch/Spanish Hartog quartet standing and smiling over him. His eyes opened in surprise when he realized his wards were wide awake and out of bed! He was supposed to have them in bed by nine o'clock!

---

[42] Cell phones were a thing of the future.

Noticeably embarrassed, the poor guy sat up quickly and apologized.

We assured him that all was fine. After all, he had followed our directions well. The boys had eaten their supper, had gone to bed, and had fallen asleep quickly and soundly. And so had he!

Happiness is
Trusting God
And sleeping soundly.

—John Hartog II

55

Ichabod, the Oilaholic

50,000 miles—that was the engine guarantee that GM promised on our brand new Kammback Vega. Since we lived in Maiden Valley, sixteen miles from Lewistown and 120 miles from Billings, it didn't take long for the miles to pile up on the Vega's odometer. Our whole family was happy with our brand new car. As we rode on the sparsely traveled highways, our lime-colored Kammback blended nicely with the green scenery of pine trees, quaking aspen, berry bushes, clover, and grass lands. Most importantly, our little Vega got good gas mileage.

General Motors named the Vega after the brightest star in the constellation Lyra. At its unveiling in 1971, the Vega was praised for its design and engineering excellence. *Car and Driver* magazine named it "Best Economy Sedan" in 1971, 1972, and 1973. *Motor Trend* included the Vega as one of the "Ten Best Cars of 1971" and as the "Car of the Year for 1971." Its brightest moment was at its unveiling. However, soon after it left the show room, it became a falling star.[43]

The "brightest star" had a dark secret hidden under its hood—its engine was junk! An inline four-cylinder engine with a lightweight, aluminum alloy cylinder block powered the Vega. Before long we fell victims to the effects of the junky

---

[43] The car had problems related to engineering, reliability, safety, rust, and engine durability.

Ichabod, the Oilaholic

engine. As the miles on our car's odometer went up, the oil gage began to go down unexpectedly. By the time our Vega had only 12,000 miles, it was burning up oil.

The Vega went through a series of recalls and design improvements. However, Vega-bamboozled-consumers, like us, in Central Montana never heard about the recalls! We were spending the gas savings on the oil and were hauling heavy oil cases in our trunks, thereby diminishing the gas mileage!

Disenchanted, we and all the other Vega owners tarnished the reputation of the "brightest star" as well as that of General Motors. From that 12,000-mile point, our Vega got worse and worse. By 30,000 our lime-colored "bright star" had metamorphosed into an oil drunkard—a "dark lemon."

About that time, in the summer of 1975, we decided to take a trip to Central America to visit Martha's parents. Her nephew, Dennis Lee, flew from California to Montana to travel with our family. When I asked him why he wanted to travel with us, he responded, "Because your life is full of surprises!" Surprises were to abound on this trip!

All five of us were traveling by land in the compact Kammback from Montana to Miami, then by air to El Salvador. We packed lightly, but I brought sixty (60) quarts of oil along for the round trip. I figured our car could go about 125 miles before needing a two-quart swig of oil. Martha was still a green driver, and as soon as we crossed the Montana border, she refused to drive!

We drove to Dallas, where we stopped overnight at Aunt Ruth and Uncle Jack's. Then we journeyed through Arkansas, Louisiana, Mississippi, Alabama, and dipped down to Miami. Every so often we stopped for gas, but more than every so often, we stopped for stretches and oil-fill ups. I was an optimist and thought that sixty quarts of oil would satisfy the Vega's craving throughout the round trip. Wrong! The sixty quarts were gone before we even got into Florida!

During the trip, we decided that our car was not living up to its name-sake, "Vega," the brightest star of Lyra. On one of our stops, our Vega baptized itself with oil, and we renamed it Ichabod, which means, "No glory" or "the glory has departed."

The original Ichabod was an Old Testament character whose mother, father, and grandfather all died the day he was born. Moreover, the Israelites were defeated in battle on that same day. It was an inglorious day to say the least.[44]

It was a slow trek through the southern Gulf States, but the oil guzzler did get us to Miami, where we let it *rust* for two weeks. We visited Martha's sister, Blanca, for a couple of days and took a high-speed, one-day tour of Disney World in Orlando Florida.

It was time for Ichabod to *rust* in peace for a while! Glad to leave our oil guzzler behind, we flew across the Gulf of Mexico to El Salvador on Transportes Aéreos Centroamericanos.[45] Our ten-day tour through El Salvador and Guatemala went by faster than we could say, "*¡Ola! Mucho gusto de conocerlos. Adiós!*"

Loaded with souvenirs and fatter from eating so many frijoles and tortillas, we flew back to Miami. Unfortunately, we didn't leave any family member behind. Ichabod still had to haul five passengers—and plump ones at that! When we arrived at Blanca's, we found our lemon-lime Vega right where we had left it. I had bought 60 more quarts of oil for our return trip. I opened Ichabod's big, hood-mouth, and poured two quarts down its dark, eager throat.

We crammed into the compact car full of souvenirs. Then, Blanca stuffed sandwiches, chips, cookies, and fruit wherever there was a cranny. Also some of her hand-me down clothes

---

[44] This account in found in 1 Samuel 4.
[45] TACA airlines is the flag carrier of El Salvador.

for Martha found a place in there. We were packed worse than sardines, but happy to be going back to Big Sky Country.

It had taken a long time to pack, and we didn't get off till ten in the morning, later than we had planned. I was hoping to drive about six hundred miles on the first day. The boys were too tired to horse around in the car, plus they could barely breathe. They slept most of the time, and they only took stretch breaks when we stopped for gas, not for the multiple oil-fill ups.

We went through Florida, cut across a corner of Georgia, and headed north through Alabama. We watched for motel vacancies, but no such critter existed. I drove through western Tennessee. Everybody and his uncle must have been on vacation, because we found no vacant motel rooms.

Then we came into Missouri, and finally at ten o'clock the next morning, we found a motel vacancy in Cape Girardeau. In twenty-four hours, I had driven 1,111 miles by myself. I still averaged 46.3 miles per hour in spite of scavenging for motels and stopping for gas and oil. Ichabod needed a drink of two quarts of oil every two hours and forty-five minutes. The shameless "oilaholic" drank about nineteen quarts of oil in that twenty-four hour period—one quart every 58 miles!

At Cape Girardeau, we slept for three hours until checkout time. Then we drove to northwest Iowa where we said, "Hi!" to my mother and slept for a whole day before taking off for Montana.

During the round trip from Montana to Miami, our Vega had guzzled over 135 quarts of oil! Yet according to the '74 Vega brochure, its engine oil filter was supposed to last for 50,000 miles. I think the reason for this claim was because there was no *old* oil ever left behind in the filter to change!

At 43,000 miles, Ichabod's engine gave up the ghost. We could not get anything for the car, so I paid to have the engine rebuilt with steel sleeves. Years later, I learned that GM would have paid for the expenses; but by the time I heard this, it was too late. We drove Ichabod another 80,000, which meant that we got a total of 123,000 miles out of it.

The other problem with a Vega was rust, and rust won the battle against poor Ichabod. In time, the door locks were so rusted that they adjusted to whatever "key" was put into them. When our son Paul wanted to get in the car before any of us, he used the end of his jacket zipper to unlock the door!

Another "bright star" had fallen to its engineering fate! I tried to sell the pitiful old car to junk dealers, but as soon as I mentioned the word "Vega," they hung up on me! Finally, I found a one-man junk yard whose owner was willing to give Ichabod a decent burial among all its relatives, of which there were plenty. I was ready to pay for the funeral services, but somehow the junk man knew I had been bamboozled.

He gave me $25 and hauled Ichabod to its final *rusting* place where it could *rust* in peace!

56

Far South of the Border (El Salvador)

While our Vega *rusted* in Miami, our family and Dennis Lee flew to San Salvador. Among the hundreds of eager people waiting for loved ones at the airport, we saw the faces of Papá Toñito and Mamá Sarita, Martha's parents. They greeted us with vigorous Latin embraces and kisses.

From the moment we landed, Martha started talking in Spanish non-stop at thousands of words a minute. The boys and I smiled and nodded our heads a lot. That first night, all of us went to bed with sore jaws and stiff necks! After a day or so, the boys and I ventured to try out what little Spanish we knew.

Our headquarters in San Salvador was a "hotel" owned by one of Martha's uncles. It is a big house with many rooms and several bathrooms surrounding a courtyard with beautiful tropical plants and flowers. A few families lived there, but they also had spare rooms for visiting relatives.

Someone new showed up daily at mealtime; and, of course, introductions went along with every meal. Food was plenteous, but water was rationed. House rules regarding water usage were these: turn off the faucet while brushing your teeth, and limit your shower to five minutes.

San Salvador ("Holy Savior") is the capital city of El Salvador and is also the country's largest city. In the early sixteenth century, the Spanish conquistadores called this area *"Provincia De Nuestro Señor Jesus Cristo, El Salvador Del*

Mundo" ("Province of our Lord Jesus Christ, the Savior of the World"). In time, this long name became, "El Salvador" ("The Savior"). The shortened form matches the nation's size much better.

El Salvador is the smallest country in continental America, and its citizens affectionately refer to it as *"Pulgarcito de América"* ("Tom Thumb of the Americas"). My wife's favorite label for her native country is *"Chiquito pero Matón"* ("Tiny but Mighty"). Having known her for over fifty years, I can say that she is definitely the product of such a country.

As we traveled through this small country, one of the features that caught my attention was its dense population. The city traffic was a picture of mass confusion. People were packed in cars and buses. We saw thousands of people walking up and down the roads—even on the country roads to and from the cities.

Though it is the smallest nation in Central America, El Salvador is the most densely populated country of the Americas—North, Central, and South. It has a density of 870 people per square mile. In contrast, Iowa has 52 people per square mile; Montana, only 5.

El Salvador is also overpopulated by volcanoes. A total of 22 volcanoes rise above the landscape of this tiny country, and 6 of them are considered active. One of our excursions included a beautiful drive to Cerro Verde. From this extinct volcano we could see clearly the highest volcano of El Salvador, the Santa Ana, which erupted as recently as 2005, and Izalco, the youngest of the 3 volcanoes. From the early nineteenth century to the middle of the twentieth century, Izalco erupted so regularly that the sailors, traversing the Pacific Ocean, nicknamed it "Lighthouse of the Pacific" and used it as a beacon.

As we stood on Cerro Verde admiring the beauty around us, the possibility of an eruption from either volcano was alive and well in our minds. We could have been blown to smithereens if either volcano had decided to start some fire works!

Santa Ana is Martha's native city and the second largest city of El Salvador. Here we went to visit the house where Martha's maternal grandparents, Papá Teódulo and Mamá Tanchito, lived until they passed away. Mamá Tanchito lived to be 99 years old. Papá Teódulo died twenty years earlier, but lived a full life doing what he loved most: planting trees.

His orchard included many varieties of mangos, bananas, avocados, citrus, and other tropical fruit. He also had chickens but not a chicken coop. Because of the warmer climate, he nailed small boards in ladder fashion against a big *almendra* (almond) tree. At dusk, all the chickens went up the ladder and spent the night roosting in the tree. For obvious reasons, the grandkids did not play under that tree after dusk.

We also visited Martha's paternal relatives who were still living in Santa Ana. Her paternal grand-parents, Papá Julio and Mamá Lolita, had also passed away. Mamá Lolita outlived her husband by several decades. Her five children were all born at home. She never saw the inside of a doctor's office or a hospital. She did not have health insurance in her entire life, and she never needed it. She lived to be 102! When Martha and I got married, Dad Nuñez told me that I would be stuck with his daughter for a long, long time.

On another excursion we went to a beach of the Pacific Ocean. The Pacific, *"Pacífico"* in Spanish, got its name from the Spaniards, who first saw it. The term means "peaceful." Compared to the Atlantic with all its storms, the Pacific seemed much more peaceful to the Spaniards who first crossed Panama. One of Martha's cousins had a beach house. This made it possible for us to enjoy a private beach all to ourselves.

After making the rounds visiting Martha's relatives in El Salvador, we went to Guatemala. I had come to El Salvador on a tourist visa, not a passport. It was no problem in El Salvador, but when we crossed over into Guatemala it proved to be a major hitch. Martha had come with a provisional passport, and that also proved to be an obstacle.

At the border crossing, the attendant took my visa and refused to give it back. He also declined to approve Martha's provisional passport. This happened after we had crossed the border and had just entered Guatemala. Therefore, I was left without any legal identification at all. And the attendant did not allow Martha to go any farther into Guatemala.

What he wanted was "*una mordida*." (a bite of money). Martha was not about to give him even "*un centavo*" because she saw it as government corruption. He insisted that he had no official papers to let us into Guatemala. Martha knew better and said the papers were in his desk drawer.

The two of them went on and on, and neither one was about to back down! Finally after a couple hours, the officer got tired and hungry, and he opened the drawer. Sure enough, the papers were there!

Martha was happy she had won and had exposed corruption! However, her parents were not happy with her. They called her, "*necia*," a word that sounded familiar to me because her mother often called me "*necio*." It means "stubborn." Being stubborn goes along with being Dutch and apparently, Spanish, too!

57

Far South of the Border (Guatemala)

Guatemala known as "The Land of Eternal Spring" ("*El País de la Eterna Primavera*") is the country where Martha spent her early childhood. Guatemala is five times as large as El Salvador, but the lower 48 states of the U.S.A. are 100 times as large as Guatemala. The Indian population of Guatemala is greater than that of El Salvador. Fifty per cent of Guatemalans are descendants of the Maya Indians. The Mayans had a highly developed civilization, hundreds of years before Columbus landed in the West Indies.

Like El Salvador, the landscape of Guatemala is dotted by many volcanoes, about 30 in all. From Guatemala City alone, we could see four volcanoes: Agua, Acatenango, Fuego, and Pacaya. Two of them, Fuego and Pacaya, are active. Guatemalans go about their daily lives completely ignoring the beauty and the time bombs that surround their cities.

Guatemala City, the fourth capital of Guatemala since 1776, is the largest city of Guatemala. It is also the largest capital of the Central American countries; its metropolis numbers about 4,000,000. It takes forever to travel through the city because of the heavy traffic, but we were able to visit the central market, the national palace of culture, and the national cathedral.

After visiting some of the tourist attractions in the capital, we focused on the outskirt sites. Since we had spent a week in El Salvador, by the time we arrived in Guatemala, I was more used to hearing Spanish and was brave enough to barter in Spanish. I bartered down to at least half the asked price. However, later I learned that a native could have cut the price down to one-third. This didn't bother me at all. The shop keepers got a little extra cash, and bartering was a lot of fun!

One day, I went into a shop to barter for a sweater, and I asked how much it cost. When the merchant told me the price, I said *"Muy barato."* He looked at me with a surprised expression (I had said, "That's very cheap!"), instead of *"Muy caro"* ("That's very expensive"). My bartering in that shop ended swiftly.

In Guatemala we visited two of Martha's favorite sites: Lake Atitlan and Antigua Guatemala (Ancient Guatemala). Antigua was the third capital of Guatemala and was founded by the Spaniards in 1543. It became famous for its lovely Baroque architecture. But in 1717, an earthquake destroyed over 3,000 buildings. Then in 1773, another earthquake hit the city, so the capital was moved to the present site of Guatemala City.

Antigua is a spectacular Spanish city from colonial days. We walked on narrow sidewalks flush against brightly painted buildings that followed along its quaint cobblestone streets. Exquisite flowers landscaped the entire city. The three volcanoes, Agua, Acatenango, and Fuego, which are visible from Guatemala City, are on Antigua's backyard—they are so close! Main Street presented a remarkable view of Volcán de Agua. Everywhere we turned on Main Street, we ran into interesting restored buildings and also ruins.

Then, we went to Lake Atitlán, which is known as one of the most beautiful lakes in the world. The lake is surrounded by mountains, and by three majestic volcanoes: Tolimán, Atitlán, and San Pedro. They form the natural dam of the lake, whose forest is the habitat for the Quetzal, Guatemala's national bird.

Martha with Guatemalan Hat by a Homestead Flowering Bush

The fruit variety was wonderful and *"muy barata."* Pineapples, mangos, coconuts, papayas, bananas, and other topical fruits cost only pennies. I also learned that a cashew nut, the real fruit, grows on the *outside* of the accessory fruit (the cashew apple) which the people call *"marañon."* It tastes somewhat like mango and citrus fruit combined. In Central America, most people throw away the cashew nut and eat the cashew apple!

Martha taught me to lean over when eating the luscious *"marañon."* because its juice leaves a terrible stain on clothes. When she was a child, Martha enjoyed all kinds of tropical fruit by the bushel full. No wonder she likes fruit better than American pies and cakes!

Guatemala, "The Land of Eternal Spring," is one gigantic flower shop! As if saying, "Look at me!" gorgeous flowers caught my attention everywhere we went. They made me homesick for my beautiful flower beds back home and prompted me to ask this question, "Do all Guatemalans have a green thumb like I do?"

Back in Guatemala City, we visited the campus of the school where Papá Toñito taught and where Martha spent her childhood years. When Martha lived there, the school was called Instituto Biblico Centroamericano (IBCA). Mamá Sarita also taught there several years.

In the 1960's IBCA expanded its academics and developed into Seminario Teológico Centroamericano (SETECA). It rivals many North American seminaries in size and academics. Martha's father started teaching at IBCA/SETECA when he was about 20 years old and taught there a total of 65 years!

More importantly, Papá Toñito and Mamá Sarita ministered together in Guatemala for fifty five years, until she died! Both of them will hear their Savior's commendation: "Thou good and faithful servants!"

58

Of Diamonds and Gold

Winters in the Judith Mountains were cold and long. A killing frost in the spring might blanket Maiden Valley as late as June 8 and pay an unwelcome visit as early as August 28. Winter daylight in the valley was brief. On December 21, the shortest day of the year, the sun crawled its way up behind the mountains at ten in the morning, shone brightly over the snow covered valley for a mere four hours, and went to bed for a long nap at two in the afternoon.

The flip side is that humidity was low. This made cold air feel warmer, because low humidity decreases the conduction of heat from the body.[46] Moreover, Chinook winds raced down the valley at high speeds and raised the air temperature by 25° to 35° in a matter of minutes.[47] At times, our January temperatures went up to the 50s!

After long winter nights, the sun was ready for summer. The temperatures went up to the 90s, but the low humidity enabled us to take full advantage of the beautiful outdoors. We lived in concert with the sun—early to rise and late to bed. We worked long hours intermingled with play. By five in the

---

[46] Conversely, the low humidity in the summers made the warm air feel cooler because of the decreased conduction of heat to the body.

[47] Chinook is an American Indian word that means "snow-eater." The wind that races along the east side of the Rocky Mountains at 100 mph can be as warm as 60 °F in January. Snow in the path of the wind melts fast!

morning, it was bright enough for me to work around the yard, and I could pick strawberries as late as ten at night.

Summers in Montana were truly delightful! We often rode our bikes up and down the road that followed the valley. One day our nephew, Dennis Lee, jammed a finger in the spokes of a bike wheel and nearly lost his fingernail. He ran into the house for help. Martha washed his finger and was ready to smear antibiotic ointment on it, when suddenly his face turned white, and then he fainted! Martha put first aid into practice, and soon he was ready to go back outside.

One of our favorite family activities was hiking through the BLM land that surrounded us. The melting snow from the mountains created small streams along the roads. Though the water was cold, the boys liked to take off their shoes and wade in the flowing, clear water. As we became acquainted with the mountains nearby, a few spots became favorites for family picnics.

Martha packed peanut butter and jelly sandwiches, blankets, and books for us to read while the boys hiked to their hearts' content. One day, as we hiked farther up the valley from the college, we "discovered" abandoned gold mines; some were quite small others were large and deep. Timbers that once had held up the ceilings of some mines now lay half fallen, blocking the entrance. Obviously, as a family we were cautious when we came upon those areas on our hikes.

Hiking up and down the roads became a rewarding pastime. We picked wild strawberries, raspberries, and serviceberries (a.k.a. Saskatoon berries). The wild strawberries were small, but they made up for it in flavor. Martha made delicious pies out of the service-berries combined with rhubarb. One summer she made twenty-four pies and froze them for the winter.

Martha was especially thankful for summers and ice-free roads. She learned to drive on Montana roads because of the

Of Diamonds and Gold

light traffic.[48] However, to this day, she dislikes winter driving. She thinks of the numerous times when she went into the ditches because of icy roads. Thankfully, she never got hurt, and the car suffered no damage either.

One road was different. It was closed in the winter, and Martha did not drive on it until she had more driving experience. It was the road up to "the dome." The dome was a relic of the old radar base that was on the top of Judith Peak at 6,400 ft.

The road to the mountain top was gravel and steep. One of the extra-curricula activities of the college was the Dome Run. On the day of the Dome Run all classes were cancelled. The students who participated lined up at the exit gate of the campus. At the given signal, they raced up to the dome, and the winner received a trophy.

A fascinating aspect of Judith Peak was the fabulous view of the valley below, the tree-laden mountains around us, and the big blue sky above us. It was truly a breath-taking spectacle. Thus, the drive up to the dome became one of our favorite activities when relatives or friends visited us.

Thinking that my Mother would enjoy the Dome Tour as much as we did, we took her along on the gorgeous scenic ride. Unfortunately, Mother hated it! The thought of the car sliding off a ravine frightened her, and she was miserable during the whole trip. When we reached Judith Peak, she refused to leave the car. The mountain-top expedition turned out to be the low-point experience of her vacation with us!

When my sister Marj, her husband Bob, and their two daughters (Tammy and Liesl) came down from Great Falls, we took them on the Dome Tour. The whole family enjoyed the steep mountain drive and the beautiful scenery.

---

[48] See "I Beg You, Have Mercy on Me," story #52.

Another interesting aspect of that mountain top was its "Montana diamonds" or "adobe diamonds." According to the area residents, Judith Peak was one of only two places in the world where these "diamonds" were found; and they also claimed that the other place was somewhere in Africa. Sometimes I wonder if they were trying to pull my leg!

At any rate, adobe diamonds were small rocks perfectly shaped like diamonds. They were certainly a novelty but had no commercial value. Many of these "diamonds" were embedded on the mountain side and some were scattered on the ground. It was not difficult to find a handful of them once you knew what they looked like. John and Paul were thrilled every time they found one of these "diamonds," and we joined in their fun.

Hiking, picnicking, and hunting for "diamonds" in the Judith Mountains cost us nothing, but God used these simple experiences to enrich our family times and to strengthen our family ties.

Happiness is not found
In getting what you want,
But in wanting what you get.

—Author unknown

59

Ice Fallies

Montana truly is a beautiful state. Glacier National park is one of the spectacular sights to behold in Big Sky Country. The Judith Mountains cannot compare to Glacier, but they provided a lovely setting for Maiden Valley, regardless of the season.

One year the spring semester was over about May 23. As usual, all the students left immediately after graduation day. The next day we got a heavy snow storm that knocked out our electric power and blocked Maiden Canyon Road. This was our only exit to U.S. Hwy 191, which went to Lewistown.

Since it was spring, the temperatures were bearable without a furnace. We also opened the garage door and cooked hamburgers on the grill. Then, we called the Forsbergs, our elderly friends down the block. We invited ourselves over and told them that we were bringing the food. That evening, we had a picnic by candlelight in the middle of a snow storm.

A whole week went by before our power was restored. As soon as Maiden Canyon Road was passable, we drove the sixteen miles to Lewistown to buy much needed groceries. Then on June 1, a second snow storm blanketed the valley and left us stranded again without electricity until June 8.

Being snowbound in Maiden Valley was not an unpleasant experience. The mountains with evergreen trees, laden with snow looked like Christmas cards. A picture taken from any direction in Maiden Valley was worthy of a ribbon in a photo contest. Along with the snow, however, sometimes came freezing rain and ice. Ice made the sidewalks and roads slick and created driving problems.

Snow-ice storms also affected the people on foot; so we had our own *"Ice Fallies"* season on campus. One day, a student went ice falling and ended up in the doctor's office, was treated, and released. Since the student was under the school's health insurance, it covered his medical costs. When I told a coworker about the mishap, he said, "That student should have been more careful. His accident will raise our rates."

I bit my tongue and didn't pursue the subject. One of us might be next! A few days later, my coworker went ice falling and ended up in the hospital. His injuries were minor, but he had to stay there three days. I was not overly critical of either the student or my coworker and was careful as he had recommended.

However, I was next! While walking between my office and the classroom building, I also went ice falling. I did not sustain any bone fractures, but my humeral head and scapula got off track because my rotator cuff muscles did their stretching exercises too aggressively and tore (something to that effect). It was difficult for me to understand the doctor's medical jargon when he was describing my injury. Anyway, as a result, I had to wear a sling for six weeks.

That year, the *Ice Fallies* were a popular school function, but the season had to end. Our *Ice Fallies* fell victim to the warmer temperatures, and we all watched in amazement, as Spring gradually closed the curtain on Winter's last act.

60

Hanging on for Dear Life

"What's happening to Billy?"[49] That's what all of us who knew him were asking. He just was not acting like the Billy we knew. Martha and I were good friends with Billy and his wife. We had much in common with them and often visited their homestead. Billy was friendly but somewhat reserved. Then one week, Billy started to change. He became talkative. He even spoke in the church-mid-week service for about half an hour. That was not like Billy.

As the next few days went by, other changes became evident in Billy. When his wife told us that he had stopped eating, we became concerned. Billy loved fried chicken; so we went to Kentucky Fried Chicken and got a bucket of chicken. We took it to Billy's place and convinced him to eat some. During the meal, Billy told us that the Devil lived in his van and that his dog was a Christian. Hearing his claims convinced me that something was definitely wrong with Billy!

Later he locked himself in the basement of his house and refused to come out. When his wife called, it was obvious she was desperate. His poor wife was at her wits end. She let me know that she was ready to call the police. She was certain they could coax Billy to come out. However, she was worried about where he might end up. She was afraid that the officials

---

[49] Not his real name.

would put Billy in a padded cell (not in jail). I called our pastor, and we agreed to go to Billy's house.

The pastor and I finally convinced Billy to let us take him to the hospital to see a doctor. The hospital was about 150 miles away in Billings. The only way Billy agreed to go was if he could drive. We were uneasy about the whole matter but had no alternative. So Billy drove! For the sake of safety, Pastor and I sat in the back seat. Anxious about our driver, we prayed silently with our eyes open!

It was a wild trip! Billy drove fast, like a typical Montanan. He detoured through another town and stopped to talk a while at a country store. It seemed like one of the longest drives in our lives, and also one of the longest prayer meetings in a car! A trip that should have taken three and-a-half hours took five hours. When we finally arrived, the staff admitted Billy and put him into a special section of the hospital.

The doctors instructed us not to visit or call Billy for a week, but they promised to call his wife daily with updates. The doctors' first report was not encouraging. They told her that Billy's condition had worsened at first. Also, he had tried to break out of his room by shoving his bed through the window. Finally, the staff had to tie him down in the bed.

When we returned a week later, Billy was back to his own self. The change and the speed at which it took place surprised us. The doctors told his wife about the treatments and medications Billy had received.

Many people who knew Billy asked the pastor and me how we dared ride to the hospital with Billy at the wheel. We did it because he was our friend, and we did it with the backing of everyone's prayers, which God graciously answered.

Billy got better, and Pastor and I lived to tell about it. That was the scariest-wildest ride I've ever taken!

61

That Low Sinking Feeling

The move of the Bible college from Billings to beautiful Maiden Valley produced great excitement, and enrollment took a turn upward. The old air force facilities were adequate at first, but the effect of increased enrollment was the need for a new building. After a few years, the school built a large multi-purpose structure that included administrative offices and classrooms. One of the rooms was large enough for chapel, conferences, banquets, and other events.

The large room was long and narrow, making it difficult to see the speaker from the back rows. The solution was a platform. Maintenance staff faced two problems: (1) The room did not have a high ceiling; the platform could not be too tall. (2) The room was multipurpose, and sometimes a platform might be a hindrance instead of a help.

Maintenance tackled the challenge, keeping these matters in mind. They built a large platform to raise the pulpit—not too high. A song leader could stand straight and not scrape ceiling paint with his head or raised hands when leading music. This applied as long as he was not over seven feet tall. The men also put the platform on small wheels. Then, when a function did not call for a platform, it could be rolled away easily to a side room behind a folding wall.

Maintenance had tackled the platform project eagerly and had overcome the problems. When the project was completed, people in the back rows were able to see the speaker much better. Also, the platform was spacious enough for a pulpit and for a row of folding chairs at the back of it.

The platform worked well for a while until one night during a week of special meetings. Someone set up the row of chairs a little too close to the back of the platform. After Dr. Longenecker, the school president, gave his opening remarks, he sat on a platform chair. In the process of sitting down, the chair legs moved over the edge of the platform and sank down a little bit in the crack between the platform and the wall.

That made sitting in the chair uncomfortable because the seat now slanted down to the back. The president moved around on the chair a little bit, and that caused the platform to roll forward a little more. In turn that caused the president's chair to sink again a little lower. Each time the president moved around on the chair, he sank lower and lower! Our poor president was slowly disappearing behind the platform as it rolled farther and farther away from the wall. Finally the folding chair collapsed, and the president disappeared from view!

From the audience perspective, he seemed to disappear from sight in slow motion. Each time he sank lower, the people snickered a little louder. His slow motion disappearance behind the platform that night affected people in two conflicting ways: they all laughed every time he slid; while at the same time, they felt extremely sorry for him.

He took it all in stride. It was obvious he was not hurt, and he got up and continued to lead the service. He was one of the best school presidents under whom I have ever served. He mentored me in many ways about life and school administration. Everyone loved him!

62

On a slippery slope

Have you ever heard of "cleechie"? Or maybe you've heard of "kleechy." If you haven't, don't bother to look it up in a dictionary—the word doesn't exist! But the substance it represents does. Believe me!

I had never heard of kleechy, until we moved to Montana and ran into Corky[50] and Leola; except, that they call it "Gumbo." Most likely by now, the only person who called it kleechy has slithered into his hardened-concrete-like-cleechie grave!

The word "gumbo" does exist in the dictionary. The problem is that you have to go down far enough to find the definition for that cleechie-like substance. According to the dictionary, "gumbo" is:

1. Same as okra [Nope! Gumbo is not that slimy veggie that slides down your throat—but it's like it!]

2. A soup thickened with unripe okra pods [Gumbo is not thick soup with those slimy veggies either—but you're getting warmer!]

3. A fine, silty soil of the Western prairies, which becomes sticky and nonporous when wet: also gumbo soil [Bingo! That's it!]

---

[50] His real name is Jerry, but he goes by "Corky." I wouldn't be surprised if that was Leola's idea; the names of their three children all start with a "J." When she called her hubby, she didn't have to think of the right "J."

Those Western prairies lie directly beneath Big Sky Country, and Corky's child-hood slithering grounds were in the middle of the "Gumbo Capital of Montana." Since Corky had grown up with gumbo, he was familiar with what some folks called kleachy (I forgot. This is another way to spell the slimy goop. Since it's not in the dictionary, you can be as creative as you want to when spelling the sticky stuff).

One day when we were visiting with Korkee, (I mean Corky) and Leola, I asked him, "Is kleechee something roads are made of, like blacktop?"

"Oh! No!" replied Corky, with that boisterous, deep laugh of his. He went on, "I can't describe to you what gumbo's like, unless you've been stuck in it."

I could hardly wait to be stuck in it! Martha and I didn't have to wait long. That spring-school break, following that gumbo-kleetchee lesson, Corky and Leola invited our family to his father's ranch. We went in two cars, and Corky and Leola lead the way.

It was a beautiful sunny day, but the temperatures were still a tad below freezing. The road we traveled was clay; it was frozen and free from bumps—smooth as glass, and we could move right along. Since I grew up in Iowa, winter-icy roads were not a threat.

As I drove along, I thought "This is not bad! We'll slide into the ranch in no time at all!"

Then, the temperatures began to rise, and the road began to thaw. Our smooth-glass-like road, turned into mud; but we kept plodding along and followed Corky, as he calmly maneuvered his car. Suddenly, we came to a little hill; half-way up it, our car came to a complete stop. This was no ordinary mud! It was gumbo!

We could not make it up the hill. We were stuck in thick gumbo soup—sort of like the kind thickened with slippery okra pods. Unfamiliar with this goopy mud, our car decided to have some fun. It sent its tires on a wild spin. Corky and I decided that with a push we could get over the top of the little hill; then slide down the other side. Leola volunteered to help push as well.

Martha was to drive; she had no experience driving a car stuck in the mud, much less in gumbo; but she was eager to try it. With two husky guys and one brave woman pushing the car while in neutral, and a go-ahead woman at the wheel, we would be on our way soon.

With Leola in the middle, the three of us got behind the car and pushed; but our feet kept slipping out from under us on that slimy cleechee, and the car did not budge! Corky instructed Martha to be ready to start the engine, and then shift it into drive while we pushed as vigorously as we could. The moment Corky shouted "Go!" she was to drive ahead.

We grasped the back bumper. Corky was on one side and I was on the other, with Leola still in the middle. We heard Martha start the car. At once we tried to lift the back end of the car a little and throw our weight against it. Then, Corky shouted, "Go!"

Right away, Martha shifted into drive and floored it. The engine roared, but the car did not move, and the tires instantly splattered *plen'y* of kleechy! Corky and I were plastered with a five-inch-wide streak of gumbo, from the top of our faces to the bottoms of our boots!

On that gumbo-kleetchee-lesson night, Corky also told us that when Gumbo is dry it is hard as concrete—an excellent road surface. But when it is wet it is SSS (soft, slippery, and sticky)—resulting in awful roads. Gumbo reminded me of the little girl with the little curl.

There was a little girl who had a little curl
—right in the middle of her forehead.
When she was good, she was very good.

But when she was bad, she was horrid.

That pretty much describes kleetchee, kleechy, kleachy, kleechee, cleachie, cleechee, cleechie, gumbo! Whatever people call it! I'll never forget what it is!

*Because You have been my help,
Therefore in the shadow of Your wings I will rejoice.
My soul follows close behind You;
Your right hand upholds me.*

—Psalm 63:7-8 [NKJV™]

63

Sunset Galloway Ranch

Christmas in the Winter Wonderland of Sunset Galloway Ranch! Corky and Leola Harkins made this possible when they invited us to go with them to Corky's father's ranch in the Chalk Buttes, fourteen miles from Ekalaka.[51] This was a small town with about 300 people, located in the Powder River basin of southeastern Montana. The Powder River, a tributary of the Yellowstone River, was so named because the sand along some of its banks looked like gunpowder.

The Harkins' ranch spread over 7,000 acres. When I was young a 160-acre farm in Iowa was a good sized family farm. But, the Powder River area does not get nearly the amount of rain that Iowa does; it takes more land for a family to make a living.

We left home a few days before Christmas. The weather was not good, but we all wanted to be there by Christmas Day. Our plan was to get ahead of a snow storm that had been predicted for that day. We met the Harkins in Billings and continued our southeastern trek together. Our entire trip from our house to the ranch was about 400 miles.

Partway into the trip, the storm caught up with us. The highway began to ice up, and the roads got worse and worse. Since he was pulling a trailer, the drive was especially difficult

---

[51] Ekalaka was named after a Sioux Indian girl who married David Harrison Russel, a scout and frontiersman.

for Corky. As we rode behind him, we could see the trailer sliding back and forth, down the road. My fear was that it might jack knife. It was so bad that Leola got carsick from the swaying of the trailer and the car. We stopped, talked it over, and we all decided to go on. Driving cautiously and slowly, we finally made it to the ranch tired but relieved.

We had a wonderful time at the ranch. The home atmosphere was certainly original-western style. The chandeliers were wagon wheels with attached lights, the coat hooks were deer antlers, and so were the door "knobs." The mornings started out with a huge breakfast—steaks, pancakes, eggs, homemade bread, and other wonderful goodies.

After their hearty breakfast, the Harkin men (real cowboys) headed out for the day. They took hot baked potatoes wrapped in aluminum foil in their pockets for warmth and for lunch. A delicious supper awaited the men who had worked rigorously all day. They kindly shared it with us, though we had not labored like them.

Normally, the men went on horseback to check on their cattle and the enormous watering tanks. However, when the snow got too deep, snowmobiles replaced the horses. Martha and I enjoyed our first snowmobile ride on the wide open spaces—7,000 acres is 11 square miles. We didn't have to worry at all about running into barbed wire fences!

That was a lot of land to cover by horseback or snowmobiles. I imagine it took several days to check all the different sections of the ranch. Instead of riding off into the setting sun like western novels have it, they came riding home as the sun set.

Since it was Christmas time, the church was having a cantata. The people were extra friendly, and they asked Corky, Leola, and Martha to participate in the cantata, and they did. As for me, I excused myself, of course. The choir director did not mind that the willing visitors had not practiced with the choir. After all, Corky and Leola had come home for Christmas!

Corky has an impressive, low-range-bass voice; Leola plays the piano and sings nicely, too; as for Martha, she will try anything that is wholesome and fun. A few years later, Corky's splendid bass voice boomed beyond "Big Sky Country." He toured several states across the Lower 48 as a "singing cowboy," with Leola accompanying him at the piano. They also recorded some of their songs.

To this day, whenever we listen to their music, we think of our Christmas in the Winter Wonderland of southeastern Montana.

Cherish all your happy moments:
They make a fine cushion for old age.

—Christopher Morley

64

Oh Where, Oh Where Has My Little Dog Gone?

A cute, black pup joined our family while we were in Montana. He was a mutt, a cross between a cocker spaniel and a poodle that cost us $20. He had the curly coat of a poodle and a cocker's sweet temperament. Actually, he looked like a miniature old English sheep dog. His outstanding quality was his loving disposition reflected in his big, black, tender eyes, which he kept hidden under his curly, black bangs.

We called him Tar Baby, in memory of a black cocker spaniel my family had when I was a young boy. In no time at all, our new Tar Baby adjusted to our family life; he liked company, and we liked to have him around. Martha has a knack at training dogs, and Tar Baby was house broken within a week.

When he needed to go outside to do his business, he rushed to the door and whined. The fenced back yard was his realm, but he longed to stake out more land. If we happened to leave the gate open, he satisfied his longing by wondering off, but he always came back promptly. He knew where his home was!

Although the winters were cold in Maiden Valley, Tar Baby did not mind the cold so much because of his thick, black fur coat. After one of our blizzards, the snow in the back yard was piled higher than the four-foot chain link fence; and I had to shovel a spot for him.

Our Sons and Tar Baby

Now, Tar Baby had a place to go! I let him out, went back into the house, and waited for his "I want in" bark. Several minutes went by—much longer than usual—before any one of us realized that the pup had not barked. I rushed outside, but Tar Baby was gone!

Then, I noticed his paw prints. He had walked right out of the back yard on the top of the snow over the fence. I called for the family "troops," and we searched for him throughout the college housing. None of the neighbors had seen him. We went to the farmer across the road, but he had not seen Tar Baby either. This was somewhat of a comfort because that farmer shot stray dogs whenever they came on his place. Nevertheless, he knew our dog and liked him; we were not too worried about that.

A black dog against a snow-white expanse should have been clearly visible, but no one had seen him. We looked and looked for him until dark and could not find him. The next day we searched again and asked our neighbors if they had seen him, but no one had. We began to think that a stranger driving through the valley might have picked him up and taken him away. Or maybe he had wondered into the BLM land and had become an easy meal for a hungry bear or cougar.

By the third day, we decided that Tar Baby was gone for sure. That thought saddened the entire Hartog household. We hoped and prayed that he was not lying somewhere suffering from frost bite. We wished him a speedy death.

On the fourth day when I went outside and opened the door, there stood Tar Baby! He was wagging his tail and was eager to come in. He was alive and well! We certainly were thrilled that Tar Baby had found his way home. We never found out where he had gone or how he had survived four days out in a Montana winter.

That was a secret that our loving dog kept from us!

65

Pie in the Sky—and Everywhere Else!

It was not supposed to end that way, but end that way it did! It was a pie-eating contest for selected participants at the Bible college in Montana. They had signed up to eat cream pies without using their hands. It was an "in your face" or more accurately a "your face in" the pie recreational activity.

On a couple of rectangular tables set up together lengthwise were dozens of cream pies: chocolate, lemon, banana, and coconut. Each participant stood in front of a pie with hands clasped behind his or her back. Leaning against the walls stood a crowd of onlookers who were cheering for the contestants. The excited crowd included students, staff, faculty, administration, and their children.

Suddenly, the pie-eating event took a chaotic turn. One of the contestants broke the rule. He reached into his pie with his hand and grabbed a big handful of gushy-pie cream. He aimed it directly at the contestant across the table and hit him right on the forehead. Before the judges could step in, the victim, half-blinded with cream pie dripping from his forehead, grabbed a handful of his gushy-pie cream and threw it deliberately across the table. He wasn't a good shot! He missed the contestant directly across from him. Instead, the flying-gushy-pie cream went smack into the open mouth of a cheering onlooker.

Before we knew it, pandemonium broke lose. Both contestants and onlookers were reaching for the cream pies and were throwing handfuls of sloppy cream across the room.

For a few moments it was like sticky-sweet-fluffy "manna" raining down from heaven! Chunks of gushy-pie cream were flying through the air in all directions. The cream pies ended up splattered on the walls, on the doors, and on people who were ducking and trying their best to get out of the way. But the flying-gushy stuff was bound to hit somebody! No one had planned the "pie shower." It was a spontaneous event once it got started. All the students who were in the middle of the pie war let off a lot of pent-up energy, and no one got angry. If there was a face with a frown, I certainly did not see it. I should say, I could not see it. More accurately, it could not see me—it was covered entirely with a white, fluffy mask.

The onlookers could not help but laugh at what was going on. The whole thing did get out of hand, but those who got hit looked hilarious. I didn't laugh—I don't know how to make those ridiculous throaty noises. Evidently, they come along with singing talent.

When it all quieted down, the administration ordered all those who had slung slushy cream to clean up the mess. To tell the truth, that pretty much included everyone in the crowd. We had to leave the room the way it was before the pie "shower"—spick and span!

Two factors helped us in the clean up effort: The windows in the room were few and were high above the firing line. The walls were cement blocks painted with waterproof latex paint—the sweet goop came off easily.

The pie-eating contest gone awry was one of those rare occasions that no one could have predicted. Folks like us who were there, and participated in some way or another, cannot help but smile every time we remember pie in the sky and everywhere else!

66

School in a Box

Regardless of where a U.S Air Force base is located, children of airmen must be educated. This was true of the kids at the Air Force radar base in Maiden Valley. When the government constructed the buildings to run the radar on Judith Mountain Peak, a new elementary school was part of that building project. The school property that was next to the Air Force base, included a playground and a red brick, modern building with two classrooms, a kitchen-dining area, and bathrooms. On the property was a wooden frame house, which the Air Force left intact. This small white house was adequate for a single teacher. Over time, it had been the home of several teachers.

The elementary school in Maiden Valley was part of the Fergus County rural public school system that was headquartered in Lewistown, Montana. The few children of the ranchers in the valley attended this school, along with the Air Force children. Before the Bible college bought the vacated radar base, enrollment had dropped to only about three or four students. With the move of the college to Maiden Valley, the attendance jumped to about a dozen children.

The teacher, Miss Walters, was faced with a new challenge: teaching a dozen children in at least four different grades. With the help of an assistant hired by the school board the students ended the 1973-74 school year successfully. John finished second grade with flying colors! He scored way ahead in the national tests. Paul was too young to attend school. When the time came for him to attend the Maiden Valley elementary school; he also surpassed his national tests.

Miss Walters got engaged and informed the school board that she was not returning the following year. She kept her promise to them and to her fiancée. She got married and flew the small white "coop"!

The board initiated a search for a new teacher and found one that summer. A month before school started, Miss Kephart[52] moved into the little white house. She was a product of the sixties with an appreciation for artistic expression. Her jovial, friendly personality endeared her to the children right from the beginning.

That fall, Miss Kephart worked tirelessly with the children on a special Christmas program: a presentation of *A Christmas Carol*. We knew that the children were busy and excited because John kept us updated on the progress of the whole endeavor. The teacher and the children, with the help of some of the parents, made the costumes and the props.

The news about the play had traveled through Maiden Valley. On the day of the big production, the residents crammed into the school to witness the greatest drama ever staged by elementary children. All of us were awed by the young actors, their costumes, and the props. The children had memorized their parts well, and the drama went on without a hitch! That night, the little school was transformed into the "Maiden Valley Little Theater."

Winter gave way to spring, when the children's energy blossoms fully. Miss Kephart came up with a creative tactic to contain that in-full-bloom energy. She instructed the children to ask their parents for a large cardboard box, like a refrigerator or stove box, and bring it school. John came home

---

[52] Not her real name.

and asked us to please go to town and find him a large box. He was thrilled about the new upcoming school project.

That whole school year, our son was as high as a kite! Anyway, Martha and I dutifully went to town and asked for a refrigerator box at the local appliance store. The other students' parents were also successful. It's a good thing that the students were so few—the appliance store was small. None of the parents, including us, bothered to ask why the children needed the boxes. John told us that the teacher had directed the children to keep their boxes at home and decorate them to look like houses. After completing their project at home, they were to bring their "houses" to school.

Martha provided the materials needed, including some colorful remnants for the window curtains. When his "house" was completed, John dragged it to school. He was happy as a lark. If a strong Chinook had come through while John was walking, the wind would have sent John and his "house" flying across Maiden Valley!

A few weeks later, John forgot his lunch; so Martha and Paul walked to school to deliver it. When Martha opened the door to the classroom, she was greeted by "houses" sliding and swaying on the floor. The students had moved their desks into their "houses" and were free to work there.

Martha and Paul stood wide-eyed for a moment. Then Martha blinked and identified John's house; she walked to it, but it was vacant. Martha asked Miss Kephart if she knew where the "tenant" happened to be. Smiling, the teacher pointed to the closet behind the room. Martha opened the closet door.

There, sitting on a desk flanked by two other desks, sat John with a great big grin on his face. Enthusiastically, he informed Martha that he was tired of roaming around the room in his "house." He noticed some empty desks around the room;

thus, he dragged three of them into the closet. Now, he had his own private office with a desk for each major subject!

Speechless (truly a miracle!), Martha kept her mouth shut, dropped John's lunch pail on his "Health and Science" desk, shut the closet door, and grabbed Paul's hand. Shaking loose her temporarily paralyzed tongue, she said to him, "Let's get out of here!"

One day, a board member came to the school and found his child in his "house." The parent was so upset about it that he called a board meeting to discuss the shocking school behavior. Soon after the meeting, John came home gloomy and with his "house" in tow. The school board had decreed that all the "houses" be vacated and hauled away from the school grounds.

Since the children had to give up their nicely decorated "houses," Miss Kephart decided to involve the children in redecorating her own little white house. She wanted to spruce it up a bit and convert it into a work of art. She bought cans of paint in rainbow colors: red orange, yellow, green, blue, indigo, and violet. She also supplied the children with brushes and turned them loose in her house. They had a jolly time splattering paint on the walls and on each other.

When the children completed their painting project, both the house and they themselves looked like pieces of modern art. In comparison, their creations made Picasso's art look like children's play!

67

Tar Baby and the Goose

We moved back to Iowa after teaching for five years in Lewistown, Montana. When we returned to my native state, we rented a duplex for a year next to Faith Baptist Bible College. We rented while we got things in place to buy land and build a house.

That left us with a problem: Tar Baby, our black cockapoo. After checking out several possibilities, we found a college-staff member who lived in the country, about three miles from school. He offered Tar Baby a temporary "home" until we moved to our acreage.

Tar Baby's short-term pilgrimage was an open spot on the yard, close to the house. I built a large fenced pen to keep him safe and added an insulated dog house. Our family went to visit him daily, watered and fed him, and cleaned out his yard. Most importantly, we petted him, played with him, and let him run lose.

Tar Baby's host family had a number of children and a menagerie of animals: chickens, geese, goats, and even a pet raccoon. One day when we went to visit Tar Baby, one of their boys asked if he might take the pup for a walk around the yard. I had Tar Baby on a leash and thought he needed a little romping around. So I handed the leash to the lad.

As he walked Tar Baby around the yard, the lad came upon a gaggle of geese eating grass. The resolute dog pulled hard on the leash, wanting to go after the geese. The lad let the leash slip out of his hand, and Tar Baby made a mad dash for the gaggle. In that split second, the geese noticed the "bat-dog" in his black curly coat, darting towards them. The frightened geese took off in all directions. If they had flown in their usual V formation, they would have *aVerted* a disaster.

The host family's acreage was on a corner where two busy roads meet. Some of the crazed geese flew over one of the roads. At the same time that a man in a pickup came driving down that road, a panicky goose flew right smack into the pickup windshield and cracked it from top to bottom!

The goose landed in the ditch, stretched out its neck, and looked around to see what had hit it. Then, seeing that the coast was clear, it shook itself, and waddled off. I caught Tar Baby and put him in his pen.

The driver stopped his pickup and wanted to know whose goose that was. I replied, "Not mine!" Politely, I told him the goose belonged to the people living in *this* home. I did tell him that the dog was mine, and that he had scared the gaggle.

The man looked bored. He knew "the rest of the story!" What he wanted to know was who was going to buy him a new windshield. I said, "Not I!" I suggested these options: *his* comprehensive insurance, *this* home owner's insurance, or *my* home owner's insurance.

It seemed far fetched to think that my home owner's insurance might cover a freak accident like this, but I was ready to investigate it. He wrote down my name and I took his. I went to our insurance agent and told him what had happened.

He said, "I have never had a claim like this! But, we will cover the damages!"

So it went from the dog to the goose, from the goose to the pickup, from the pickup to my home. And my home owner's insurance policy paid it!

68

Few Bees or not Few Bees

What do you do when you don't have much money? You do what you can do in line with what you have to do. The acreage I had found when we moved back to Iowa made it possible for me to do just that. Truly God had helped us purchase that land. First, small acreages were difficult to find; and second, our finances were extremely limited. The twenty-acre plot that I found was priced at $25,000, but the owner took as down payment the only money I had—$200!

The acreage had no utilities or buildings. It was just land—perfect for rearing two active growing boys. The rugged rolling acres, landscaped with hickory and black walnut trees and a little creek, were a perfect sanctuary for wild life like song birds, deer, raccoons, possums, squirrels, bull snakes, and even a ground hog.

According to the real estate contract, the seller was to survey the land. However, the trees were so thick that the survey had to wait until the late fall, after the trees had shed their leaves. When the survey was completed, it revealed that parts of the land were on our future neighbors' side of the fence, and parts of their land were on the piece inside the fenced area I was in the process of buying.

The contract also stipulated that the seller was to give me a free and clear title. He had to secure quit claim deeds from the land owners around the twenty-acre plot. This required exchanging all the parcels in order to relocate them on the right sides of the fences; this process took over a year. Consequently, sixteen months after signing the contract to buy the land, the deal was ready to close—finally!

In the meantime, the seller sold a ten-acre piece from his farm to another buyer. Both of us closed the deal on the same day in the same lawyer's office. The cost to both of us was $25,000. I acquired twenty acres, and the other buyer received ten acres. In the sixteen months it took to close, our land had doubled in value. We now had $25,000 equity with our piece of property.

After living in a small duplex, we were eager to homestead on our acreage. Martha could hardly wait to clean a new house; the boys were dreaming of playing cowboys and Indians on the rugged land; and I was anxious to get back to gardening and bee keeping. We began clearing the land; and I decided to order a bee colony, even before we built the house.

Some days later, I received a call from the post office that my bees had arrived. It was late in the afternoon; so I zoomed out of the house, drove to the post office, rushed in and asked, "Where are my bees?"

The postman said casually, "They're not *in* here."

Surprised, I exclaimed, "I just received a call that the bees had arrived!"

He smiled and waved me to follow him. He took me outside to the back deck and pointed to the box. Because every one in the post office was afraid of bees, the delivery man had to unload them outside.

It was late when I returned to our duplex with the bees. In the fading light of day, I opened the package and shook the bees into the open hive that I had set by the back door. Soon it was dark and quiet, and my bees were resting peacefully. I looked forward to the next morning and the twelve-mile ride to their new place.

I woke up to a beautiful sunny day. There was not a cloud in the sky. After one of Martha's hardy breakfasts, I picked up the hive and set it in the back of our little-old-green Vega. With its back seat folded down, it turned into a station wagon. To put plenty of distance between me and my humming friends, I placed the hive back by the hatch door. Happy and rested, we (thousands of bees and I) headed for the country. What more could a human being or a bee want?

To get to the acreage, I took county blacktop roads. Because Iowa is pretty much laid out in square miles, I encountered a gravel road crossing at each mile section corner. That was no problem, of course, since the gravel roads have stop signs, and the paved roads have the right of away. Then five miles after leaving town, as I drove merrily down the road, I saw a moving cloud of dust off to my left. That was a common sight in Iowa. Anyone driving down a gravel road always leaves a cloud of dust behind, unless it has rained the night before.

About half a mile from where that gravel road met the blacktop, I saw the dust maker. It was a white truck coming down the mile road at a fairly high speed. The driver had half a mile to stop; so I did not give it a second thought. As we both got closer to the crossing, I became a little worried. The truck driver did not seem to be slowing down enough. I started to slow down a little even though I had the right of way. When the truck driver came to the stop sign, he did not stop at all, nor did he even slow down!

Instead, he shot onto the blacktop ready to cross it. I knew we were headed for a crash! I hit the brakes hard as the windshield of the little Vega turned a blur of white in front of me. Immediately I heard a loud thump, which jarred the driver's seat. And then it was all over. The white truck crossing in front of me had missed me by about a foot and was still barreling down the gravel road now to my right, throwing up a cloud of dust behind him—oblivious of the fact that both of us had missed by a split second turning into "ashes to ashes and dust to dust."

I breathed a prayer of thanks, started the engine again, and began to move forward. Then, I sensed that my honey buddies were no longer humming softly. At first the noise was muffled, but it quickly grew louder and louder, and closer and closer! Dark blotches were swirling around my head, and all the windows began to darken as well!

Instantly, I realized what had happened. When I jammed on the breaks to avoid the crash with the white truck, the beehive shot forward and slammed into the back of my seat. My formerly contented, humming, sweet buddies had turned into annoyed, buzzing bees. They zoomed out of the hive by the thousands!

That near-car-collision had turned my little Vega into a beehive with a terrified "King Bee"! Like a Queen Bee in a normal hive, I was a prisoner in my own kingdom! Irritated bees were flying all around me! Buzzing Angry Bees! VERY ANGRY BEES! Of course, since I was driving, I did not have my veil on.

I pulled over and sat still to consider my options. If I started swatting them, I could never win. Any escape attempt involved movement. Obviously, what-ever I tried might anger my bees even more and provoke them to sting me—thus commit mass suicide.[53]

Besides, if I escaped unscathed, the bees would end up sizzling in the hot car; and if I left the doors open, I was bound to lose all of them. Then, I remembered what my friend Willie, the beekeeper, had taught me in Montana.[54] "When you are around bees," he calmly admonished, "move very slowly." I

---

[53] When a honey bee stings, it leaves its barbed stinger behind, along with its abdomen—digestive tract muscles and nerves.
[54] See "Where Has All My Honey Gone?" story #53.

acted upon my only sensible option: I sat still without moving a muscle—not even my eyelids. I noticed that the buzzing buddies were settling down. Not as many of them were covering the windshield and the other windows. Consequently, my vision scope was enough for me to drive safely.

S—l—o—w-l—y, I reached for the steering wheel, and I turned on the ignition. Steering the Vega at about 5 mph, I drove onto the blacktop and took my time avoiding road bumps and sudden stops at the stop signs. As my Vega crept along, I could see the countryside more clearly—the number of bees on the windows was declining! Humming happily and quietly, they were flying back into their cozy hive.

When I arrived at the acreage, "only" hundreds of bees, not thousands, were buzzing around the windows. The rest were buzzing in the hive. I slipped out of the car and left them alone for an hour or two. Eventually, almost all the bees flew back into the hive, and I was able to move it to its permanent place.

Thankfully, that day I had escaped two deadly disasters: death because of a reckless stranger in a white truck and death because of irritated buddies from a white hive. I had driven seven miles with thousands of angry bees in my little-old-green Vega but not one had stung me!

69

Our White House in the Woods

Waiting for the closing of our acreage had paid off. Our piece of property now came along with $25,000 equity! It was time to begin the process of building a house. We went to the bank for a home loan. The banker was willing to grant us only a construction loan, not a final house loan. Nevertheless, that was a step forward, and I took the next step straight to our kitchen table, which became my make-shift-house-designing station. I became our family's "architect," and things began to move fast! I found an excavator to put in a drive and dig the basement.

Our twenty-acre plot was considered agricultural land, and we were exempt from the regular bothersome building permits; thus things moved ahead even faster. Next, I located a construction company and hired them to build the house from my rough architectural drawings. They framed up our house with windows and doors and surprised me with a bill for their work. I had planned for them to finish it all. But they only framed houses, and their bill reflected just that!

That meant I had to become our family contractor, minus the white-hard hat—we couldn't afford one. In November, we moved into the house, just as it was; and we lived in the basement while we finished up the main floor. I contacted subs: electricians, plumbers, and trim workers. That year, hammers were part of our Christmas presents for the boys. With their help, I did much of the other work myself: flooring, dry walling siding, shingling, painting. Within three months, we were able move to the main floor. In the process, we had gained a considerable amount of sweat equity.

Spring time arrived—time to finish up the outside of the house, including painting the siding. On a sunny day, I grabbed my paint bucket and climbed to the top of my ladder. I was eager to transform our house into a white house in the woods. Then it happened!

One second I was painting merrily away from the top of the ladder; the next second I was desperately hanging on a sliding ladder, while grabbing tightly the paint bucket with the other hand. Thankfully, when the bucket and I crashed, we hit soft ground, and I did not get hurt; but paint splattered all over the windows and nearby door. I quickly cleaned up all the paint before that entire wall became a continuous white canvass.

Spring turned into summer. With the house almost completed, the boys could enjoy their big back yard. They got a lot of exercise and fresh air, built forts, and pretended to be cowboys. On clear nights, the rural setting granted us a blessing: dark skies speckled with millions of shining stars! A few years later, one of those dark nights almost turned into a tragedy.

We were enjoying a relaxing summer evening as a family when some of John's classmates showed up at our door. John was a senior at a small Christian high school in Des Moines; we knew all of his classmates well and welcomed their unexpected visit.

John joined his friends outside where they were talking and laughing. Paul, Martha, and I had stayed inside and let the older kids have fun. They were good kids; Martha and I were not worried. Then, about an hour later, the kids came to the door. John was not with them, and his classmates looked awfully somber.

We asked them, "What's the matter? Where's John?"

They replied, "We don't know!"

Then, they went on to tell us that, just for fun, they had kidnapped John; and they had dropped him off a couple of miles down the road, by an abandoned farm place. They had planned to return later and pick him up. However, when they went back to look for him, they could not find him. What worried them, they told us, was that a car had slowed down near the place where they had dropped off John. Now, they were worried that maybe strangers had picked him up.

We jumped in our car and joined the kids in their search. We drove up and down the roads looking for him, but could not find hide or hair of him so we returned home. We were about to call the police for help, but I decided to go back by myself and look for him again.

The dark country nights had both an advantage and a disadvantage. On the one hand, these nights revealed clearly the millions of beautiful shining stars against the dark sky. On the other hand, the nights hid completely any human shadows fleeting through the ditches, which lay along the lush corn growing in the summer fields.

With my window open and driving slowly and closely alongside the ditches, I shouted, "John! John!"

I went up and down at least two miles either way from the abandoned farm place where the kids had dropped off John. I did this several times and was about to give up and drive back home. All of the sudden, I saw a dark shadow slither out of a corn field into the ditch! The figure stretched out its arms and waved them vigorously. My heart just about jumped out of my rib cage!

I drove closer and called to him. Sure enough, it was John! He jumped into the car, and we sped straight home. As we drove, he told me what had happened. He had decided to walk home by staying close to the edge of the corn fields. Every time a car drove by, he threw himself on the ground. That way, no strangers would see him and try to pick him up.

Then, a big dog spotted him and barked at him. (The dog's loud-rumbling bark triggered off the image of a huge, ferocious dog in John's mind). Immediately, he scampered farther into the cornfield to put a greater distance between him and the dog. Consequently, the people looking for John were unable to see him.

Moreover, the dense cornfields made it impossible for him to recognize familiar voices. However, when he heard my shouts, they sounded familiar. He left the safety of the fields and walked out into the open ditches, which made it easier for me to see him.

When we arrived home, his classmates, even some of the boys broke down and cried. They felt bad for having abandoned him in the dark. However, now John was safe and sound—just cold and drenched from the dew on the corn stocks.

That dark-summer-night incident had a good ending: our white house in the woods exploded with rejoicing, and the stars shone brighter against their black canopy!

Rejoice with me;
For I have found my sheep which was lost.

—Luke 15:6b

70

Just a Matter of Time

After trading off my 1964½ Mustang for a red pickup in 1972,[55] the possibility of owning another Mustang became a mere fantasy. But in 1979, my dream became an unbelievable reality.

Living on twenty acres afforded us the opportunity to take care of four children for almost the whole summer. Martha's sister, Blanca, was having major surgery that was to restrict her from lifting her toddler for six weeks. Blanca and her husband had planned on boarding their four children at different relative's homes. When we heard of their plan, we offered to take all four children. It was only for the summer—the perfect season for kids to play outdoors.

Blanca delivered her happy, noisy, and energetic children in her Cadillac. Up to recently, she had hauled the kids in her 1972 Mustang. Understandably, her husband purchased the Cadillac to replace the "pony." In passing, I mentioned that I loved Mustangs and hoped to own another one some day.

During that time, Martha was working full-time at a bank in Ankeny, but as a college teacher I had the summers off. With the help of our two sons and Blanca's oldest girl, I became the "nanny" for three children. I set up a daily work, play, and nap schedule according to the children's abilities and needs.

---

[55] See "Apartment Living (part two)" story #46.

Since we had just built our house, there was no grass on our lawn. A farmer friend had leveled roughly about an acre around the house, but the only things that grew on our lawn were dandelions and stones of all sizes, from half the size of golf balls to tennis ball size.

Each morning I laid out a plot, ten feet by ten feet for the kids, except for the youngest one. I gave them the task of picking up the stones and putting them in buckets to prepare the ground for grass seed. After working for about an hour, the children could play the rest of the day. The toddler took an afternoon nap.

Our hilly grassland and forest provided them *plen'y* of room to play. To them, it must have seemed as if they had the whole world to themselves. However, often they found enough to keep them occupied within shouting distance of the house.

Each day when Martha came home, she asked me if the children had behaved. I always said, "Yes, I could hardly even hear them."

Since happy, robust children make a lot of noise playing outside, Martha found it hard to believe that they were so quiet. One day she came back sooner than usual, and she discovered the secret of the silent, peaceful children.

When I greeted her with the usual hug, she hollered (to make sure I could hear her), "Oh! No wonder the children are quiet!" Still imbedded in my ears were the cotton balls, which I stuffed into my sound-detecting organs every morning after she left for work!

The summer went by with no problem. The kids and I got a lot of exercise, fresh air, and sunshine. The older ones had fun cooking up dishes from dandelions, which were plentiful, and dared the younger ones to eat the odd-looking but safe concoctions. If the younger children misbehaved, the older ones threatened to sic the geese after them.

My '72 Mustang

At the end of the summer, four suntanned, happy children boarded the Cadillac and returned to Michigan with their parents. About a month later, Blanca's husband called. After the usual greetings, he asked me, "How would you like to have our old Mustang?"

Nonchalantly, I responded, "Sure!" We said our good-byes, and I thought nothing more about his offer.

Another month went by, and we got a call from Michigan again. Blanca's voice on the other end said, "When are you going to pick up the car?"

Still not taking it seriously, I replied, "Oh, some day soon," and asked, "You're not serious, are you?"

Blanca said firmly, "Yes, we really mean it!" She convinced me; so I promised to pick up the car. And I did! I caught a ride to Blanca's place with a teaching colleague who was going to Michigan for a conference.

The Mustang had 48,000 miles on it and was loaded with everything a car of that era could offer: bucket seats, power brakes, power steering, four on the floor, a 351 Cleveland engine, power convertible top, leather seats, and more.

For title registration purposes, Blanca and her husband sold me the car for $1. I became the proud owner of a beautiful 1972 Mustang convertible. When I returned home, I completed the title transfer. Sales tax at the time was three percent; the state of Iowa slapped me with a 3¢ tax.

Nine months later, I was asked to speak at the annual faculty retreat. To kick off the new school year, teachers and spouses were having dinner at a restaurant on the south side of Des Moines. Since we lived in a northern suburb, we had to drive through the city. As usual, Martha and I talked as I drove. Suddenly, I saw flashing red lights on the car behind me.

Immediately I pulled into the parking lot of a gas station—a spot where every driver going down that street could see us. Obviously, the Mustang had a lot more "get up and go" than my old Vega did, and I was not paying particular attention to the speedometer. According to the friendly patrolman, his radar clocked me going ten miles over the speed limit. He issued me a well-deserved ticket, but he was gracious and wrote down my speed at less than ten over.

However, a Hartog saying goes like this: "If things are looking bad, cheer up, because they are going to get worse." And that evening things got worse. The problem was that Martha and I had started off early hoping to arrive before everyone else.

While the patrolman was ticketing me, one by one the other faculty members and their spouses drove by the gas station. One by one they did a double take when they saw the flashing lights of the patrol car; the cop standing by the shining Mustang convertible; and their colleague sitting at the wheel!

We waved a cheery, "Howdy!" We were confident that things were going to get worse, and they did. But Martha and I were prepared. We talked over the matter while the friendly policeman was writing out my well-deserved ticket. We decided to play it cool.

Martha and I were the last to arrive at the restaurant; but we had a good excuse, and every body knew it! Naturally, we were expecting a lot of friendly teasing from my fellow teachers about going too fast. They did not disappoint us, and Martha and I took it in stride—as planned. We played it cool and smiled big!

However, as we expected, matters got even worse. After the meal, I had to get up and bring the "keynote speech." The retreat theme that year was "Take Time!"

71

The Jaws of Death!

Tar Baby's happiest day was when we moved to our house in the woods. He became familiar with his future home soon after the land deal closed, and we began clearing the building site. He tagged along whenever we went to the acreage to cut down brush. This meant taking a detour to the country place where he was boarded while we lived in the duplex.[56]

On moving day into our unfinished house, our dog moved with us along with his insulated house. He had been used to living outdoors in a temporary pen, and he became more of an outside dog. But, since we spent much time outside working or playing, he loved it!

Tar Baby was fond of each member of our family. We purchased him for the boys, but I was his "alpha dog." We were soul-buddies, and our whole family knew it. Tar Baby was at my side wherever I went. He watched every move I made; and when I spoke to him, he listened attentively and wagged his tail.

One of his favorite activities was running back and forth ahead of me on my strolls through the pasture. However, Tar Baby's true delight was to chase rabbits and squirrels—his hunting instincts took over when he saw one. In a flash, he went after it! Therefore, he did not stay at my side all day long. On a particular day, I was just taking a peaceful hike around

---

[56] See "Tar Baby and the Goose," story #69.

the pasture. A week earlier, I had sprained both wrists and was unable to do much manual work. I was just relaxing.

I was admiring some delicate wild flowers, when suddenly I heard the sound of something snap, followed by a sickening scream. I ran as fast as I could in the direction of the scream, which was the area where I had seen Tar Baby wander off. I saw no dog, but as I approached the barbed wire fence along our property, I heard a frightful, gasping sound.

I crawled over the fence, and there in the tall grass of an abandoned pasture was Tar Baby with his head caught in a big, rusty old trap! I tried to free him! But my sprained wrists did not have the strength to get the trap jaws open enough to release him!

I had to pull each of the jaws side ways and then push down on both jaws at the same time. That left me with no free hand to lift him out of the deadly trap, and he was too weak to crawl out by himself. I could barely open the jaws and only long enough for him to take a quick breath; but immediately the ugly jaws snapped around his head again and blocked his wind pipe.

This happened time after time. I worked out on that pasture for nearly half an hour trying to rescue my dog from the jaws of death. We had no cell phones in those days, and no one could hear my shouts for help.

Tears were running down my face as I cried out, "No, Tar Baby! No, Tar Baby! Don't die on me!"

Tar Baby was not making any sounds anymore, and each time I tugged at the trap, my wrists weakened more and more.

I shouted, "Oh, God help me!"

At once, God helped me. A thought come to my mind, which let me figure out a solution. I got one jaw half way down one more time and put one knee on it to keep it down. After that, I worked with both hands on the other jaw and got it half way down. Next, I put my other knee on the second jaw and

The Jaws of Death!

put my full weight on both jaws. They went completely down, and I heard a click. Finally, they stayed open!

Now, with two free hands, I lifted Tar Baby out of the trap. He was limp and did not move. I laid him down tenderly in the tall grass and sat down beside him for a half hour. I was too sad to do anything and too weak to walk back the quarter mile to the house.

As I looked down at Tar Baby through my teary eyes, I finally noticed a little movement in his chest. There was still a small sign of life in that limp little body! I petted him and massaged his chest gently. We were out there alone together for another half-hour.

Finally, Tar Baby opened his big, brown, gentle eyes! He looked at me lovingly, and gave his tail a tiny little wag!

"You are going to make it, Tar Baby," I whispered to him. "You are going to make it!" I then yelled joyfully and thankfully.

The small breaths of air, which he had breathed each time I was able to get the jaws partly open, carried him through until I could deliver him completely from that deadly trap. After another half hour, I picked him up carefully and carried him to the house. From that day on, he clung close to my side constantly, even in the back pasture.

Tar Baby, one of the great joys of my life, had survived the jaws of death!

Happiness is having a loyal dog.

—JH II

72

Fire! Fire!

"We are planning an overnight camp-out with our guys," our church youth leader said to me. "May we have it at your place?" His request sounded reasonable. After all, twelve of our back eighteen acres were wooded—perfect for camping. Recently a farmer friend had put his cows back there, but for now, they were pasturing at his place.

Martha and I agreed to let the youth have their special outing at our place. Our sons were in the youth group, and they were in full agreement with us. I got back to the youth leader with our reply, "Set a date and plan the overnight camping."

Our part was to lay out a treasure hunt. We hid small trinkets in clumps of grass, in hollow trees, on low tree branches, and under small rocks. On the appointed day, about twenty-five youth and their leaders descended on our place before dark. The kids scattered out on their treasure hunt, which was a big success. We had put out about thirty-five "treasures," some of which the kids never found. In our later hikes, we ran into a few of them; others are still hidden in the woods to this day. Even Martha and I could not find them—we forgot where we hid them!

Then it was time to build the fire for their cookout. The youth had to gather the wood, but they found plenty of dead, dried wood lying under the trees. Soon, the air smelled of hot dogs and S'Mores. Food cooked outdoors is so much tastier!

From our house, we could hear the gleeful shouts of the youth as they participated in their fun and games. They threw more wood into the fire and gathered around it for singing and devotions. It was a beautiful night under the stars, and eventually it was time to hit the sack. The youth had brought sleeping bags, and some had pup tents. Talking and giggling went on until the last few eyelids finally closed.

Early in the morning, the first ray of dawn began to bring life to the woods again. The campers woke up to a joyous serenade—compliments of the song birds! (Our woods were habitat to at least forty varieties of song birds, and their singing was a feature that struck first-time visitors to our acreage). The rest of that morning was consumed with normal camping activities. Then the tired but happy campers left. As they waved their thankful goodbyes, we turned our thoughts to other things.

About seven o'clock that evening while we were eating supper, an anxious neighbor called to tell us, "Your back acreage is on fire! You better call the fire department!" I informed him that unfortunately it was impossible for a fire truck to access that portion of our land. Behind our house was a deep ravine with no way to cross it.

I thanked him, turned to Martha and the boys, and yelled, "Let's grab some buckets and shovels and get back there right now!" With four buckets and a couple of shovels, we hurried to the back acres. We went down, then up the deep ravine, straight toward the area where the youth had camped the night before. When we arrived, we found a lot of burnt over pasture and smoldering stumps of dead trees that had gone up in smoke. Thankfully, there was no wind that evening.

Soon, the nice neighbor also joined us. The only equipment we had to battle the blaze were four five-gallon buckets. One by one we filled them half way with water from the small creek that ran through our acreage. It took us until midnight, but we finally got the fire put out.

Later, we learned that a couple of boys had started a fire inside a hollow dead tree after the others had gone to sleep. The draft immediately took the fire up into the tree like a chimney. The boys tried to put it out and thought they had succeeded. But they hadn't and didn't know it. Throughout the day, the fire had spread from the stump over several acres of pasture grass and fallen branches as well.

When they heard about our predicament, the boys approached us the next day at church. Without doubt, God had enabled us to avert a potential disaster. As we tried to put out the fire, I was reminded of these words, "See how great a forest a little fire kindles!"[57]

> *Happy is the man who finds wisdom,*
> *And the man who gains understanding.*
>
> —Proverbs 3:13 (NKJV™)

---

[57] James 3:5

73

Preach It, Brother!

Earlier in the week, I had received a call from a church without a pastor. They needed someone to fill the pulpit for Sunday. It was a somewhat short notice; but I was going to be free that Sunday. I accepted the invitation, and began to study right away.

All prepared for preaching on Sunday, I was able to work outdoors all day that Saturday. I hauled and stacked wood for winter, raked leaves, and took in some of the last garden crops. All day long I wondered how much honey the bees had been able to gather for the winter.[58] Now it was late Saturday evening; I needed to do one more thing: open the hive and take a look before the sun went down.

Since I was to preach the next day, I decided to put on my bee protection veil—just to be safe. I had grown used to my sweet buddies and often opened their hive for a look without wearing the veil. As long as the weather was nice, and I did not make quick moves, the bees minded their own business—gathering nectar.

Because it was late in the evening, I hurried to put on the veil. When I opened the hive, I could see that the bees were busy at work; they were buzzing as usual. However, this time it seemed a little louder, a sign that the hive was prospering. I

---

[58] See "Where Has All My Honey Gone?" and "Few Bees or not Few Bees," stories #53 and 68.

put the lid back on the hive and headed for the house, but the buzzing sound tagged alongside of me.

I realized that a bee had made its way inside the veil and was trapped. I took the veil off to free it; but in the process, it stung me above my upper lip. I did not think much of it. After all, I had been stung before, and the result had been little or no reaction. I continued to work outside for another twenty minutes, putting away tools. It was now dark—time to turn in for the night.

I came in the house and stood tall at the kitchen entry waiting for my, "Hello kiss." Instead, Martha walked up to me and exclaimed, "What in the world happened to you?" And then she broke out laughing. She continued, "You look so funny!" Still no kiss.

"Oh, it's nothing," I said calmly, "A bee got into my veil and stung me on the lip. It's nothing." I was beginning to understand why no kiss.

Still laughing she said, "You ought to see yourself! Your cheeks are all puffy and your eyes look like you're squinting! I can hardly recognize you! You really do look funny!" She burst out laughing again. Now I understood fully. Martha doesn't kiss strangers.

When she calmed down, she said, "What are you going to do about tomorrow? Do you think you better call the church and tell them you can't come?"

Before she continued her interrogation, I looked at the clock. It said "10 o' clock." I calmly told Martha, "It's too late to call the church. They won't be able to find anyone else at this hour."

I decided to get some rest and wait to see how things were in the morning. After a nice warm shower, I hit the sack. I did not have to close my eyes much. They were already half way shut because of the bee sting! When I woke up in the morning, my cheeks were still puffy and my eyes were still squinty. Martha suggested that I call someone to fill in.

A little offended I said, "I would if I knew whom to call. Besides, I have my message ready, and I can still talk." Looking funny certainly didn't mean being speechless! Words could still flow out of my mouth!

By the look on Martha's face, trying to mimic my own face, I realized that it was my looks that bothered her. I should have been more precise in writing our wedding vows: "Do you take this man even if he ever gets squinty little eyes and puffy cheeks!"

As a Dutchman, I was determined to go, even if I had, squinty . . . you know what! Resolutely, I said to Martha, "I've never been there before. They don't know what I'm supposed to look like. They'll just think that this is how I always look!"

We went! When we arrived at the church, they welcomed us warmly, and I preached as planned. Martha smiled at me as I preached, she always does. It encourages me. But this time it was different!

Since the church was within an hour's drive from home, we went home for dinner and a restful afternoon. During that time, the swelling subsided. I practically looked like my old real self again!

Martha said, "Now what are you going to do? They won't recognize you!"

She had a problem when I looked different and also when I looked like myself! Figure that one out!

I replied, "Don't worry. I'll think of something!" For one thing, I decided to wear the same tie.

That evening when I walked into the church, I saw a lot of surprised faces. The few puzzled stares didn't faze me at all because it was nice to feel and look like my old self again. In case you're wondering, I did confess why I looked so different. It was my first and only confession in front of a church congregation!

74

What's in a Name?

We were happy teaching at the college in Iowa, and we were thankful for our peaceful, country living. However, God called us out of our serene surroundings to the edge of a hustling and bustling metropolis. After teaching in Iowa for seven years, I was called to teach and be the head librarian at Calvary Bible College in Belton, Missouri, a suburb of Kansas City.

My philosophy is that one of the greatest teaching tools is to know the students by name. Thus, before the beginning of every semester, I try to learn the names of all the students who are registered to take my classes. I usually teach freshmen, and their number varies from year to year with highs of 130 to lows in the 80s.

Each year, it takes me about six weeks to connect the names with the faces. I don't have to learn the names of all the sophomores, juniors, or seniors because I already know them from the time they were freshmen. After teaching in a school for four years, I know the names of most of the student body.

Teaching at Calvary that fall meant teaching all new students. As usual, I put a plan into action. First, I requested the latest yearbook from the college, and I resolved to learn the names and faces of the freshmen, sophomores, and juniors pictured in the year book.

I choose those three categories because these students would be the sophomores, juniors, and seniors in the upcoming fall. I had to memorize 200 students by sight and name. This was also an excellent memory exercise to keep my mind sharp. Of course, I also had to learn the names of the incoming freshmen when they arrived on campus. Still, I had a jump start in recognizing by name the upper classmen.

About a month before school started, I made copies of the year book pages, cut out the students' pictures, and wrote the designated names on the back side of the pictures. I studied the students' pictures and names daily. I played the memory game "Go Fish!" by mixing up all the pictures and trying to guess the right name for each picture. It got to the point where I could read the names and remember the corresponding pictures, or I could glance at the pictures and say the names.

When I arrived on campus, a bulletin board across the Registrar's Office caught my attention. It had pictures of the incoming freshmen. Right away, I asked permission to make copies of the pictures. My future students were no longer faceless and nameless! On the first day of classes, I would address them by name.

In the meantime, during the few days before classes started, I met some returning students and greeted them by their names. As you can imagine, they were surprised and asked me, "How do you know me?" Or, "Have we ever met before?" Each day I met more students, and I greeted them by their names.

The first day of class, I called on "Peter" and asked him to open our session in prayer. Next, I called up "David," "Elizabeth," "Sally," and "Andrew,"[59] and asked them to help me hand out the syllabi. The students were amazed that I knew all their names. They whispered to each other, "How does he know us?" It was a lot of fun to surprise the students this way!

---

[59] Not their real names.

Soon, word got around about the new professor who knew every student by name. Since I did not have all the students in my classes, I did not meet every student during the first few weeks. However, each time I met returning students, I greeted them by name.

Two months into the semester, a student I had not met yet came walking toward me on the sidewalk. "Wonderful!" I thought, "Another chance to astonish a student!" Cheerfully and confidently, I exclaimed, "Hello! Bill!"

With a big smile, he replied, "I'm not Bill."

I was sure he was, but he said he wasn't; and I was not about to argue with him or give him a new name! Totally taken back, I asked, "You're not Bill?"

He laughed and exclaimed, "No! I'm not Bill! The yearbook has my name wrong!" Still laughing, he continued, "By the way, I've been waiting for this day for two whole months to hear you call me, Bill!"

He had heard that I was calling all the students by name, and that I had learned their names by studying the yearbook pictures. It made his day when I called him by the wrong name!

For the first time that fall, a student had to introduce himself to the new teacher. And both of us got a big kick out of it!

*Happiness is knowing
That God loves you
And knows you by name.*

—John Hartog II

75

The Raymore Police

Fall semester was done and so was our new house! Upon arriving in Missouri, we found a reputable Christian builder, chose our building site, and waited eagerly for our house to be finished. In the meantime, we lived in a duplex owned by our builder. The duplex was in Belton (the location of the Bible college), and our house site was in Raymore, the town next door and a peaceful suburb of Kansas City.

Now, the house was ready. It was time to move. The Hartog household became as busy as a bee hive. This would be one of the easiest moves we have ever made. Most of our things were still packed since we knew we were renting the duplex for just a few months. Moreover, the moving distance was only about three miles. Also, since it was semester break, our sons were free to help us as usual.

We waited to move after Christmas, and then things began to progress quickly. Having such a short distance, we were able to haul all the small things in multiple car trips. For the last few loads, we borrowed a pickup from the college to transport the large furniture pieces and the major appliances.

It was at the end of December and first part of January, but the weather was fairly warm at first. Then, the morning of our last moving day, the weather changed, and light snow flurries began to fall. As the day wore on, the snow became heavier, the wind blew stronger, and snow drifts piled higher.

By noon, as we were taking the final load, the snow storm had become a blizzard. The school pickup had no topper—we had to deal with the snow covered appliances as well as slippery roads. Also, it was difficult to navigate the roads because the snow was piling up deep on them. Thankfully, before the roads became impassible, we were able to unload and squeeze the last load into the garage. Then, we took a break and enjoyed a relaxing moment in our cozy new house.

When we first built our house, we were at the edge of the housing development. Beyond us lay farm fields. The morning after our move, I was standing by a window when I saw a police car driving slowly down our street, which ended by a corn field. The officer was having a difficult time because the wind was still blowing and the snow drifts were getting higher.

With nowhere to go, I invited the family to the "police show." Curious, we watched to see what would happen next. Suddenly, the car stalled right in front of our house. The policeman tried to go back and forth, but he could not get out. After a while, he knew it was hopeless. For one thing, there was no one to help him.

Though the view was entertaining, the boys and I bundled up and went outside to help the stuck-in-a-huge-snow-drift policeman. We grabbed our shovels, trudged through the snow to the street, and went to work. That snowdrift was a big one, but the three of us were able to dismantle it. We gave the car a strong push and sent the officer on his way. He was a thankful policeman, and we had made a valuable contact.

Winter gave way to spring, and spring to summer, and more houses started going up in our development. The city police patrolled our street a little more than usual. This gave us a sense of security. Whenever we were outside, we waved at them and smiled big! They always waved back, but didn't smile every time.

The Raymore Police

Some kids, who lived several blocks away, biked to our area and decided to loiter around the building sites. On one of their escapades on a site behind us, we caught them turning on the water and leaving it run. They ran to their bikes, which they had left by our house. I snatched the bikes and was about to lecture the kids, when our friendly policeman drove by. I walked the frightened kids to the police car, and the officer lectured them instead. The kids never played in the building sites or turned on the water ever again.

A few months later, we went to visit some friends for the evening. Upon our return home, I realized that in the last-minute rush, I had left the house key on the kitchen table. Unfortunately, the garage did not have a remote controlled opener—we couldn't afford one!

I was about ready to break a basement window, when I thought, "Great! What if the police drive by just when I'm trying to break into my house!" I backed out of the driveway, drove to the police station, and informed the officials of my plan. They assured me I would not be arrested if the police patrol saw me. Assured, I returned home.

As inconspicuously as possible, I broke that little basement window, reached in, opened it, and Martha crawled in—that was her expertise.[60] It was a single pane window that did not cost much to repair. After that incident, we started a "garage-door-opener fund." When we had enough money, we bought a remote controlled garage door opener, which turned out to be a blessing and almost a curse.

Not long after we had the opener installed, I heard a loud crash in the garage, and I rushed down to see what had happened. As soon as I stepped inside, I saw that one of the huge opener springs had broken off and had gone flying through the garage. However, no one was in it, and both cars

---

[60] See "Wedding Bells (part two)" story #25

had escaped the damage of a zooming spring. One of the cars was parked outside, and the boys had the other one.

Later on a beautiful fall night, Martha and I were at home enjoying a relaxing evening. Paul, a high school senior was already in bed, just as his soccer coach had ordered. Our peaceful evening was broken by a multiple ringing of our door bell. I ran to the front door, turned on the porch light, and peeked through the ornamental window. Standing on our porch, right under the light, was a burly policeman.

I opened the door just enough to squeeze my face through it. Flabbergasted, I asked him, "Is something wrong?"

He responded, "Come out here!"

When I stepped outside, I noticed that he was not alone. Behind him was a large group of young people who looked embarrassed and a little terrified.

The officer said, "I caught all these young folks TP-ing your house, and I have confiscated their driver's licenses." As he said this, he showed me the licenses stacked neatly in his hand. "Do you want to press charges?" He asked.

I glanced at the teens in the semi darkness and recognized several of their faces; I realized that they were Paul's classmates. Immediately, my apprehension disappeared and I decided this could be fun. I was capable of being just as mischievous as the teens were.

With a serious look on my face, I replied, "Hmm. Let me think about that for a few minutes." The culprits could not see it, but the policeman winked at me. Slowly and deliberately, I walked up to them, one by one. Then with a stern face, I gave them a good looking over.

Having completed my inspection, I turned to the policeman and told him, "Nah, I guess I won't press charges. It looks like these are my son's classmates. I know their parents well." A little shook up, the kids responded with a big sigh of relief.

The policeman turned around and gave them back their driver's licenses. Then, looking at them straight in the eye, he admonished them, "The next time you TP someone's house, be sure you don't park your cars right in front of the house. Park a block away!"

With a big smile on his face, he continued his instructions: "One more thing. Wear black clothing!"

*Helping the helpless
Affords happiness for both parties.*

—John Hartog II

76

The Disappearing Act

Tickets went on sale for the spring banquet at the Christian high school. The boys were wondering whom to invite, and the girls were looking forward to be invited. Our son Paul was a ninth grader, and this was to be his first date. He and his friend Tim planned to make it a four-some. Neither Paul nor Tim had their driver's licenses yet, but that minor matter was included in their plans. Paul takes after his father in this area.

Tim had his eyes set on a particular young lady; she was hoping he would invite her. And Tim did. Paul had several girls in mind. One of them, Kristy,[61] happened to be sitting at the ticket booth when Paul walked by. How convenient! He stopped and said to Kristy, "I'll take two tickets . . ." As Kristy reached for two tickets, Paul continued, "If you go with me."

Surprised Kristy looked up, paused, and replied, "Sure!" and handed the two tickets to Paul for payment. Now it was a four-some.

Next, Paul and Tim had two more ladies to ask out—their mothers. They were crazy and a lot of fun; but, more importantly, they could drive. Tim was to provide the limousine—his parents' old-beat-up station wagon. It sat six comfortably: two in the front, two in the back seat, and two in the wagon cargo bed.

---

[61] Not her real name.

To ensure that they arrived promptly at the various destinations that evening, the boys decided to ask Tim's mom to be the limousine driver—an excellent decision. I have experienced personally the dreadful results of Martha's problem: She was born directionally impaired! However, the boys could count on her to keep the atmosphere lighthearted. Their bait for their moms was dessert after the school banquet. Any sane woman would go for that delicious bait. The insane mothers consented. The four-some became a six-some.

On banquet night, Tim and his mom stopped by our house first. Martha sat in the front passenger seat. The two boys, decked out in their fancy suits and ties, sat in the back seat. Next, the limousine stopped at Kristy's house where Tim's date was also waiting.

Paul and Tim went to the door and escorted out the girls who were wearing pretty formals. The boys opened the car doors, helped the girls get in, and then shut the doors. The girls slid to the center of the back seat, but the boys did not sit beside them. Instead, Paul and Tim walked behind the vehicle, opened the tailgate and squeezed into the cargo bed. Tim's mom got out and closed the tailgate, got behind the wheel, looked at Martha, who rolled her eyes and smiled. No one said a word all the way to the banquet!

The silent limousine headed to the high school, where the gym had been decorated for the spring banquet; and a special meal awaited the young guests. When they arrived, the boys crawled out of their "floor seat" and opened the car doors for the girls. Now in familiar territory, the four-some talked and laughed as they greeted their peers going to the banquet.

While the youth banqueted, Martha and Tim's mom ate at a nearby fast food place and replayed the evening events. At the arranged time, the limousine returned to school to pick up the four youth. When they approached the vehicle, they were jovial and relaxed.

This time, after opening the car doors for their dates, Paul and Tim joined the girls on the back seat, and they talked and laughed non-stop. The noisy limousine then headed toward downtown in Kansas City. Icy rain had fallen that day, and the roads were slippery; but Tim's mom maneuvered the vehicle well.

The next destination was dessert at the Skies—a restaurant located at the top of the Hyatt Regency Hotel. The neat feature of the Skies is that it rotates slowly continuously. Over the span of 90 minutes, the Skies provides a stunning panoramic view of the city, especially at night, when Kansas City's lights look like millions of bright stars shining on the ground!

When they arrived at the Skies, Paul and Tim got out first, opened the car doors for *all* the ladies, and waited for their dates to get out of the car. In a matter of seconds, Tim's date got out, and so did Paul's date. But as soon as Kristy's feet hit the ground, she slid on the ice, and she disappeared under the parked station wagon. Dressed in her pretty formal, Kristi landed flat on her back and slid halfway under the car!

Every one hollered, "Oh, no!" and asked her, "Are you okay?" Her voice echoed softly, "Yes!" Paul stood by her head—with his eyes wide open wondering what to do next. Martha gave him one of her "help her out" looks. Bashfully, Paul reached down and pulled out Kristy, who looked fine but a little embarrassed.

Kristy's disappearing act under the car soon took a back seat that night. The stunning view from their booths in the Skies, the delicious dessert, and the cheerful conversation, all made it possible for the young people to conclude their first date as planned. The evening turned out to be a smashing success!

77

A Sign of the Times

In contrast to their mother who learned to drive in her thirties, John and Paul obtained their driver's permit as soon as they turned fourteen. Back then, we were living in Iowa, which issued permits to fourteen-year-olds. When we moved to Missouri, Paul had already been driving for half a year. However, as soon as we established residence in Raymore, Missouri, he had to relinquish his Iowa permit.

In Missouri a person had to be fifteen years old to obtain an instruction permit and sixteen to qualify for an intermediate license. Because our driving included the Kansas City heavy traffic, we decided to wait and apply for Paul's intermediate license.

Soon after Paul turned sixteen, I drove him to Harrisonville, our county seat, to take the driving test and apply for his license. Everything was new to us in Harrisonville—we had never been there. However, it was a small town, and we found the courthouse in no time at all. Paul went in by himself. I spotted a bench on the courthouse lawn and waited for him. It was the perfect spot to enjoy the unusually warm January day.

Soon, a patrol officer came out with Paul, and they got in our car for the driving test. The officer had Paul drive around town, beginning and ending at the court house. When Paul returned after the test, I asked him, "How did it go?"

He replied sadly, "Not well, I failed the test." I was shocked because he knew the laws. Also, he knew how to drive well since he had already driven before we moved to Missouri.

Surprised, I asked him, "What happened?"

"You won't believe it," Paul answered, "I drove the wrong way down a one-way street!"

I could not believe it! It was difficult to understand how he could do that in such a small town! When I asked him to point to the street, he said, "Right here on the side of the courthouse. It was the last block of the driving test."

Frustrated, I said, "How could you do that!"

He looked at me straight in the eye and responded in his typical calm demeanor, "I did not see the sign." Then he added, "The patrol officer said I could come back in two weeks and try again."

To make sure he saw it next time, I directed my disappointed son to join me and said, "Paul, let's go look at that sign."

Since we were right there by the courthouse square, it was only half a block away. When we got there, we saw no sign. If my sons do something wrong, I do not try to defend them, but this was different. We had looked around carefully. However, there was no "One Way" sign posted anywhere on that corner or on any corner in that intersection.

Puzzled by the whole thing, I told Paul, "Let's go talk to that patrol officer."

We went back into the courthouse, and I asked the officer why Paul had failed the test. He said "Because he drove the wrong way on a one-way street, the one on the west side of the courthouse."

Respectfully but confidently, I responded, "That's not a one-way street!" He replied, "Yes it is."

I could not believe it; so I exclaimed, "There's no sign anywhere near that street that shows it is a one-way street!"

"It *is* a one-way street!" The patrolman declared with all the authority granted to him by the state of Missouri! Then sheepishly he admitted, "The sign fell down six months ago, and we just haven't gotten around to puttin' it up yet."

I guess the locals knew that road well enough to know that it was a one-way street, but anyone coming in from the outside, like us, had no way of knowing this crucial information. The officer, however, did not show mercy!

Two weeks later, we decided to pay the stubborn patrol officer another visit. Once more, we drove the fifteen miles from Raymore to Harrisonville. This time, Paul passed the test with flying colors, and he was issued a Missouri intermediate driver's license.

Harrisonville may have been only a short distance away from the bustling Kansas City suburbs, but culturally it was much closer to the laid back life of the Ozarks!

The U.S. constitution only guarantees
The American people
The right to pursue happiness.
You have to catch it yourself.

—Benjamin Franklin

78

Hillbilly Bean Soup

Cooking is not one of my talents. To survive, my body depends completely on Martha's cooking, which is always pretty good, unless her spicy Latin blood takes over. Once in a great while, I have wandered into the kitchen and have prepared some edible delicacies.

One day while Martha was at work, I got brave and cooked up a huge batch of homemade soup. I happened to be home with not much to do, except to go grocery shopping for Martha.

I was going up and down the aisles looking for the stuff on her list, when I ran into a "Hillbilly Bean Soup" box. The colorful dried beans in it caught my eye. These were supposed to make a delicious soup. The directions looked easy. I thought, "Since Martha is working hard, I will surprise her with homemade soup for supper! She can just relax when she gets home."

We had tomatoes and onions from the garden and had ham in the fridge. I bought garlic and the package of beans, as well as the items on Martha's list, and drove home. Excited about my cooking endeavor, I put the groceries away, dove into the sink, rinsed the beans, and proceeded with the label directions.

I put the beans in the biggest pot I could find—a canning pot—covered them with water, and soaked them for about two hours. I figured that was enough time. Then I turned on

Hillbilly Bean Soup

the fire full blast, brought the beans to a bubbling boil, and simmered them for about an hour.

In the meantime, I diced two cups of ham, chopped up a whole onion and enough tomatoes to fill up two cups, and peeled the crackly skin off from the three garlic cloves. I checked the beans, and they were still quite hard. I reckoned the additional cooking with the other ingredients would take care of that.

I dumped the other ingredients in the pot. After it came to a boil, I let it simmer for several more hours. This was turning out to be an all-day project, and I ran into a minor pesky problem: the *krazy* soup kept boiling over, and Martha likes to keep her stove spic'n span.

I could hardly wait to sample my prize master-piece. After all, the chef should be the first to sample the broth. I waited two hours; then I helped myself to a big bowlful. Relishing its rich, full taste, I thought, "I bet Martha will be surprised at my cooking."

I looked at the clock. It was time to pick up Paul at his school. I knew that when I told him about my cooking project, he would be thrilled! But as soon as he opened the car door, he yelled with a hand over his nose, "What in the world did you eat?"

"Why?" I asked. He replied, "This whole car smells like garlic!" And he quickly opened his window to let in some fresh air. As we drove home, Paul looked at me every so often, turned up his nose, and winced.

By the time we arrived home, Paul's sense of smell had been desensitized, and he himself smelled like garlic. The kind, considerate boy that he was, he decided to stay outside and shoot baskets.

Soon, Martha came home. The moment she opened the front door, she hollered, "Hi! Good looking! What's that you've got cooking? This whole house smells like garlic and *frijoles*!"

I smiled and stated proudly, "I made some Hillbilly Bean Soup. It has sixteen different kinds of beans in it, ham, tomatoes, onions, and three cloves of garlic."

She asked, "Where did you get the garlic?"

I replied, "I got three cloves at the grocery store."

Surprised, she interrogated me, "You bought three cloves?"

"Yes, I did." I felt like a defendant in a court of law. I kept my answers brief, and did not provide any information that was certain to incriminate me.

Prosecutor: "What did they look like?"

Defendant: "Like three onions."

Prosecutor: "You put them in the soup?"

Defendant: "Yup, just like the directions said."

Prosecutor (absolutely shocked and talking fast with a Spanish accent): "No wonder this place smells garlicky! A clove is one little piece of a garlic bulb, not the whole garlic bulb. You must have put at least fifteen cloves in that soup with *frijoles*!"

Any judge would have asked the clerk to strike out the last statement or at least called the prosecutor out of order. However, the garlic had convicted me!

In my defense, I must confess that my sense of smell does not work well. It was affected by the head injury I sustained in Winona Lake in 1973.[62] I could not understand what all of the hullabaloo was about!

The court proceedings over, we sat down for a quiet supper of Hillbilly Bean Soup. John did not join us—he was not home.[63] So he missed out tasting my rich, full flavored concoction. Too bad! Hot, spicy foods top the list of his

---

[62] See "The Black Out," story #48
[63] John was working late at the college library.

Hillbilly Bean Soup

favorites. As our firstborn, he received a double portion of his mother's Latin blood!

Martha was kind and had a bowl of soup. But then, she exclaimed resolutely, "I can't eat any more of this!"

I thought to my self, "The soup must be *plen'y* garlicky if Martha won't eat it." I didn't respond audibly. I knew I was about to receive my sentence.

Sure enough, all that spicy soup was making Martha speak her Spanish-accented-thousand-a-minute word talk. Even more resolutely, she declared the verdict: "And, if you want me to kiss you, you shouldn't eat any more of that garlicky soup with *frijoles* either. The soup will have to go!"

Sensing an opportune moment, Paul jumped in, "I can't eat any more of it either." He didn't say anything about the kissing.

Convicted and sentenced, I dejectedly said, "I'll put the rest of it in the freezer."

To which Martha, back as a prosecutor, replied, "No way—all the freezer stuff will taste like garlic!"

However, a determined Dutchman, I was not about to waste all that Hillbilly Bean Soup. Accordingly, as head of the Hartog household, I put it in the freezer anyway. The next morning when I went to check on my delicacy, I noticed that the freezer had quit—evidently the motor had burned out, and it never worked again!

I'm sure it was a mere coincidence, but to everyone else's delight, the Hillbilly Bean Soup went to the junkyard along with the deceased freezer. And so did my career as a master chef!

Happiness is
Reading this krazy book.

79

The Great Library Makeover

Library work requires attention to detail. One of the librarian's intricate tasks is to keep straight one library catalog corresponding to one collection of books and to avoid misshelving them. An impossible intricate task is to keep straight two catalogs corresponding to two separate collections of books intermingled on the shelves in one library. Forget about shelving errors—they are as difficult to find as a needle in a haystack!

The latter task awaited me as head librarian at Calvary. For two years, the college had been after me to come. After saying *no* for a year and a half, Martha and I agreed to make the move and help them out.

Before we came, the extent of the chaos that awaited me was not obvious to us. The problem was a long standing one. Twenty-three years back, two Bible colleges had merged. The Kansas City campus assimilated the other college's student body, its records and its assets, which of course included a library.

The great hurdle I faced was that the two libraries had not become one. Instead, both collections of books were put into one library building without taking proper steps. A specialized librarian always takes certain steps before adding *one single* book to the existing collection. Simply dumping a whole college library into another college library, with two card catalogs, but inter-shelved books, proved to be incredibly bizarre!

To adapt a familiar term, the two libraries were "separate but not separated." Because both were Bible college libraries, the books were similar and often duplicates. Moreover, both collections were cataloged according to the Dewey Decimal system, which allows more leeway to the cataloger, and is not as precise as the Library of Congress method.

Thus, two copies of the same book ended up on different shelves instead of side by side on the same shelf. Therefore, when a person checked out a book and returned it, there was no way of telling which of the two collections it had come from. Shelving could be done with one eye closed!

If the shelves were a massive chaos, the card catalogs were even worse. Cards went into the catalogs at random, sometimes into one catalog and sometimes into the other. Each passing year, the whole system became more and more confounded, and the mingled collection became still more mixed up. To make matters worse, over the years more and more books were added. Which card catalog became the greatest beneficiary of the additions was any one's guess.

When I arrived on campus, one of the professors said to me, "Nobody can find the books by using the card catalogs. I tell the students, 'Just look through the shelves and try to find the books you need!'"

On my first day as head librarian, I met the two full-time library staff ladies, Marilyn and Dawn. Their greeting to me was, "All the student library helpers have quit. We are also quitting at the end of the week."

I said, "Please stay with me. We will get all this organized. It will take time, but we will get it done." They were doubtful but they did not quit.

My first decision was to switch the cataloging classification from Dewey to Library of Congress. Since it was a different system, when we re-catalogued a book, we could tell it was done and ready for the "new library." We put the re-cataloged books in a separate section with their own card catalog drawers, and we kept tract of every re-cataloged book.

The challenge we faced must have seemed hopeless to the ladies. We had over 55,000 books and some 600,000 catalog cards to re-do. As a motivating tool, I posted a sign to show our progress. Month by month I posted the number of books that we had changed over to the new system. At the end of the first month, we had about 1,000 books done.

I also hired some new student helpers to work part-time. We had to re-do all the catalog cards as well. Since this was before the era of computers, and we had to use manual typewriters, I figured it would take about five years to complete the changeover.

In the meantime, another problem that contributed to the chaos plagued us daily. Our current library facilities were too small, and we were packed full. Halfway through the project, I noticed a large structure across the road from the administration complex. It was a storage building, but I determined to turn it into an efficient library facility. Again, I became an architect. The opportunity to design a well-laid out library was a great pleasure, and is the dream of any librarian.

That spring before graduation, we cleared the junk out of the building. By the end of that summer, with the help of maintenance, library staff, and volunteer help, our new library facility had become a reality. When school started that fall, the library was set up, and the changeover of the books continued in much better surroundings. In the process, we found books in the collection that had been "lost" for years but were on the shelves the whole time.

The entire library staff worked diligently on the project. They looked forward to the tally of completed books posted monthly. Every time we processed 5,000 books, we had a snack party. When we reached the half-way mark, we had pizza. At the completion of the project, we had a big celebration at a nice restaurant.

Three years after we had begun the changeover, just when we thought we were making good headways, a Bible college in Arkansas closed. Its assets, including its library, became our property. Thankfully, the new library building included a big storage area that became home to the "new" books. This time, we took the proper steps before integrating those books with ours.

With an administration that was one hundred percent behind me, the two full-time ladies staying with me, and capable student help, we were able to overcome against great odds. In less than five years, we had a new library facility, a unified, fully organized library, plus two experienced librarians with MLS degrees to carry on.[64]

I like challenges. Most of all, I like challenges that entail problems that have possible solutions. It was time for other challenges! Our family moved back to Iowa—my beloved home state.

---

[64] Within a couple of the library-change-over years, I approached the administration with the idea of having the ladies work on a library degree. The administration approved the funds, and the ladies began taking library science classes. In time both of them earned their Master in Library Science (MLS) degrees.

80

Life in the Slow Lane

It was early summer when the phone rang. Blanca was on the other line. "We're having a family get together this fall," Blanca said; then she went on, "Sara and Dennis are flying from California. She's running the Chicago Marathon, and Dave and I are going to join her." Blanca finished with this plea, "Please come!"

Blanca is Martha's younger sister, and Dave is her husband. Sara is Martha's older sister, and Dennis is her husband. Sara is a marathoner who is a breast and colon cancer survivor. She has run thirty-one marathons, including the New York, Chicago, Boston, Los Angeles, and the Grandma's Marathon in Duluth, Wisconsin. She has run some of these many times over.

Sara has completed every twenty-six-mile race, even if it's not at the head of the pack. Her goal is to finish each race in a time worthy of a medal. Blanca and Dave have run with her several times, and they have finished most races. Now that you know who's who and what's what, I can go on with my story.

Blanca's tune the day she called was this: "You guys don't have to run. We can just visit at the hotel afterwards." Her song sounded reasonable. We were not into that kind of rigorous exercise! We walk a lot because Martha enjoys it. I think it's a big waste of time; but I walk because I do not want Martha walking alone. Martha and I decided to make the trip from Des Moines to Chicago, strictly for the reunion.

Life in the Slow Lane

Summer turned into fall. Martha and I made the trip to Chicago, and we arrived the day before the marathon. We looked forward to spending a couple of days with the family. When Blanca greeted us, her tune had changed. She and Sara tried to convince us to run with them. Our retort was, "No way, Jose! We have not trained, and we have no shoes! The answer is, NO! Period! End of song!"

Soon afterwards, Blanca and Dave sang sweetly, "There's a big special sale on running shoes here in Chicago. All the top brands will be on sale. We need to get shoes to run. Come along with us!"

We had no problem accompanying them to the big sale. After all, we did not make the trip just to sit alone in a hotel room. So off we went—happy as larks.

They were right—it was a great sale! Thousands of people were milling around, looking at running shoes; and lots of merchants were displaying their footwear. The prices were incredible. They were such bargains, that Martha and I bought sneakers as well. It is difficult for a Dutchman to turn down a real bargain if it is something he can use. Those shoes were made for running, but we bought them for walking.

The next morning, Blanca, Sara, and Dave sang one more tune: "You have running shoes. Run with us." Determinedly, we both said, "No!" We told them of our plan was to watch them get started and cheer for them. Then we were going to walk around and gawk.

By the way, Dennis doesn't run. He just comes along to cheer Sara at the starting line; then he bums around—smart man! Also, a minor reason why he doesn't run is that he has heart problems and has undergone by-pass surgery. This time, Dennis was not able to cheer Sara because he was visiting his mother in the hospital. She had flown with Sara and Dennis from L.A., had suffered a stroke on the plane, and was hospitalized the moment they landed in Chicago.

Dave and Blanca auditioned for a new tune, "Come on! Come with us! We won't run real fast, we will stay with you, and you can quit at any time."

Martha had heard about people getting bloody feet during marathons. In fact, Blanca got them when she ran in the Grandma's Marathon. Sara had a solution. She lent Martha some runner's socks and also a t-shirt inscribed with, "I ran the Granny Marathon!" Martha was neither a granny nor had she ever run a marathon. As for me, Dave offered me some of his running socks.

Though not trained, decked out in the borrowed outfits and brand new sneakers, we looked like professional marathoners. This convinced us that we were ready for the event. They say, "Looks can be deceiving." Deceived or not, we were excited about it!

Before we took off, I needed to take care of an important matter. I slipped out; raced into our hotel room; and snatched the bag of bite-size Snickers we had brought to munch on the trip. I also grabbed the bananas—the healthy food Martha had packed for us. Now we were ready!

We walked swiftly to the starting area, just to warm up. Our early arrival put us toward the front of the pack. By starting time, literally thousands of people had milled around us. Then the bell rang! And off we went! In no time at all, we had lost sight of Sara, Blanca, and Dave. My main concern now was to keep track of Martha, who is short and tiny; and I feared I might lose her in such a huge crowd.

Martha and I ran as fast as we could for about a mile. Then we slowed down. Nevertheless, we are not quitters. We persevere once we start anything. The side walks were jammed with people cheering, "Run! Run! Run to the finish line!" Some runners took it seriously and ran past us, but we walked fast instead.

After about six miles, we noticed that the people around us were now slowing down; but they were still moving toward the finish line. We did the same. The crowds were cheering us on. We kept going.

As we moved along at our pace—walking fast—I downed a banana and shared the other one with Martha. The Snickers also came in handy for extra energy. By now, no more runners came by, only walkers. They asked me where I had gotten my Snicker bars. I told them I had brought them along. We saw several water stations and a few fruit stands along the way, but none of them sold Snicker bars.

Pretty soon, even the fast walkers had left us in the dust. That didn't bother us at all. We started walking at the pace of our daily walks at home. Instead of bird watching in the country, Martha started gawking at the pigeons nesting on the tall buildings; and she just about walked into a wheel chair. Yup! Someone passed us in a wheel chair! And then another! We looked back to see how many people were still behind us. There were a few dozen who were walking, and behind them was a pack of people in wheel chairs.

We reached the eight-mile marker. Those hardy folks in wheel chairs were now passing us right and left. At mile nine, the crowds were no longer *plen'y* but scanty. By mile ten, the final wheel chair passed us. We were dead last.

A quarter mile farther, the police took down the barriers; and the cars began coming down the street. The marathon marking route signs went down; so we took to the sidewalks. We were somewhere in Chicago, but where? Not walking toward the finish line for sure! It was time for "Plan B."

We had planned to run only a mile with Blanca and Dave and then return to the hotel, which was within walking distance of the starting line. Since we had heard of pickpockets in Chicago, we had taken no money along and could not hire a taxi. Martha, my directionally impaired wife, was relying on me completely to get us back to the hotel.

I knew we had run north; then the loop had turned west a little and then south. Also, I had gone to Moody Bible Institute, which is in the heart of Chicago; so I recognized some of the main streets. I calculated that we were about two miles from the hotel. Hungry, tired, and bored, we started plodding toward the hotel.

About two hours after the marathon was over, we made it back to the hotel. We had blistered feet from our new sneakers, shin splints from walking on the pavement, and we didn't make it to the finish line. Worse yet, we were out of Snickers.

But we awarded each other a big hug and a big "A+" for effort and an "F-" for insanity!

> *The grand essentials of happiness are:*
> *Something to do,*
> *Something to love, and*
> *Something to hope for.*
>
> —Joseph Addison

81

Living with an Angel

The year was 1988. Five years had passed since Tar Baby had died; it was unusual for us to be without a dog for such a long stretch. In the meantime, Paul had graduated from high school and was about to go into college. He kept begging us to get a dog—a black lab.

Martha and I gave in to Paul's pleas, but not all the way. Paul was leaving home in a few years, and Martha thought that a big dog was alright for Paul but not for her. After talking it over, we settled on a half-dog high and a-dog-and-a-half-long dog—a miniature black dachshund! To this day, whenever Martha sees one, she does a double turn and smiles.

We heard of a college girl who had dachies[65] for sale. I called her, and set up a visit. John was attending seminary but was home for the summer; so we made it a family outing. When we arrived, the young woman and her mother welcomed us into their neatly-kept home. We went into the kitchen where two dachies were playing with their mother. Pretty soon, a German shepherd and two cats joined them. The pups frolicked fearlessly with the big shepherd. It was clear that the pups were healthy, alert, and well-socialized.

We picked out the little female, paid the owner, and promised to keep in touch. The dachie rode between our sons in the back seat and slept peacefully. Martha commented, "She

---

[65] An endearing term for dachshunds

is small enough to fit into your shirt pocket." When we got home, I tried it. She did fit into my shirt pocket! Smiling, Paul said, "She looks like a rat!" He had wanted a black lab, but before long, the black dachie had won the hearts of all of us.

As usual, I had the privilege of naming the new member of our family. Since dachshunds originally came from Germany, Vinzigar Schwartz Engle became her registered name. In broken German it means "Tiny Black Angel." To us, she became simply Vinsy.

Dachies are known to be difficult to housebreak, but Martha had her trained within a week. She also trained Vinsy to do the usual tricks: sit, shake "hands," and roll over. Inside the house, she also obeyed the command, "stay!" Outside, it was a different story. The sight of a rabbit or squirrel made that command go into one long-floppy ear and out the other. Vinsy's hunting instincts came to life! With her long ears flapping in the air as she chased those critters, Vinsy looked like a flying angel!

You guessed it. Martha became Vinsy's mistress. She found Vinsy's stubborn trait a delightful challenge. When Martha's mother and father visited from Central America and saw the dog, Pappy Nuñez said, "The reason you got that dog was to have someone to order around after your sons left home!"—a good insight!

Right from the beginning, we had Vinsy sleep in a pet carrying cage or a "pet taxi." We put a blanket over it, and she slept quietly in her taxi, regardless of where it was. Thus, she traveled with us wherever dogs were allowed and also were welcome (There's a difference).

This turned out to be useful in another way. Whenever we had an extra activity after school and had to be gone from home longer than usual, she went to school with us. I kept her in her covered taxi in my office and let her out between classes. I even did this for a whole semester when I taught a small class in my office. The students didn't know that another "student" was present until the semester ended. On the last day, I uncovered the taxi and let Vinsy out. As usual, the dachie brought big smiles to their faces.

One day, we happened to be in Walmart during a baby-picture-taking promotion. As we walked by the photo table, we noticed that the photographer was sitting around doing nothing. Martha turned to me with her ornery smile and exclaimed, "Let's ask him to take Vinsy's picture!"

The photographer was surprised and hesitant when Martha asked him, but replied, "I'm willing to do it if the store manager allows the dog in the store."

In no time, I found the manager and asked him. His answer was, "Sure!"

We ran to the car, grabbed Vinsy, rushed into the store, and sat her on the table. She posed nicely for the photographer, who said, "She's more cooperative than most babies!"

In a few weeks we received the notice that our "baby's" pictures were ready. We eagerly rushed back to Walmart, and waited in line as proud parents viewed the proofs. When our turn came, I told the saleswoman, "Ours is the cutest. She has a tail!" She frowned and looked surprised, but her expression changed as soon as I told her about our "baby." To this day, a collage of Vinsy's Walmart pictures hangs on the wall in our back hallway.

Our pets receive good, loving care. This entails yearly visits to the vet for regular tests and shots. When Vinsy was only a couple of years old, she decided that vet's visits were not for her. Somehow she knew when a car trip was ending up at the vet, and she became distressed. The moment we walked into the clinic, she began to blow white-frothy bubbles with her mouth, and her little body stiffened—Vinsy displayed her displeasure with the vet's office by having a seizure!

The vet did not seem too pleased when Martha told him, "Something in your office provokes Vinsy to have seizures." This was not good for public relations! The vet did what doctors usually do with distressed patients. He prescribed a tranquilizer for Vinsy. From then on, each time Vinsy went to the vet, she got one of those pills, which transformed her into a sloth.

Vinsy had a good life and lived to be almost fifteen and a half years old. Toward the end, she became deaf and blind. However, she was able to get around, and her loving disposition did not change. Then, she developed a tumor in her abdomen. Although she was more loving than ever, it was obvious she was in pain.

The time had come for Vinsy to leave us. We gave her a tranquilizing pill and petted her all the way to the vet's office. Martha wrapped Vinsy in her favorite blanket and held her as the vet stroked her head tenderly. Then, he gave her an injection that sent her into a peaceful sleep from which she never woke up. All of us cried in that office, including the vet. We went out through the back office door and drove home.

For the first time in fifteen years and three months, an excited dachie did not welcome us home. Martha and I hugged each other and cried. Then, I put our sleeping angel in a box. Since we lived in the country, I buried her under a flowering crab apple tree in our backyard. It was a sad day when we had to put her down, but the framed pictures on the wall remind us of all the pleasures she brought to our household.

Living with our miniature dachie was truly like living with an enchanting little black angel!

Vinsy and Rex Resting on the Deck

82

Rex

He was homeless, and his life was in danger. Earlier, he had tried to lead the college life as a drifter. But as an illegal, he had been expelled from college. Then, my wife and I took him in and let him stay at our place. He went by Rex, the tag that his former buddies had pinned on him in his younger days. And the label had stuck.

Rex was a rabbit. One of my college students had seen him at a pet store during Christmas break. Fully aware that it was against the college rules to have pets in the dorms, the student bought the bunny and named him Rex. Upon his return from the break, the student talked his roommates into the exciting proposition of keeping Rex in the dorm and keeping it a secret. That made Rex an illegal.

The guys worked out a deal with the lady students in one of the women's dorms. On the days when the guys had scheduled "room check," Rex moved to the gals' dorm. When the coast was clear, the rabbit went back home to his buddies. Rex became a drifter.

There were a few close calls when he was almost discovered. One time, the girls had him and put him under a laundry basket. Then, an unexpected visitor showed up, and Rex started hopping and making the basket move. One of the partners in crime saw the movement out of the corner of her eye, reached out quickly, and held down the basket before the visitor saw it! Otherwise, for several months, things went well as planned. Rex was the best-kept secret on campus that spring semester.

A couple of weeks before graduation, the resident advisor (RA) of the guys' dorm did an unscheduled "room check." The sole resident in the room that day was Rex, who surprised the RA when he opened the door and walked in the room. Rex, sensing trouble, hopped away and hid. The secret was out! The boys tried to talk the RA into keeping the matter confidential; but loyal to the vows he had taken as resident advisor, he did not relent. He followed the prescribed procedure for such a crime.

He reported the incident to the dean of students, who called in the culprits. The students begged this higher power to let them keep Rex since the semester was almost over. But their pleas went into deaf ears. Right before graduation, Rex was expelled from college. Downhearted, the fellows returned to their dorm, picked up Rex, and put him on the grass by the door. Rex was now homeless! However, the guys thought Rex might stick around; so that they could continue to feed him.

Nevertheless, Rex, sensing freedom for the first time, hopped away and began munching on tender spring shoots. The big problem was that Rex was tame and had never encountered an enemy. Cats and dogs loitered freely around campus. Rabbits, particularly domesticated ones, were easy targets for such loiterers. Rex's life was now in danger. He hopped around campus and escaped impending danger that day.

The next day, a married student saw Rex hopping around by the library. The student thought it was interesting that the bunny did not hop away but kept coming toward him. Then, he realized that it was not a wild bunny as he first had thought. Rex's fur was the color of a cotton tail, but he had lopped ears. Immediately, the student realized this bunny was someone's pet.

Rex did not remain expelled for long. The married student picked him up and took him to his homiletics class.[66] Rex lay patiently on his lap through a whole class of amateur preachers. Rex's benefactor, however, was not in a position to help him any further. A little research on survival might help Rex; thus, the student took him to the library. The assistant librarian at that time was Martha, who was about ready to kick out the student with his bunny.

However, Martha has a tender spot for animals, and Rex's gentle nature and his big brown eyes won her heart. Rex had found a permanent home at last—maybe. She told the student she had to check with me before adopting the bunny. The bunny had to attend a second class with the to-be preacher. In one day, Rex was trying to qualify for graduation!

In the meantime, another student showed up at the library. He knew all about the cute bunny whose name was Rex. When I showed up at the library, Martha welcomed me with the sob story about the lopped-ear rabbit and told me that she had just adopted Rex. Before I had a chance to remind her that she should have checked with me first, she asked sweetly, "Please go to the lumber yard and get materials to build it a hutch." Warning! This is how wives function who fall in love with cute lopped-ear rabbits!

When we came home with Rex, we didn't have a safe place to contain him. Martha put him on our deck and fetched Vinsy, our dachie, to bunny sit. Martha trusted Vinsy to protect Rex from the neighbors' cats and dogs. Whenever they visited our place, Vinsy chased them away with her tenacious bark.

However, it definitely did not work out according to Martha's plan. No cats or dogs came by that day, and Vinsy didn't bark at all. Rex, a sheltered college dropout, didn't know

---

[66] This is a class where young preachers learn how to pound the pulpit, without splitting it in half!

any better. All it took was a look at Vinsy's long floppy, black ears, and the chase began. Rex, a flopped-ear Dutch rabbit, relentlessly chased his new-found German love all around the deck. Martha ended up rescuing the dog from the rabbit!

While all that commotion was going on, I got busy throwing together a temporary cage for Rex. That's the only thing I could do in such short notice until school was out in a couple of weeks. After graduation, I had the whole summer free and the time to make a permanent house for Rex. In the meantime, I became an "architect" again. I drew the plans for his hutch-in-a-yard homestead, which eventually became a rabbit-chicken condominium, with an attached enemy-critter proof, fenced yard.

Rex loved being with people. This went back to his early days in the men's and women's dorms. He had an unusual way for showing his exhilaration when we visited him in his fenced yard. As we stood there, he made figure eights around our legs! Every now and then, he jumped up about three feet in the air, and then he went back to making figure eights again.

We kept Rex to the day of his death when he died of old age. That homeless lopped-ear rabbit, turned comic, brought special laughter to our home!

83

Abraham

His original name was not Abraham. Frankly, I don't even remember his first given name, nor if he even had one at all. He spent his first growing months in a far different place than his later life.

Abraham started out in life as an Easter chick, which a grandfather bought as a present for his little granddaughter. Since I don't know what she called him, I will call him "Chicken Little." He was a soft and fuzzy, little fellow. Within days, his soft baby fuzz fell off, and in its place prickly, feather stumps popped out of his skin.

Two months went by before all the homely stumps exposed beautiful shiny feathers and what looked like rooster feather markings. At three months, the beautiful decked out young bird confirmed this matter. He let out a hesitant crow-like sound followed by a loud confident crow. Something else happened throughout this process, the rooster realized who provided his dinners; and he switched his allegiance from the granddaughter to the Grandpa.

I first heard about Chicken Little from Grandpa who was one of my students in an evening school class. Generally, evening school students are older than the college students. One night at the beginning of the semester, I told the class about the rabbit house I was building for Rex. Grandpa came up after class and told me about his Easter chick. During the subsequent weeks, the students asked me to give a progress report on my construction project. I finished the rabbit house in October, and the students cheered when I told them.

Having heard the news, Grandpa approached me and informed me that his rooster was up for adoption—it needed winter lodging. I took pity on the young cock and consented to take him. The next time we met for class, Grandpa waited around afterwards until I packed up my teaching paraphernalia.

We walked together to the parking lot. He opened his car door and took out a gunny sack. He handed it to me and said, "Here's the young rooster." When I got home, I opened the sack in the garage, and a confused but handsome rooster strutted out.

I decided to call him "Abraham" certain that he was destined to become the "father of many chickens." At first, all went well in the Hartog homestead. Abraham had his run of the coop, and Rex had a nice rabbit cage in it as well. The rabbit house-chicken coop was top quality. It was well insulated and had south windows for solar heat. A heat lamp kept it nice and cozy on the bitter cold days of January and February.

Rex and Abraham came through the winter in great shape. That spring, I built an enclosed yard. It was ten feet by ten feet with fencing around it and on the top as well. This was to keep out hawks and other harmful predators. Rex had a large outside cage in the fenced pen, and Abraham had the run of all the rest.

Abraham was no longer a young rooster. He was a mature cock with long spurs and a proud carriage. It also became evident that he was a man's rooster. I figured that his bond with Grandpa promoted this curious trait. Abraham liked me, but he did not like Martha or any other woman. Martha fed him, watered him, and talked "baby talk" to him. It didn't matter!

His dislike of Martha became more obvious as time passed. He was fine when I went into the fenced yard, but he tried to attack Martha when she went in to feed him. One day she decided to set him straight as to who was boss. She was able to grab him, and she took him into the kitchen. When I walked in, Martha was standing in front of the stove with the oven door open. She was holding onto the rooster tightly. Something was cooking in her brain! I could see it on the determined grimace on her face.

I asked her, "What are you doing?"

She replied sternly, "I wanted to teach Abraham a visual lesson. So I opened the oven door and told him, 'If you don't shape up, you will end up in there!'"

Turning to me, she said, "I cannot have a rooster like this around!" "By the way," she went on, "I thought of showing him the big pot and threatening to cut him up into little pieces and making soup out of him; but roasted rooster sounded more delicious!" Martha talks fast and when she's upset, she talks faster.

Abraham, like Martha, had a mind of his own. During the daytime, we often left him out into our big back yard that ran into farm land. A few days later, Martha opened the chicken pen to let him roam the back yard. Abraham flew out, did a speedy turn-about-beak, and began to attack his mistress viciously. She jumped into the chicken yard, and he parked himself in front of the gate and stood guard.

It was impossible for Martha to step outside; her only option was to scream, "Help! Get me out of here!" She was calling for me, but I'm sure that her hollering echoed throughout the whole neighborhood. I ran toward the chicken yard, shooed the rooster away, and let Martha out. I put Abraham on good behavior and grounded him in the chicken pen with this warning: "If you bother Martha one more time, I will invite you over for dinner."

The "feather" that broke the rooster's neck happened the following Saturday when I had to go to the bank. Abraham was still grounded. I certainly did not count on any Abraham-Martha problems. While I was gone, Martha took pity on Abraham, and she left him out into the back yard

As soon as Abraham flew out of the chicken pen, he ruffled his hackles, flew at her, and spurred her legs. She ran away from him, but he chased her and continued to spur her legs. Just when she was about to reach our property line that bordered a soy bean field, I came home. As I drove up our driveway, I immediately saw my screaming wife being chased by a rooster.

I wish I had a video of the whole episode. It was a hilarious sight to behold behind the steering wheel. However, although funny to behold, it was not fun to experience at all.[67] I ran out of the car and rescued my rooster-pecked wife. Then swiftly but benevolently I executed Abraham.

He had no trial. He was not represented by a lawyer. I did not read him any Miranda rights. But he was the guest of honor at our dinner table the next day!

Happiness is sharing a meal with
A special guest of honor.

—Martha Hartog

---

[67] That night, I noticed that the back of Martha's legs were dotted with round, purple spots—bruises left by the rooster's spurs!

84

The Silver Bullet

It was a pre-owned vehicle and the best car I have ever had. Its previous owner was a most trustworthy individual—my brother Paul. He is a car enthusiast and gives his vehicles top notch care. When he sold me his '81 silver Honda Civic, it was about two years old and had 25,000 miles on it; but it looked almost brand new. Unfortunately, hidden under that shinny silver body was a tin worm that got hungrier by the years.

Nevertheless, I knew that the Honda's engine was reliable and tough! This feature appealed to me greatly because I am auto-mechanically challenged. The reliability and durability of these little "Hondoos" made my own resilient Honda worthy of its nickname, "Silver Bullet." More often, however, it simply went by "the Honda" or "the Bullet."

Immediately upon arrival from Tulsa, the Honda became the favorite vehicle of the family. The Mustang convertible took a back seat because it had succumbed to rust.[68] Wherever we went, the Silver Bullet took us, and we expected it to serve us for many years; I took care of it the best I knew how.

I used synthetic oil. According to the directions, it is good for 25,000 miles. However, I changed the oil every 15,000

---

[68] By the way, eventually, I had the Mustang restored and repainted in a fire engine red. I am its sole driver, with a few exceptions.

miles, just to be sure. The Silver Bullet appreciated this greatly; just like the Eveready Bunny, it kept going and going.

I thought the Honda was performing superbly when it reached 100,000 miles. At 200,000, it was still going strong. By 250,000 the engine and the transmission were still in top shape. At that point I set a goal of 300,000 for my Silver Bullet!

In the meantime, the tin worm hidden under the silver frame became ravenous. It survived extremely well on a high sodium-content diet, provided by the DOT. Honda Civics were notorious for rusting in less than three years, especially in locations where salt was used on winter roads.[69]

I did my best to keep the rust at bay. When a rust spot showed up, I treated it and then sprayed paint over the spot. On its tenth birthday, the Bullet received a new silver coat from Dave, Blanca's husband. He was enjoying his own new purchase—a professional auto painter's kit.

Nevertheless, our stay at Blanca's was only for a weekend. Consequently, Dave and I did not have time to endow the old Honda with a much-needed undercoat. As a result, the tin worm morphed into a glutton, and the Silver Bullet provided more than enough rust for that ravenous tin devourer.

But time was taking its toll on the rusty silver Honda. The gas gage indicator quit working at about 200,000 miles. I solved that problem by filling up every time it reached another 200 miles on the odometer. I had learned that it could go 250 miles on a tank-full.

Then, one day, I hit a bump on the road only three blocks away from school. Frost had raised a section of the concrete two inches. When I drove over the bump then dropped down

---

[69] In 1972-1979 Honda's recall by the FTC and the National Highway Traffic Safety Administration was the largest safety action among all the imported brands. Civics were known for their typical Honda rust, and my 1981 model was no exception.

to the next concrete piece, I heard a big bang. I had no idea what had caused that big boom, but the car kept running. I did not think much more about it.

Then after a block the Honda died. I started it up again and drove two more blocks. At that point it died again, and I could not get it started. Thankfully, I was right by the college. I coasted to the curb and parked the old Hondoo.

The school mechanic looked it over and opened its hood, but he could not find anything wrong with it. Then, he looked under the car and exclaimed, "Your car is about to break in two!" The ravenous tin worm had ravaged the Silver Bullet!

After the mechanic left, I got curious and opened the trunk just to take a look. Immediately, I discovered the source of the big bang. It was not the "big bang theory" either. It was an actual event in time. The spring had come up through the rusted trunk floor and had made all that noise. This still did not explain why the Bullet did not run, however.

I called the auto junk yard, and its owner offered me $25 for my dead car. I accepted his offer readily! When the junkyard truck driver came to haul away the '81 Honda Civic, he pointed to the car and looking at me in the eye, declared emphatically, "That car doesn't owe you anything!"

My Honda had about 280,000 miles on it—just 20,000 short of the goal I had assigned for it! Several months later, I learned why the Silver Bullet had missed its 300,000-goal. The gas line from the gas tank to the engine was designed to go through the rear spring. When the spring shot up through the rusted trunk floor, it severed the gas line.[70] The car ran the last two blocks on the gas still in the line ahead of the break, but that was as far as the car could go.

---

[70] Rust, caused by exposure to salt, weakened the Civic's lateral suspension arms, the front crossbeam, and the lower supports of the strut coil spring.

The Honda was an excellent car even to the end. I never had to touch its engine or its transmission. Before sending it to its grave, I should have stopped by the morgue and taken out its engine. I could have sold it separately because it was still working with no problems.

Its engine was willing but its body was weak!

*Happiness is
The natural flower of duty.*

—Phillips Brooks

85

An Unwanted Guest in the Coop

More tenants moved into the rabbit-chicken coop. Rex, our sociable bunny, had been living alone. Elated, he welcomed his fowl friends with open floppy ears. Steadfast to her word, Martha had roasted Abraham. Delighted by his delicious flavor, we decided to purchase and raise a dozen chickens for meat and eggs. The hatchery where we bought the chickens required a minimum order of twenty-five. Since we already had a coop, we planned to keep seven hens and one rooster as pets and feast on the others.

We picked up our twenty-five, day-old chicks and waited for three months or more until their sex identity and their temperament were indisputably established. Martha refused to do battle with another Abraham! Over half of the chicks turned out to be roosters, and we focused on a couple of bantam Cochin cocks because this breed is known for being gentle. True to his breed trait, a bantam Cochin with slate-blue feathers endeared himself to Martha. This cock was to live and bear the name Solomon—the name I gave him because he was destined to have many wives.[71]

We selected seven of the hens and invited the remaining roosters and hens to dinner. It was time to name the surviving hens. They were also purebreds of different varieties and

---

[71] Our Solomon outlived all his wives. He died at the ripe old age of 10 ½ years.

An Unwanted Guest in the Coop

colors. Some had single combs, while others had rose combs, and a few had feathered feet. Some were Amerauncanas, which lay green shelled eggs, and one was a tiny black hen that laid tiny white eggs. Taking into consideration their physical characteristics and personalities, Martha assigned silly Spanish names to five of the hens: *Chiquita*, *Chulita*, *Conchita*, *Ronquita*, and *Bonita*. I assigned dignified names to the other two: Sheba (after the Queen of Sheba) and Duchess (after Dutch nobility).

The flock depicted a serene picture as they clucked contentedly and kept busy scratching in the enclosed back yard. More importantly, they entertained Rex. This peaceful atmosphere changed drastically one day that summer.

It was the day before I was to leave for Perú to teach for a week in Trujillo. Just as I was washing our car so that I could leave it nice and clean for Martha, she emerged from the house carrying the egg basket.

Walking past me, she smiled and said, "Hi! I'm going for eggs!"

I grinned and replied, "Ok. Have fun!"

Martha stopped in front of the chicken yard and greeted the chickens sweetly. Then she went into the coop to gather the eggs. As she reached for an egg, she saw the shape of a fat U curled up against the nest wall. It scared her out of her wits, and she let out a blood curdling scream, which the neighbors heard for sure.

Startled, I looked up and saw Martha and eggs flying out of the coop. She was running and flailing her hands and hollering like a wild woman, "I hate living in the country! Don't you ever leave me alone again!"

Martha did not hate the country. I knew the exact reason for her irrational behavior: She had seen the unthinkable! She confirmed my conclusion when she zoomed past me like an arrow straight into the house.

Pointing back to the coop, she hollered, "There's a huge snake in the coop! Get it out of there! I hate snakes!"

There you have it! By the way, the neighbors heard Martha's shouting, but they didn't budge. They had heard a minor edition of it before—every time she saw a garter snake. Once inside, Martha watched me from a kitchen window. She saw me going into the coop and coming out of it with a six-foot-long bull snake, which I resettled across the road near the Four Mile Creek.

That bull snake had to go. Lately, we had noticed that the egg production was down. Now we knew why. If allowed to stay, that snake would keep returning for more eggs. Moreover, I was leaving for almost two weeks and did not want Martha and the snake to meet again while I was gone.

No poison snakes live in this area of Iowa. We have big bull snakes, which are beneficial since they eat field mice. Whenever I catch a bull snake, I cart it away to a field far from our house. We also have harmless little garter snakes.

However, snakes are snakes. Martha does not welcome any snake at our place. If I hear a scream, I know that it is either Martha or the next-door lady. That scream is a signal that one of them has seen a snake, usually a garter snake. Like a knight of old, I always go and rescue the "victim."

Martha does not lose it often, but a snake, any snake, has a way of getting her unraveled!

86

Oh, Mi Pawpaw!

The picture of the fruit in the seed catalog looked luscious! Pawpaw was its name. The short blurb under the picture stated the following: "It is also known as the Nebraska Banana, and the fruit is yellow when ripe." I thought to myself, "No need to guess if they are ripe like with watermelons!" The blurb continued, "It is easy to grow, is disease free, and is not bothered by insects." Pleased, I said, "Hardy little thing! Can't go wrong with it!" The blurb described its taste as that of custard—smooth and creamy. "That convinces me!" I exclaimed, "I'm getting one plant!"

However, as I read on, in small print it said, "For proper pollination plant two pawpaws. The plants are shipped in dormant stage." "Okay," I said to the catalog, "I'll get two plants." (I always talk to my beautiful seed catalogs when Martha is not around!) In the past, when I had received dormant plants, they looked like they were dead; but I had planted them anyway knowing plants typically spring to life after I give them a good drink.

Without any further ado, I called in my order. My pawpaws were arriving in April. I had to be patient—a difficult thing for a Dutchman to do. April was only three months away! Winter dragged on, but spring was certainly coming soon, and so were my pawpaws. By fall, I could pick some luscious, golden fruit.

The days were getting longer now. The bitter January cold was slowly becoming a thing of the past. February was short.

Then wicked old March delivered a blizzard. Finally it was April! April fools day arrived. No matter. Pawpaws were fool proof; you couldn't go wrong with them. Right before the end of April, the UPS man delivered a package.

When I opened it, the label of the inside plastic bag said, "Pawpaw Trees." Trees? All I saw were two straggly twigs with a few dry roots, surrounded by a handful of dry peat moss. Oh, well! I was planting them anyway. A good drink was all they needed to spring them to life!

"Make the hole twice the size of the roots," the directions said. "That won't be hard," I thought, "They don't have many roots to begin with!" After digging the two holes, I carefully placed each tree in its underground home. Then, I packed dirt neatly around the plants and poured a bucket of water around each one. Standing tall over my scrawny twigs, I ordered them, "Do your thing! I expect pawpaws this fall!" Somehow I got the feeling they weren't listening.

"Be patient," I told myself. A month went by. This surely wasn't the "green revolution" I was hoping for. Summer turned to fall, and both of my poor pawpaws were still dead twigs. D. O. A. How could it be? I got out the plant encyclopedia and looked up "Pawpaws." I was struck with the first few words: "Pawpaws do not transplant well." And so ended my first year as an expert on pawpaw trees. Fall gave way to winter. Snow. Ice. Bitter cold.

January had barely made its appearance when a barrage of seed catalogs assailed my home. Let me warn you! All it takes is one order, and your name and address become viral among all the seed companies in the United States and Holland! I don't mind it, because I enjoy looking through all of them and dream about their promises: the beautifully landscaped flower beds in the spring and summer, and the luscious fruits and vegetables in the summer and fall.

Oh, Mi Pawpaw!

I opened that first catalog, and the picture of a pawpaw immediately caught my attention. There it was, BIG and golden! The Indiana Banana! Aha, it changed its name! It's not a Nebraska Banana anymore! But it couldn't fool me. A pawpaw is a pawpaw under any other name. I wondered, "Had it spent some time with a rose?"

Two dead pawpaws were not going to defeat me. I searched through the pile of seed catalogs until I found the solution to the problem. One seed catalog said, "Pawpaws are very hard to transplant." I told the catalog, "Every body knows that!" Then I noticed that this company sold potted pawpaws.

All I had to do was put the rascals in the ground, pot and all. It was a win-win situation. Wonderful! How could I go wrong! I called in my order for two potted pawpaws. They were arriving in May. Only four months away! Winter dragged on, but spring was certainly coming soon, and so were my pawpaws. By fall I could pick some luscious, golden fruit.

The days were getting longer again. The bitter cold of January was slowly becoming a thing of the past. February was a short month, which helped. And March came and left without a blizzard. Showers swept April away, and May was bringing in my pawpaws! Half way through May, the UPS man dropped off a package. My pawpaws had come!

I eagerly opened the package. There they were—nice and green and full of life and vigor! Well, one of them was. The other was kind of golden green. Golden green sounded better than pale yellow green. This was going to be a long lasting happy relationship—*mi* pawpaws and I!

By the end of June, Green Boy had grown an inch and was looking strong. Goldie, however, wasn't doing too well. Sickly yellow described that poor pawpaw more accurately. July's hot weather was too much for Goldie. She went into shock and gave up the ghost. Year two ended with one living pawpaw and no luscious fruit. Somewhere in the back of my mind, I remembered the words, "For proper pollination plant two pawpaws." That was a half truth! The whole truth and nothing but the truth is this: "For proper pollination plant two pawpaws *that survive*."

The spring of year three, I attempted to start a second pawpaw, but it ended in failure again. However, the summer of the fourth year brought some good news. A friend of mine said he had planted a few pawpaw seeds, and one had germinated. Because he was moving, he had to leave behind his pawpaw; and he offered it to me.

I jumped in the car and drove the few miles to his home. When my friend handed me the small tree, instantly I saw it was a pawpaw in disguise—it was an ash tree that had sprung up from a random seed. My friend's pawpaw seeds had not germinated! I went back home to my one and only pawpaw, which was taking its good old time to grow. When I started my pawpaw project, I did not know that pawpaws do not transplant well at all or that they are hard to start from seed. They are also slow growers in their early years. Year by year my one and only pawpaw grew slowly.

On its seventh birthday, my pawpaw finally bloomed. Beautiful, purple blossoms that looked like little lanterns appeared beneath the canopy of its shiny green leaves. At last! Smooth custard on a stick was going to smear my lips. Alas! After a few weeks the little purple lanterns all turned brown and fell off! They needed another pawpaw to pollinate them.

My little tree was a stubborn Dutch pawpaw and did not give up. On the spring of its eight year, little flower buds appeared under its shiny leaves. Winter was just as stubborn and decided to make a last fling. A late spring frost killed all the little purple flower buds just as they were beginning to bloom. I thought, "No wonder they don't sell pawpaws in the fruit section of grocery stores!"

My Pawpaw Fruit

Not as eager to taste the luscious fruit, I thought, "Oh well, maybe next year." I did some more reading, and came across the secret of having a lone pawpaw bear fruit: simply pollinate the blossoms with a cotton Q-tip. I could not wait until year nine arrived. This was bound to be "The Year of *Mi* Pawpaw!"

By mid-May, my pawpaw tree was loaded with little purple lanterns. I reached discreetly under the leaf canopies and hand pollinated each blossom with a Q-tip. I expected a bumper crop! All my nine years of hard work and waiting were to be repaid richly. As summer wore on, one by one and two by two, the little pawpaw blossoms dropped off the tree. By the end of the summer, only two tiny-green pawpaws remained on the tree. I checked it regularly.

As the days went by, the two pawpaws grew into little-banana-looking fruit. One day in late September, I checked on their progress; but instead of two plump pawpaws, only one was hanging from the tree. One had fallen and had become rabbit food for sure—clusters of black "seeds" were lying under the tree.

Now, my only hope was the one pawpaw that was still hanging on for dear life. I continued to check it each day. At the end of another week, it was almost perfect. One more day, and I could reach for it and pluck it! Twenty-four hours to go! Just thinking of that smooth, creamy custard flavor made my mouth water. I was harvesting it first thing in the morning—for sure!

I got up early and went straight to my pawpaw tree to enjoy the fruit of my labors. To my horror, I saw that someone had peeked under its leafy canopy, and had confiscated my pawpaw! Evidence of the culprit lay all around on the ground. A deer had invaded my yard the night before and had feasted on my one and only sweet golden pawpaw!

The next year, the old pawpaw tree started sending up little pawpaw trees from its roots. So many came up that I had to mow down over fifty of them but left five as pollinators. By then, I was sick of the whole pawpaw project. I gave up on pawpaws, but they did *not* give up on me. Five years later, when the pollinators had grown and spring had sprung, beautiful purple lanterns adorned mi pawpaw trees, and the blossoms formed fruit.

That fall, I reaped a bumper crop of golden pawpaws. After fifteen years, my dream of scooping smooth and creamy, delicious custard out of pawpaw "cups" came true at last.[72]

     Fruit at last—Fruit at last!
   I can't believe it. I got fruit at last!

---

[72] Pawpaws were President George Washington's favorite dessert.

87

The Day I Got "Nailed"

It was time to become an "architect" again and to revive my block-laying abilities. Our older son John, who is both a teacher and an administrator, was able to purchase a house on an acre in the country. The location is beautiful. The house sits on top of a hill that overlooks a pretty valley, but the kitchen-dining area was extremely cramped. So he asked me, "Would you design an addition with a dining area?—that's all!"

However, as it often happens, the more we thought and talked about the project, the more complex the addition became. This is no problem as long as the plans are still pencil lines on paper. In the end, the final design included the dining area, a three-quarter bath, a laundry closet, a bedroom, and the back-hallway stairs going down to the basement.

My architectural work was done. It was time to turn the pencil lines into solid walls. John had a friend dig out the basement with a backhoe, and the dirt became a large hill by the building site. I donned my cement-block-layer cap. I put in the foundation and laid the concrete block walls. John then hired a contractor to frame up the addition.

One day, John climbed the dirt hill, and he called me to take a look. The view was magnificent! He turned to me and exclaimed, "Wouldn't it be neat to have a second story on the addition! It could be a big den—that's all!"

The framer agreed to do it. I went back to the drawing table and put in the few needed details, mainly windows and

The Day I Got "Nailed"

the stairway; which was easy. I placed the stairs going up from the back hallway. The two-story addition was framed by the end of November.

That year, Blanca and Dave, Martha's sister and her husband, were with us for Thanksgiving dinner. Afterwards we went to see the addition. All of us were impressed, except Martha. When we returned home, she said, "I have a suggestion—that's all!" I thought, "Oh, no!" But as a good husband, I listened.

Martha depicted her suggestion clearly, and asked me to picture the setting of the stairway going up to the den from the front dining area instead of from the back hallway. My first reaction was one of disbelief. The stair case was already nailed in. But I could imagine the alteration. The picture in my mind was of a warm, welcome ambiance. My disbelief turned into belief!

The project was at the point where the change could still be done. The whole stairway needed to be taken loose, turned around, and nailed back in place. I talked to John about it, and he agreed to the change. Friday morning after Thanksgiving, Dave, John and I took the stairway loose in one piece; carried it outside; turned it around; brought it in again; and nailed it down.

Blanca and Martha cheered during the process, and they clapped enthusiastically when we were all done. Then, the ladies suggested that we go outside and come right back in to see what it was like. The stairway with its railing going up was a lovely welcome!

We left satisfied with our work and went home. After a light lunch, I got some long, strong, pointed spikes and returned to John's house. I just wanted to make sure that the staircase was securely reattached. I re-nailed the side planking of the stairs to the floor joints—of both the main and the second floors. It was Friday evening by the time I finished. The stairway-turning around project had taken a whole day!

When I came home, my "hat" changed instantly from that of a builder to that of a preacher. I emptied my pockets and put their contents on my computer table. Then, I sat down by my computer to put the finishing touches on the message, which I had started earlier that week. I found the sermon passage in my Bible, read it, put a marker in the Bible, and turned in for the night. Saturday morning arrived too soon.

That morning I had to drive from Des Moines to Omaha to catch the plane to Connecticut. As usual, Martha had packed my suitcase and carry-on. I stuck my Bible in the carry-on, jumped in the car, and drove to the Omaha airport. When I went through security check, the alarm went off.

Immediately, a TSA officer grabbed my bag and escorted me to the side. I was stunned since I thought my bag had nothing in it that should create a problem. The officer asked me, "Who packed your bags?"

I answered, "My wife did, except that I put my Bible in it at the last minute."

The officer asked me to open my bags, and he took out my Bible, which then opened automatically to my sermon passage. With a sober look, he demanded sternly, "What's this?"

I looked up, and at once I knew I was in trouble. "Oh!" I replied absolutely astonished, "That's my Bible bookmark! That's all!"

My Bible bookmark happened to be one of those long, pointed, stairway spikes! Somewhat panicked, I thought, "Now, I'm really in deep trouble." As I stood waiting, for what seemed like an eternity, images of shackles and iron bars passed before me.

The TSA officer's voice startled me out of my "visions" when he asked, lifting up the spike in front of my face, "Do you wanna keep this?"

The Day I Got "Nailed"

With as much confidence as I could muster, I replied, "No way!"

Then he searched through the rest of my bag and found commentaries and sermons, as well as the usual stuff that Martha packs for me. I breathed a sigh of relief. The officer said, "Put everything back in your bag, and we'll scan it again."

I dutifully packed my bag neatly, and he scanned it. He stopped and stared at me with a "You are hiding something from me" look. Frustrated, he said, "There *is* something else in this bag!"

Dumbfounded, I simply gave him a blank look. Then, I found my vocal chords and said, "If there is, I have no idea what it could be."

Déjà vu! "Who packed the bag?" He had short-memory syndrome.

Respectfully, I said, "My wife did except that I put my Bible in it at the last minute." I was beginning to sound like a broken record.

He took everything out again and carefully went through my stuff piece by piece. I thought, "By now the guy knows exactly what I wear!" He found nothing. I felt better.

He scanned the empty bag. His face looked like a big question mark. Emphatically he exclaimed, "There *is* something in this bag!" He lifted up the built-in-flap "floor," tipped the utterly empty bag upside down, and out fell my long-lost finger nail clippers!

Delighted, I shouted, "My neat nail clippers!" Pointing to the clippers in the officer's hand I yelled, "I lost those nail clippers years ago!" Now, he was the one dumbfounded! He shook his head in disbelief.

My long-lost but now found nail clippers were special. They were combined with a can opener and a knife blade. The clippers had slipped under the built-in-flap "floor" of the carry-on bag. We had not used the bag for several years—way before the terrorist attack of September 2001. Now it was November 2002, and there I was with a spike and a knife blade in my carry-on. I thought, "I am *really* in deep trouble!"

As I stood there waiting, for what seemed like an eternity, images of shackles and iron bars passed before me. The TSA officer's voice startled me when he asked me, lifting up the nifty nail clippers in front of my face, "Do you wanna keep these?"

With much more confidence than at the first interrogation, I replied, "No sir! I did not realize they were in there, and I never want to see them again!" Of course I hated to see them go. They were my nifty clippers, but I had no other choice.

Just to double check, he sent me through security again. No alarm went off! I was padded down. Nothing there! The TSA officer nodded and said, "Go on!" Cool and collected, I thanked him for being extra careful in his search.

As I walked past him, he tore a piece of paper in two, handed me half of it and said, "Here! Use this as a book mark for your Bible!"

88

"Only a Little Bit"

Much of my professional life has involved teaching on the post-high school level. I make an effort to create an atmosphere in the classroom that makes learning an enjoyable experience for the students and me, of course.

My personal preference is to teach freshmen. When they arrive at college, life is a whole new experience for them. As high school seniors, they were the big shots in school; the lower-grade students looked up to them. Now, they are the new kids on the block. They are at the bottom of the student-body totem pole.

Our culture considers them to be adults. But, in reality, many years lie ahead before freshmen reach full maturity. I enjoy teaching college freshmen—it is fascinating to watch them mature as they progress through the first year of the rest of their lives.

They have many questions and crucial decisions to make: How will they pay for their education? Should they work, and if so, how many hours? What academic major should they choose? Whom will they marry? What is God's will in their lives regarding a career? Besides these decisions, freshmen have a host of other important matters to settle during their college years.

Freshmen also encounter nitty-gritty issues in the classroom. Some students like to have the room warm, awfully warm; others are partial to cold, almost chilly temperatures.

During the changing of the seasons, especially in the spring, some students want to have the windows open because they think it is too warm in the room. While others want the windows closed because they think the room is too cold. I try to keep a balance between the too-warm crowd and the too-cold crowd.

Most importantly, the reason freshmen are in college is academics. That is my forte. As a college professor, I afford my students several avenues for their learning experience, like reading assignments, quizzes, and tests. My favorite is the last one.

For extra credit in Old Testament Survey tests, I ask the students difficult Bible questions such as "Who were Huppin and Muppin?" "Who were Huz and Buz?" or "Who was Aunt Jemima's father?" During testing time, I do not have to say or do anything. I just sit and watch my students "sweat it out." All is quiet in the classroom. You can almost hear a pin drop.

I say, "*You*" because I certainly am not able to hear a pin drop. I am hearing impaired, and even when I wear my hearing aids, it is difficult for me to hear certain students, particularly the ladies. You may think this is a rabbit trail—I'm also good at these when I am lecturing. However, this particular rabbit trail has a purpose to fulfill in this significant account.

Now, let us go back to tests—my favorite learning tool for freshmen. If students do not understand a test question, which happens once in a while, or if they have some other request, they are free to come up and ask me. They usually speak softly to avoid disturbing their classmates who are still taking the test. Here is where the rabbit trail fulfills its purpose in this account.

A nitty-gritty matter and my hearing impairment collided one spring day. During a test, a student came to me and asked me a question in an extraordinarily soft voice. He did not have his test with him. Right on the spot, I reckoned that his question was not related to the test at all. However, the room was a little on the warm side, so I gathered that he wanted to open a window.

As a partially deaf professor, I have learned to figure out what people are saying by eliminating all the ridiculous possibilities. (Oops, I nearly got off into another rabbit trail!)

I'm back to the student whispering a question to a deaf professor. On that test day, in order to strike a happy medium between the too-warm crowd and the too-cold crowd, I smiled and whispered back to him, "Get permission from the other students first and then only a little bit."

The student raised his eyebrows (as if asking, "What?"), shook his head slightly (as if in disbelief), and then rushed out of the room.

I thought, "Something is not right here. I don't like the way that student looked at me. And now he's disappeared!"

A few minutes later, however, the student returned. I stopped him dead in his tracks, and I asked him, "What did you ask me a little while ago?"

With that initial raised-eyebrow look (without the head shaking) he replied, "Dr. Hartog, I just asked you if I might step out to use the restroom." Obviously embarrassed, he did an about-turn, and then walked swiftly back to his chair.

Sitting on my chair, watching my students sweat it out as they continued to take the test, I arrived to this intellectual conclusion, *"Get permission from the other students first and then only a little bit,"* was not quite the answer that student had expected!

89

Flying High (part one)

With great anticipation we entered the Des Moines International Airport that Saturday morning. In less than twenty hours, after a couple of layovers in Chicago and Miami, we were scheduled to land in Perú. The opportunity of being short-term-teaching missionaries for a week awaited us. Then the following week, we hoped to be see-as-much-as-you-can-of-Perú tourists.

This would be my second visit to Perú and Martha's first. A couple of years earlier I had gone to Perú to teach for a week in Trujillo. I had flown from Des Moines to Dallas and from Dallas to Columbia, where I had gone through customs with my limited Spanish. My survival kit included my Spanish Bible, which is my constant airport companion, my smile, and my innocent countenance. I endured the experience with little difficulty. It was a piece of cake!

This Perú trip should be more delightful because Martha was with me, and she is fluent in Spanish—her mother tongue. Thus, we had nothing to worry about. Our final destination was the seminary in Trujillo, where Martha was to teach a ladies' class in Spanish, and I was to teach a men's class through an interpreter.

We arrived at the Des Moines airport at 9 a.m., two hours before our scheduled flight as required for all international flights. We picked up our glossy wrinkle-free tickets, checked in our baggage, went through security, and walked merrily to our appointed gate.

Two hours was a long time to sit and wait. However, we came prepared. Martha had taken a seminary module earlier that summer and hoped to complete her required reading during the trip. I brought along my Spanish Bible and some seed catalogs. As we waited, we read, talked to each other, gawked at passers-by, and watched the clock tick the time away.

Our connecting flight between Des Moines and Chicago was scheduled on a small American Airlines Eagle, which seats thirty to fifty passengers. After a brief delay in Chicago, we were to fly to Miami. A long delay was awaiting us in Miami before we could board a plane for Lima, Perú, where we were to land the next day early in the morning. A missionary was meeting us in Lima, and together, all three of us were flying to Trujillo, 300 miles north of Lima.

In the meantime, as we waited in Des Moines, pictures of our delightful trip filled our minds. Finally it was nearly 11 o'clock. Then we received the news: our flight was delayed for half an hour. That gave us some concern because the layover in Chicago barely gave us time to catch our connecting flight to Miami.

That Saturday, we experienced one delay after another. Martha read her "exciting" module books; I read my Spanish Bible and planned my garden for the following spring. Finally, at about 1:40 p.m., we heard that our flight was leaving for Chicago at 2:00 p.m. instead; 2:00 p.m. came and went with no plane. But, our plane from Chicago to Miami left as scheduled.

Around 3:00 p.m., we heard that our flight to Chicago was cancelled. The reason given was violent turbulence in the Chicago skies. Later we heard that this was a false report. The weather forecaster probably was new to Chicago and its typical strong-wind gusts. The more probable reason had something to do with environmentalists trying to save fuel. Frequent fliers, who were sitting around us, said that there were just not enough passengers on our flight from Des Moines.

At 4:00 p.m. our flight was re-scheduled. Now we were to fly to Dallas and from there to Miami. We love Dallas and thought, "Okay! It sounds good!" But no plane left from Des Moines. The only flying we did to Dallas was in our imagination.

No plane was flying to Chicago, but Martha's reading certainly was soaring! As 6 p.m. approached, her reading came to a halt. It was time to reschedule again. Forget Chicago to Dallas and then Perú. Let's try Chicago to L.A. and then Perú. This meant going to Chicago, soaring back over Des Moines, waving, "Hi!" to our beautiful state capitol, zooming over Denver, landing in L.A., and from there flying directly to Perú.

Martha and I looked at each other in amazement. The American Airlines representative switched our wrinkled ticket packets (they get scrunched up by passengers under stress), issued us new ones, and destroyed the old ones. Forget saving the trees!

We were just beginning to imagine our exciting flight to L.A., when the airline staff shouted, "Hurry up, your flight is leaving!" Wow, this flight was for real, and now they wanted us to hurry! How dare they! After we had waited for seven hours for a plane to Chicago!

We ran down the bridge to the plane, where a flight attendant glanced at our boarding pass and shoved us hurriedly into the puny American Airlines Eagle. We were on our way! But a small matter kept troubling me, "What about our luggage?" I wondered, "Had it gone to Chicago; or to Miami; or to Dallas; or to L.A.; or worse yet, had it even left Des

Moines, and would it be waiting for us when we returned in two weeks?"

As we settled in our cramped quarters, I turned to Martha and asked her—just for the fun of it, "Where in the world is our baggage now?" Her eyes opened as big as saucers, her mouth dropped open, and she replied, "I wonder if we're going to get pretzels and pop on this puny flight?"

With that, we were on our way to Chicago and then from there to the west coast instead of to the east coast. But, these questions troubled me: Would we ever get to Perú? What about our luggage?

*Happiness comes not
From having much to live on
But from having much to live for.*

—Author unknown

90

Flying High (part two)

What do you do when you have a four-hour layover at Chicago's O'Hare International Airport? You stay awake and gawk at people! Our flight to L.A. was not leaving till midnight. By the time we finally left Des Moines that evening, American Airlines had decided to dump us in Chicago and let another airline fly us the rest of the way to Perú—we hoped.

We relied on the American Airlines Rep. in Des Moines to take care of the whole switcheroo. He had asked us for our ticket packets and had given us new ones. Everything looked fine, except that the word COPA appeared on our new American Airlines tickets. Compañía Panameña de Aviación was doing the honors of flying us to L.A. and then Perú.

When we landed in Los Angeles it was early Sunday morning, but still dark. An attendant told us we needed to go to the International Building, and we should hurry because our COPA plane was leaving in half an hour. Tired and overwhelmed by the vastness of the L.A. airport, we asked her, "Where is this building?" and pointed to our tickets.

She replied, "In Terminal bla-bla." It was hard to understand her. I asked her, "Where?" Impatiently, she told us, "Go outside; take a left; go to the corner; take a right, and you're there"—something like that! We grabbed our carry-ons and raced to that location. When we arrived, it was obvious we were in the wrong place. A thoughtful man had compassion on us, and he directed us clearly and precisely to the building.

Running, with our carry-ons bouncing behind us, we headed toward the ticket-specified location. Once inside, we had to find the COPA desk, go through security, and find our way to the gate. At the COPA desk, a perplexed Rep. scrutinized our tickets. I looked at her and said, "It's a long story," and I gave her an abridged edition of our *krazy* day.

She seemed to understand our predicament and did some quick checking. She grabbed our tickets, looked them over, and handed us our new boarding passes. Then, she said, "The plane is getting ready to leave! You've got to run!"

When we arrived at the departure desk, we heard the "last-boarding" call. We raced down the passenger boarding bridge right into the plane. A stewardess closed the door behind us just as we stepped inside the plane. She glanced at our boarding pass and escorted us to the first class section—something new to us. At last we were on our way to Perú! On first class to boot!

It was about 3 a.m., California time. Exhaustion had overtaken us. Reclined on our comfortable seats, we fell into a deep sleep. Lima was just around the corner, and our luggage was the furthest thing from our minds. No sooner had we fallen asleep than we smelled food! It was breakfast, which we welcomed with gusto. Tired but gratified we returned to Inca Land dreams.

After some hours in the air, a pilot's voice on the loudspeaker interrupted our dreams, "Fasten your seat belts" he announced, "and prepare to land!" I turned to Martha and said cheerfully, "We're here at last!" Then we heard the rest of the story: "We are now making our descent to Tocumen International Airport in Panamá City." Absolutely shocked, Martha and I looked at each other, and in unison we exclaimed, "Panamá!"

Sure enough, Compañía Panameña de Aviación was paying a visit to Panamá, its native land! I called over an attendant and asked her, "What's going on?" Kindly she replied, "We're stopping here briefly to reload and clean the plane. You'll have to disembark."

We had left home Saturday morning at 8:00 a.m. to travel to Perú. It was now 11:00 a.m., Sunday morning, and we were in Panamá City! Nevertheless, in about an hour, we were back on our freshened-up, first-class seats. The layover was worth it. COPA served us a scrumptious lunch. We were now headed for Perú with full tummies, and we were wide awake! Thoughts of Inca Land dispelled concerns about our luggage.

About four and a half hours later, the pilot's voice came through loud and clear: "Prepare for landing. We are now making our descent to Jorge Chávez International Airport in Lima." It was roughly 4:30 p.m. Originally, we had been scheduled to land almost twelve hours earlier! Our contact, who was to have picked us up at the airport, was long gone.

We did not blame him. After all the routing and airline changes we had gone through, he would have had to hire a detective to trace us down! We now had two problems: (1) Our missionary contact had our airline tickets to Trujillo, and (2) that flight had come and gone. (By now, it had made several round-trips to Trujillo. The flight from Lima to Trujillo was only about one hour and a half.)

We had the phone number of the missionary's home in Trujillo. The first thing we did was to try to contact him, but the pay phone we used ate up all our change and did not get us through. By now, our airline from L.A. was dumping its cargo unto the baggage belt; we stood by and watched as the belt went around and around, until it became empty. Our suitcases had not flown with us!

We went to the COPA desk to report the problem. The employee checked and informed us that she could find no record of our luggage and asked to see our baggage claim stubs. We looked in our ticket packet, but the stubs were not

Flying High (part two)

there. The problem went back to Des Moines. The American Airlines Rep., who did the switcheroo, goofed! He failed to transfer our baggage claim stubs to our new ticket packet.

Thirty-three hours had passed since we left home. Now we were strangers in a foreign nation, with only our passports, the clothes on our backs and a few in our carry-ons. However, we were not hungry. Besides our reading material, Martha had packed munchies in our carry-ons. She claims I have a tape worm because I eat constantly. However, the goodies were slim-pickings by now; so we bought *butifarras* at an airport café.

Food always helps my brain think better. Still savoring our Peruvian food, I exclaimed, "Let's try one more thing! Let's go to the American Airlines office and see if they know anything about our luggage."

We found their office and told the clerk about the whole switcheroo. Not having the baggage claim stubs complicated things. Nevertheless, she went ahead and typed our names and place of departure on her computer. Then, a big smile crossed her face! She could not find our baggage, but she had found our baggage claim numbers and wrote them down for us.

That was the first ray of light, but it flickered a little because she could not tell us where our suitcases had decided to hide. She tried to cheer us by telling us, "Don't worry. They're not lost." I found that difficult to believe! Halfway encouraged, I slipped the piece of paper with the claim stub numbers into my billfold.

Then I thought of my credit cards. I went back to the pay phone and used a credit card to call the missionary's house. It worked! His wife answered the phone. She told me that her husband had gone to the airport earlier and had waited quite a while for us, but gave up and left. However, he was still in Lima. She promised to call him and have him pick us up.

All the good news made me hungry! We tried some *empanadas* at a bakery booth. While we were sitting there, a security officer joined us. When we told him about our dilemma, he warmed up; and we chatted for a while. Martha's mother tongue certainly came in handy. Although he did not respond that night, the officer heard the gospel clearly in Spanish. Our short-term-mission work in Perú had begun!

By the time our missionary friend arrived, it was bed time. He drove us to a hotel in Lima, and he picked us up the next morning. Back to the airport we went! We now had another hurdle ahead of us. Our tickets to Trujillo were for a Sunday flight, but now it was Monday morning. The missionary persuaded the airline staff to honor his ticket and ours. No bribes!

Since the trip from Lima to Trujillo was during the daylight hours, we were able to view the beautiful coast of Perú as we flew along the edge of the Pacific northward. An hour and a half later, we landed at the Capitán FAP Carlos Martínez de Pinillos, the international airport of Trujillo, Peru's third largest city.

We had no luggage, but we had made it to our destination—Trujillo. A blessed short-term-teaching-missions work awaited us there, and we were eager to get started!

91

Trujillo

Faithful to its description as the "Capital of the Everlasting Spring," Trujillo welcomed us with a lovely sunny Monday. The possibility of our luggage beating us to our final destination was far fetched, but we checked anyway. Sure enough, it wasn't there, and we took it in stride—we were not about to spoil such a beautiful day! The airline staff promised to call us the moment our suitcases arrived.

Our missionary hosts welcomed us warmly into their home. Aware of our predicament, they willingly would have given us their clothes off their backs! All I needed to complete my outfit was a tie, and our host lent me one. I was ready to teach! But not Martha!

She needed a skirt to teach the ladies' class. As usual, she had packed a few extra personal clothes in our carry-ons, but she had not packed a skirt. Martha is short and thin and our hostess was taller and stouter. At first glance, borrowing a skirt from her did not seem likely at all.

All four of us went shopping for a skirt! Martha and I became tourists before our short-term-teaching-mission work had started in Trujillo. Classes started at two in the afternoon. To save time and also money, we went to the open market where the variety is greater, and the prices are negotiable. I love to barter! And this was an excellent way to freshen up my Spanish.

We checked every clothing store, and all we found were jeans and a few mini-mini skirts—way too short even for Martha! "Wow!" she exclaimed, "American culture has certainly influenced Trujillo fashions!" Nonetheless, we didn't leave the market empty-handed. I bartered for nice leather shoes for Martha and me. Our students should be thankful. They would be spared the effects of two-day-travel-worn tennis shoes!

To go with her new leather shoes, Martha needed a skirt. Our hostess poked around her closet and found just the right skirt—a black one that came down a little bit below Martha's ankles. She looked spiffy in her wrapped around-'n around skirt and new leather shoes! Now, Martha was also ready to teach!

The wacky experiences that led us to that first day of classes faded temporarily the moment we met our students. We were happy to meet one another, and they were eager to learn. Modular classes meet for about four hours every afternoon for a week, and our first class went well!

Our gracious hosts contributed to its success. They fed us, clothed us, and encouraged us. Tired, but contented, Martha and I hit the sack soon after supper. Wearing bed-time clothes borrowed from our hosts, we slept soundly our first night in Trujillo.

The next morning, we received the promised call. Our luggage had finally arrived! After breakfast, we drove to the airport and picked up our two suitcases. When our host saw how little they were, he remarked, "You travel lightly!" We did! It was nice to have our few, old clothes back. The miles they traveled and the route they took is a secret our suitcases did not divulge.

The week of our short-term-mission work went by fast! Martha thought that teaching in Spanish was a bit rough the first two days; but by the end of the week, she was speaking her usual one-thousand-words a minute. The ladies helped her when she could not think of some Spanish terms. Most of the ladies audited the class, but all of them attended faithfully—even nursing mothers!

I taught with an interpreter. Although I can read Spanish and can understand a fair bit of what Spanish-speakers say, it is more difficult for me speak it. This is typical when learning a foreign language. Since I was teaching a Bible class, I naturally specified the Bible chapter I was explaining. For example, when I said, "chapter three." The interpreter said, "*capítulo tres*."

About halfway through the week, just to keep my interpreter on his toes, I said, "*capítulo viente*." Without batting an eye, he said, "chapter twenty!" On the last day, I switched over to Spanish and read a short passage to the students. They looked up surprised, and then they laughed and clapped!

Because our classes were in the afternoon, we had the mornings free; and our kind hosts thought that we should not just sit around and do nothing. They were willing to show us some of the popular sites in the area. They jump-started us on our see-as-much-as-you-can-of-Perú tour. Every morning, we ate a hearty breakfast, and then we drove around Trujillo and beyond it.

Our hosts drove us to the coast and we dined on a delicious meal of fresh-caught fish. They also gave us a private tour through Trujillo proper, the third largest city in Perú.[73] Its beautiful colonial buildings with wrought ironwork reveal its former Spanish colonial heritage. Near Trujillo, we visited two major archaeolo-gical sites from pre-Hispanic times: the temples of the sun and moon and also Chan Chan. The latter

---

[73] Trujillo proper has a population of about 300,000 and its metropolitan area, about 800,000.

is the largest adobe city of the ancient world. It was the capital city of the Chimu Indians, who flourished from about A.D. 900 to A.D. 1400. They worshipped the moon and considered the sun as the destroyer.

We also drove way up into the Andes Mountains where we visited a Cathedral museum with artifacts from early colonial days. Then, we went back down the mountain with its winding roads, which were often steep and narrow with no railings. When meeting another car, we had to hug the mountainside for the sake of that upcoming car. Otherwise, it would have fallen over the edge of a 200 to 300-foot precipice. On the way, we saw the cutest donkey traveling in the open trunk of a car that was packed with Peruvians!

In the middle of the week, we attended a prayer meeting at a Spanish Baptist church. Because they did not own cars, many of the believers took taxis or buses, or even walked quite a distance to church. Some of the seminary students also had traveled many hours by bus to attend the modular classes. The faithfulness of the believers challenged and blessed us.

It was truly a privilege to teach the students in Trujillo and to fellowship with all the believers there. With some tourism thrown in the middle, our week came to an end too soon! On Saturday, we switched roles from teachers to tourists. We said good-by to our kind hosts, Steve and Evelyn Stillwell; and we boarded the plane to fly back to Lima and on to Cusco. From there, we planned to go to Urubamba.

Our see-as-much-as-you-can-of-Perú journey was about to begin in earnest!

92

Urubamba/Machu Picchu

Soon after we boarded the plane from Trujillo back to Lima, rumors that airline problems loomed on the horizon buzzed around us. A few passengers were chitchatting about a struggling airline, but all the buzzing sounded like a rumor, and we ignored it. Our thoughts were on the great adventures that awaited us that week on our see-as-much-as-you-can-of-Perú tour. Moreover, our upcoming journeys were to be through various means: airplane, car, train, bus, and taxi.

At the airport in Lima we were to change planes and then fly toward southern Perú to Cusco, the capital of Peru's Cusco Region. We planned to spend three days in that region and celebrate our 40th wedding anniversary. Martha and I believed we were still young and vigorous; our plans included a hike through Machu Picchu, "The Lost City of the Incas."

While waiting in Lima for our plane to Cusco, a Spanish newspaper headline caught Martha's attention. It emblazoned the news that Aero Continente was facing legal and financial problems. We looked at each other in disbelief. Continente was to fly us to Cusco that afternoon and bring us back to Lima the next week!

With her eyes as big as saucers, Martha exclaimed, "Hey, wouldn't it be something if that Continente airline went down!" (She meant bankrupt, of course.) The newspaper headline went into our new file of far-fetched travel concerns. Continente was still flying; our boarding call assured us of that; and our plane landed us safely at Alejandro Velasco Astete, Cusco's International Airport. A gracious missionary couple, who were serving in Cusco, picked us up at the airport; and they drove us to Urubamba, about an hour away.

Under the snow-capped mountain of Chicón lies the beautiful Sacred Valley of the Incas. Nestled in this valley is Urubamba, its biggest city. The scenery that surrounded us was picturesque. The altitude and lovely landscape affected our brains, and we completely forgot all about Aero Continente and its problems. As we were driving by the mountain side, Martha shouted, "Look!" and pointed to a little boy carrying a long stick for a staff. Behind him and his dog was a single-lined menagerie of animals: llamas, donkeys, goats, sheep, and geese. They were coming home from pasturing all day on the hills above.

We spent the next couple of days in Urubamba. Inca Land, our home base, was a peaceful mountain resort with quaint little cabins and a restaurant. It served delicious homemade flat bread, which Martha relished. (My weakness is chocolate, and Martha's is bread). Our first night for supper we got brave and ordered alpaca steaks; they tasted yummy! Peruvians also eat *cuy*, a.k.a. guinea pigs, but we passed on that! Guinea pigs are Peru's meat of choice because they don't require much room to raise as regular pigs do.

Machu Picchu, the highlight of our tour awaited us the next day. After a restful night's sleep, we walked the short distance to the railroad station. While it was still dark and chilly, we boarded a PerúRail train that zigzagged for about an hour through the mountains up to Aguas Calientes—the closest access point to Machu Picchu. A beautiful sunny day and a hodgepodge of international tourists welcomed us, and all of us were there for one purpose: to see Machu Picchu. Some tourists were taking the four-mile hike up the mountain; others were riding a bus. Mature individuals, like us, chose the latter.

In the midst of the throng of tourists who spoke all kinds of tongues, some sort of order prevailed.

Before we knew it, we were bouncing in a Grey-Hound-like tour bus to Machu Picchu, 7,970 feet above sea level. Machu Picchu means "Old Mountain." The Mysterious Lost City of the Incas lies saddled between this mountain and Huayna Picchu—"Young Mountain," which is 1,180 feet higher than its older sister.

The bus from Aguas Calientes up to Machu Picchu takes about 20 minutes. The ride up was treacherously steep but spectacular as the narrow track winds its way up the mountainside. It can be a bit scary at times with almost vertical drops plunging down into the Vilcanota Valley below. The bus drivers took all this in stride. I, however, was convinced that we should have taken the hike and was relieved when we arrived!

The Lost City of the Incas, built around 1450, is an icon from the Inca civilization; but they abandoned it about a hundred years later. The Conquistadores from Spain did not find it; thus they did not plunder it or destroy it as they did other Inca cities. Its existence, however, was known to the locals and to a few native explorers and missionaries. In 1911, area farmers led the American historian, Hiram Bingham to the Lost City of the Incas. It was then that the whole world became aware of its existence.

Machu Picchu is a fascinating place. As we hiked around it, we could picture clearly the daily lives of its original inhabitants. They were strong people with great skills. For their building projects they used huge rocks, which they moved without the use of a wheel and positioned them strategically. The terraced fields evidenced their agricultural expertise. The *Room of the Three Windows*, *Intihuatana* (Hitching post of the Sun), and *Torreon*, the *Temple of the Sun*, told the religious story of these people. They believed their king was a child of the sun and sacrificed children at his death.

Taking a Break at Machu Picchu

Though far removed from the Inca worshippers, some tourists deem it a spiritual experience to visit Machu Picchu. It is at the top of the list of New Age devotees. One object that attracts them at Machu Picchu is a massive rock, which supposedly emanates energy. We were surprised at the number of people who touched it, hoping to get energy from it.

We spent the whole day among the ruins of that ancient Inca stronghold. The high altitude and low pressure began to affect Martha. Halfway through our hike, she got tired. When she gets tired, she falls asleep wherever she happens to be, which this time turned out to be a smooth grassy plateau. After her brief nap, we continued our exploration through the ancient city.

We had just about reached the end of our upward journey, when Martha decided she had had enough. She sat on a flat rock and told me to go ahead. I did. Then, when I reached the mountain peak, I saw something that would make Martha smile big! A small family of llamas was pasturing right in front of me.

I shouted, "Martha, come up! You've got to see this!" She responded, "Why? Did you see a llama or something?" I pretended not to have heard her, and told her, "Just come up and look!" Curious Martha climbed all the way up. Thus, it was in Machu Picchu that Martha and I saw our first baby llama.

It seemed too soon, but it was time to make our trek back to our resort. We had left before dawn and returned after sunset. Before going to bed, we decided to confirm our flight back from Cusco to Lima, which was scheduled to leave on Monday. We stopped by the desk and asked the desk attendant to help us contact Aero Continente.

The "I'm so sorry look" on her countenance, told us right away that something was wrong. Sure enough! She gave us the bad news: Aero Continente had gone bankrupt! We were stranded on a Peruvian mountain. However, our see-as-much-as-you-can-of-Peru journey was not over. According to our schedule, we had a wonderful blessing awaiting us—worshipping with Inca descendants in the city of Cusco!

*Happiness is worshipping the Creator
And enjoying His marvelous creation.*

—Martha Hartog

93

Cusco

That night, Martha's response to the bad news about Aero Continente was, "I told you it was going to crash!" (She meant, go bankrupt, of course). We were stranded in the Sacred Valley of the Incas. However, we were tired and needed rest; for the night, we put that airline problem into our newest file of pending travel concerns. The next day, Sunday, promised to be a special day. We were going to church with Cusco missionaries, Tim and Barbara Whatley.

Cusco, the historic capital of the Inca Empire, lies at the edge of the Sacred Valley of the Incas, is 11,200 feet above sea level, and had a population of about 350,000. The kind missionaries picked us up and drove us to a village near Cusco for church. The people assembled in a make-shift building adjacent to the missionaries' humble living quarters.

The high-altitude temperature was frigid; the walls of the building were skimpy; the benches were rough, flat boards. Totally oblivious to these inconveniences, the people raised their voices in triumphant song to the true and living God. These joyful worshippers were descendants of the Incas who had worshipped the sun and had built grand structures to it on "Old Mountain."

Now in Quechua, the language of their ancestors, these native believers raised their song to Jesus—their Savior, the Son of God, and the King of kings. The name "Jesus" is recognizable in any tongue, and hearing it in Quechua brought tears to our eyes.

After church and a hearty lunch, the missionaries drove us to a hotel in Cusco. Monday morning, they came back and took us to the airport. We had to find an airline to fly us back to Lima. Unfortunately, all the flights were full. Finally, TANS (Transportes Aéreos Nacionales de Selva)[74] sold us one-way tickets to Lima, but we had to stay in Cusco until the next day, Tuesday.

Back at the hotel, the manager met us with some good news. Aero Continente was going to refund our money for the unused part of the trip, but we had to apply in person. No problem. The airline office was close to our hotel and opened at 1:00 p.m. Martha and I went right away since there was nothing else to do.

I was the first one at the door and tried to open it, but it was locked; so I remained by the door. Martha leaned against a pillar near the office and relaxed by reading one of her seminary-module books. As one o'clock approached, more tourists showed up who wanted to get in; but I stood immovable at my post.

When one o'clock arrived, the door cracked open barely enough to let someone's face squeeze through. The mouth on the face opened wide and declared, "The office will open at two sharp!" By this time, a lively charismatic throng of international tourists had gathered by the door. In their mother tongues, they were uttering boisterously their intense frustration.

At two o'clock the door cracked open again, barely enough to let a new face squeeze through. The quivering mouth on the face declared, *"Thee off—eece weel op—en at threeee."* The

---

[74] In 2006, two years after we had been in Peru, the Peruvian government suspended the license to this airline.

mob, no longer satisfied with vocalizing their anger, decided to take action. One tourist shouted, "Let's break the door!" The crowd heeded his call and began to push against the door.

Since I refused to move, my flesh and bones were being squeezed against the door. I felt as if I were ten feet tall and one inch thick. Now and then, Martha, still leaning against the post, looked up from her book to make sure I was still in one piece. Then, she smiled and went back to her reading. She took a couple of breaks to rest her eyes. She went across the street to the plaza and socialized with the local ladies. I had to stay put to save my place.

Some French people, who were standing next to me, said to one another in French, that they should be the first to go in because they had farther to go. I said *"J'ai ete ici avant vous!"* (This means, "I was here before you!") They were surprised that I knew enough French to understand what they were saying. Then they quit trying to squeeze in front of me. Soon a riot broke out. The police arrived, and eventually they were able to control the mob, somewhat.

The office door finally opened—all the way. Immediately, the crowd in one perfect harmonious mass pressed toward the entry. The police shut the door at once. With no place to go but still in one piece, I stood just outside the door. Shortly, more police came and forced their way to the door. They stayed outside by me and allowed people to go in only two or three at a time.

Once inside, I was asked to fill out forms and was assured that the funds would be mailed to my home address. They either lost my address or were making false promises to calm us. The funds never arrived. We had to pay twice for the flight back to the U.S.

Martha Socializing at Cusco

Back at the hotel, the manager met us with some bad news. Taxi drivers were going on strike at five the next morning. Our sob story in Martha's Spanish version touched his heart. He offered to call and have a driver pick us up at four a.m., before the strike began.

We got up early enough, and so did our taxi driver. He arrived on time and raced us through pre-dawn Cusco, straight to the airport. High fences surrounded it, but one gate was open. As we drove through it, we looked back and saw airport security close the gate behind us and lock it. Our driver said that they were trying to avoid impending troubles caused by the taxi drivers' strike.

Thanks to our speedy cabbie, we made it into the airport, in the nick of time. TANS airlines flew us to Lima; here we checked in our luggage and made sure we had the baggage claim stubs. Before we could board our American Airlines plane to Miami, a thirteen-hour layover awaited us in Lima,

Our see-as-much-as-you-can-of-Perú tour had come to an end. Machu Picchu, the Lost City of the Inca Empire, was to have been the highlight of our tour. However, all that changed on Sunday morning in Cusco. The Inca descendants singing in Quechua about Jesus our Savior stirred our hearts.

The church service in that humble Cusco setting—that was the pinnacle of our tour!

Serve the LORD with gladness;
Come before his presence with singing.

—Psalm 100:2

94

Homeward Bound!

We had survived an airline rescheduling fiasco, a bus trip on a treacherous mountain road, an airline bankruptcy, and a taxi drivers' strike. With all that behind us, we welcomed the thirteen-hour layover in Lima as a time to relax and recall our recent adventures. I also read my Spanish Bible, looked through my seed catalogs, and enlarged my garden plans for the following spring. Martha read her last module book. She rested her eyes from the printed page by gawking at people, and by walking up and down the airport.

As the long, awaited time for boarding drew near, more and more people milled around the departure gate area. The privileged few (the first class and disabled passengers) were beginning to take their place at the head of the line. Plebeians, like us, were sitting on the edge of our seats, ready to jump when our rows were called. The place was crowded, but order prevailed. Two hundred and thirty passengers were flying on that plane from Lima to Miami that day. Obviously, it was time for worn down summer tourists to return home.

About ten minutes before loading time, an airport announcement jarred us to attention and brought havoc to the expectant crowd. Our flight was departing in a few minutes as scheduled, but from another gate, far from where we were. In a split second, our gate area vacated entirely. Grabbing our carry-ons and also one another, Martha and I became one with the crowd that was pressing on in one solid mass toward the new gate. Strangers, who had been chatting amicably earlier, were now shoving one another rudely.

Martha and I put our body motion on cruise control and moved along with the flow of the crowd. I turned to Martha and whispered, "If we were in the U.S., this would not have happened!"

Eventually, we all boarded our plane and walked nonchalantly down the narrow isles, looking for our assigned seats as if the shoving had never happened. Buckled in our seats, Martha and I breathed a sigh of relief. At last we were in Peruvian skies! Then we flew over Ecuador and Panama and began our descent over the Caribbean. From that height, glancing down on Cuba, it was almost like looking at it on a map. Then, the tip of Florida came into view, and our pilot executed a smooth landing at the Miami International Airport. We were back on American soil!

Entering our country through one of the gates, labeled "American Citizens," was a great privilege! After he checked our passports and handed them back to us, the security officer smiled and exclaimed, "Welcome home!" It was good to be home—almost.

First, we had to rejoin our luggage and go through customs. We rushed to the baggage claim belts and stood patiently as hundreds of suitcases went past us. But, ours were not among them. Our little suitcases had played the disappearing act once again!

I thought "Here we go again!" But, the airline personnel assured us that they were somewhere in the airport. Of all the suitcases belonging to two hundred and thirty passengers, American Airlines had lost only one set, and it was ours! Fortunately, we had a two-hour layover before our plane left for Chicago. We hoped our luggage had come out of hiding by then.

And it did! Customs officials waved us through without asking us to open our suitcases. Their small size and ragged appearance probably helped. We entrusted back to American Airlines our "precious" cargo expecting to greet it in Des Moines. Then, ready for our row call, we rushed to our departure gate. We had barely sat down at the edge of our seat, when the intercom boomed with the news that our flight was now boarding at a different gate. *Déjà vu!*

In a split second, our gate area vacated completely. Grabbing our carry-ons and also one another, Martha and I became one with the crowd that was pressing on in one solid mass toward the new gate. Martha and I put our body motion on cruise control and moved along with the flow of the crowd. I turned to Martha and whispered, "This is Miami for you. If we were in Des Moines this would not have happened!"

Eventually, we all boarded our plane and walked nonchalantly down the narrow isles, looking for our assigned seats as if the shoving had never happened. Buckled in our seats, Martha and I breathed a hungry sigh of relief. In all the rush, we did not have time to grab a MacDonald burger and fries at the Miami airport. Martha turned to me and said, "I hope we get pop and pretzels, at least."

Within half an hour of flying in U.S. skies, her hopes were dashed away. A stewardess announced that the food for the trip inadvertently had been left in Miami. No snack on the flight! Martha found her air-traveling gum and chewed one piece after another all the way to Chicago. She chewed rapidly and intensely, and sweat beads began popping out on her face.

For some reason, the plane felt unusually warm and stuffy. My guess was that all of us must have worked up a sweat from all the shoving and rushing. "Oh, well," I thought, as I watched Martha chewing away, "at least nothing else can go wrong on this trip." My reasoning was founded on this fact: we were nearly on the last lap of our journey.

Homeward Bound! 383

No sooner had that insightful thought left my mind, than another announcement came through—this time from the pilot cabin: "The motor in the air conditioner of the plane has gone out. We are sorry for the inconvenience you are experiencing." I wondered if the plane had any parachutes. Just in case, of course!

We received a *warm-welcome* trip from the U.S. skies all the way to Chicago. The instant we entered O'Hare International Airport, we rushed to the nearest MacDonald for a Big Mac, fries, and a large, cold pop.

A small American Eagle flew us to Des Moines without a hitch. Martha got her pop and pretzels. Everything went right! How could that be? It just didn't seem normal anymore. We were home, and so was our luggage!

Whoever is happy
Will make others happy too.

—Anne Frank

95

It Was a Bloody Event!

My body time-clock is certainly off kilter—that's for sure! I can stay up all night; but getting up early, any day, is a challenge, especially in the winter when the sun has a tough time getting up, too. Before I went to seminary, I was a morning person. Then, when I started working the night shift at the post office as a seminary student, my nights and days switched places.

For many years, I had to teach classes that started at seven in the morning. In the winter, those classes were killers! A tired-out professor had to teach a whole bunch of dozing-off students. Naturally, if I stayed up into the wee hours of the morning, I slept in a little bit longer. On those mornings, I had to go into "tornado mode." I hustled around to get ready, and the morning activities swirled around me like tornado debris.

One slept-in-a-little-bit-longer morning happened on a test day. (Thankfully, the tests were ready—piled neatly on my desk) I jumped out of bed and began swirling: I showered; slipped into my clothes; downed a bowl of cereal; jumped into the car; raced to school; dashed into my office; grabbed the tests; whirled into class; and landed two minutes early in the midst of my students, who looked like they had been up all night long, studying for the test!

Cool, calm, and collected, I stood behind the lectern and asked a student to pray on behalf of his classmates (seventy-five plus anxious students). A few guys helped me pass out

It Was a Bloody Event!

the tests; then I sat down to relax and catch my breath. The philosophy I firmly advocate concerning tests is this: "It is more blessed to give than to receive!"

The room typically became quiet as the students "sweated it out." Taking it easy on my monitoring chair at the front, I was thinking about all those anxious students who had to take such a challenging test. Automatically, I assumed my distinguished-thinking posture—my chin resting on my hand. Instantly, I realized that, in the midst of that morning's whirlwind, I had forgotten to shave!

No big deal. The men's restroom was down the hall from the classroom and so was my office. In one of my desk drawers, I kept disposable razors for emergencies. This was one of them. In my thinking posture, the solution to my dilemma came easily. I pictured clearly everything swirling around me. You guessed it! I decided to go into tornado mode!

I scurried quietly past the students; slipped out the door; darted into my office; snatched a brand new disposable razor; whirled into the restroom, and headed for the sink; wet my face with a few water splashes, and gave it several speedy shaves. In no time at all, I was trimmed up and hastened back to class.

Just as I was dashing out of the restroom, I felt a warm trickle on my face. I touched my cheek, looked at my hand, and saw blood! I swirled back into the restroom and headed for the sink. The face reflected on the mirror was bleeding like a stuck hog. Little trickles of blood were bubbling on my mustache and beard areas. As soon as I splashed water on my face, the pesky nicks started bleeding right up again.

Never in my life had I seen so much blood coming out of so many little nicks. Hurriedly I blotted my face with little pieces of paper towels. At last, the trickling blood clotted and stopped. But, I could do nothing about the stubborn little nicks. Fifteen minutes went by before I finally returned to class.

Nonchalantly, I quietly slipped past the anxious students; sat down on my monitoring chair; and assumed my distinguished-thinking posture. After completing their ordeal, one by one the students walked to the front with their exams and answer sheets.

I sat on my monitoring chair and looked up as the students walked by. Some of them just looked at me and smiled. Others stared at me with a surprised look on their faces and exclaimed quietly, "What in the world happened to you!"

Following the suit of the smiling students, I just looked at the inquisitive students and smiled—but not too big a smile. I was afraid the pesky little nicks might start bleeding all over again!

That day when I slept in a little bit longer, the students took a difficult test, but I learned a simple lesson: Never shave in a hurry with a disposable razor!

Happiness usually comes
From being too busy
To be miserable.

—Author unknown

96

Granny, Get Your Gun!

"Sheep die first, and then they get sick." That's what shepherds say. We understood why the day after we bought our two sheep. Sheep can be robust and vivacious one day, and stiff and cold the next day.

We decided to buy two sheep on the day the bad news had reached our household! Not about a dead sheep, but that Ankeny was annexing our small country subdivision. We all had bought small acreages because we liked the farm-like living, which for many of us included farm animals. People in our neighborhood had horses and chickens. We had chickens.

When we heard the bad news, we decided to be like our neighbors and add some large animals to our homestead. In order to grandfather them in, we had to act quickly—before annexation. Martha had wanted a donkey since she was a little girl and I wanted sheep. This settled our options, and we began the search.

We heard of a homesteader who had a donkey and went to visit him. When we arrived at his "farm," it was dark already, and all his critters had gone to bed. But the fellow told us about the amazing menagerie he had on his place, including llamas. As for donkeys, he only had one old jack named "Lightening"; but it no longer was able to live up to its name. The poor old thing appeared more like a sloth, and he wasn't for sale.

We walked around and saw one majestic creature and a smaller one silhouetted against the horizon as they grazed in the semi darkness. The scenery brought back memories of Machu Picchu. We approached the fence, and the curious young male came over right away and nuzzled against Martha's cheeks. That did it! We were adding a llama to our homestead. We bought it on the spot but did not bring it home that night.

Its owner then told us of a place where donkeys were for sale and offered to transport both animals after we had purchased a donkey. We went to the donkey place the next day and bought a young jenny. As head of the Hartog household, I named the new members of our homestead. Desi, the llama, and Lucy, the donkey arrived together later that day.

Next, on our agenda was to buy a couple of sheep. We drove to the farm places around our homestead and asked, "Do you have any sheep for sale?" We sure got some funny looks! Then, a Century Farmer directed us to a sheep farm nearby. From about one hundred sheep, we picked out the healthiest looking lambs, two cute ewes. One had a black face and the other, a white face. That afternoon, the kind sheep farmer delivered them to our homestead. In the midst of all the excitement, I failed to name our newest additions.

We had obtained the animals first, and then I built temporary shelters and pens for the four of them. Soon, the "architect" in me came to life again. Within a couple of weeks, I had built an efficient barn for our animals. In the meantime, that first night, our animals bedded down in their temporary fenced pens. Assured that our animals were safe and sound, we went to bed.

The pen for Desi and Lucy was intentionally small. The llama owner had told me that crowding helps animals get along, and it worked! We stuffed them into the chicken yard and locked up the chickens in their coup—temporarily, of course. Desi and Lucy behaved well and slept in their pen through the night. However, the sheep found a way to escape and wandered off. The next morning we found them fast

Lucy, Desi, and Beula

asleep by the chicken yard. Martha said, "They were lonely and wanted company." But we hauled them back to the sheep pen.

During the day as I hurried through my building projects, I checked on them now and then to make sure that they were still in their pen. By early evening when I checked on them, the black-faced sheep had turned in early and was lying peacefully inside the temporary shelter. I went in and stroked her, but she didn't move.

No question about it, she had assumed pasture temperature and would never set hoof into her finished barn. One minute she was trying to figure out how to get out of her pen, the next minute she lay sleeping in timeless bliss. When I told a former sheep farmer about it, he said, "Oh! That's sheep for you. They die, and then they get sick!" Unfortunately, our lamb had died nameless.

I took seriously the left-over lamb and named her Eula, since she was a ewe. Then, a sweet widow named Eula visited our church. To avoid the confusion we had with our dog Julie,[75] Eula became Beula. She attached herself to Martha, and under her care grew to be the biggest sheep I have ever seen. Martha and I enjoyed watching her chase Desi and Lucy around the pasture. Beula did not run, she bounced up into the air and then came down again as she chased her two companions.

However, our robust Beula had a problem: she was a hermaphrodite. She had the characteristics of both a ewe and a ram. Sometimes, Beula displayed a gentle disposition. Other times, she was aggressive. She got a mean look on her face, put her head down, and rammed forcefully into people. Martha was the first victim of Beula's split personality. Later, Beula took on our veterinarian who was a 300-pound man. She nearly knocked him over. Understandably, he was concerned

---

[75] See "Hold Your Tongue!" story #40.

about the risks of keeping such an unpredictable pet. Later Beula went after me and got me right on my side.

One day, Martha noticed that right before Beula became aggressive she got a mean look in her eyes. Martha splashed water on Beula's face, and she snapped out of her aggression immediately. Eureka! This was the way to stop Beula's nonsense! We went to Walmart and bought water guns—enough for Martha and the grandkids. Martha tested her purchase and unloaded a couple of water guns on Beula's mean-looking face. They worked!

When the grandkids came over, they invariably asked to see the animals. Armed with their water guns, Martha and the children headed for the barn. One day, Ethan, one of our grandchildren, wanted to visit the animals. He and Martha got ready for battle. However, Ethan was not quick enough on the draw, and Beula pinned him to the fence. That was her downfall!

I determined that she had to go a different way than her sister—not underground, but into the deep freezer. I took Beula to a meat locker where she became mostly lamb-burger and leg of lamb. Martha could not bear the thought of eating Beula; thus she stayed untouched in cold storage for several months.

I often told my students stories about our animals, but I had failed to tell them the rest of Beula's story. One freezing January day, a concerned student came to me after class and commented, "Your sheep is probably very cold today." "Yes," I replied, "She's very cold and stiff!"

97

Itsy Bitsy and His Gang

Our chicken condominium is hardly ever vacant. Periodically, we order new chickens from a hatchery. A minimum order of day-old chicks is twenty five. Often half of the chicks turn out to be roosters. Because even young roosters fight and are unprofitable as adults, I butcher all the roosters, except one. Martha gets the privilege of choosing the survivor—not an easy task because she gets attached to the cocks.

All the hens escape the knife. Six months later, they begin to express their gratitude with daily tokens—their incredible edible eggs. For almost three years, they keep us supplied with more eggs than we can eat; we give away the extras to friends. Naming our poultry is a joint venture, but I usually yield to Martha's silly names. Because our chickens are pets, they live a long time. Solomon lived to be ten-and-a-half years old.[76]

Our present ruler of the roost is Itsy Bitsy. He is a tiny Quail Antwerp Belgian, but he struts like a full-sized rooster. If he thinks any member of his harem is in peril, he attacks. He even attacks Martha when she picks up a hen; but she grabs him, strokes his beautiful feathers, and feeds him sun flower seeds. Come to think of it, maybe that's why he attacks her!

Our largest hen is Blackie, a black, gentle Jersey Giant—a brown-egg layer. Green eggs are thank-you gifts from Eagle,

---

[76] See "Unwanted Guest in the Coop," story #85.

a five-year-old Amerauncana that is still laying! Arauncanas were native to Chile, and their eggs were eggshell robin blue. This color changed to green when the Spaniards crossed their chickens with the Arauncanas. The hybrids are the Amerauncanas, and the purebreds are the Arauncanas.

Hilda, our Hudain, sports an extra toe on each leg and a fancy feather hat. Martha says, "She looks like she's ready to go somewhere but has no where to go!" Her head covering hinders her vision; often, she bumps into whatever is in her path. Hilda used to lay beautiful white eggs, but her laying days ended when her egg-laying ovary stopped functioning.[77] This dysfunction affected her vocal chords as well, and now she crows. She still looks like a hen, but she crows like a rooster.

Also, when she scratches in the yard and finds some edible tidbits, she makes rooster "Come and get it!" sounds; and all the hens scurry to her, just like they do for Itsy Bitsy. Hilda and Itsy Bitsy don't fight like typical roosters; they just have crowing competitions. But it takes Hilda a little more neck stretching to let out that crow. Undoubtedly, Itsy Bitsy is still king!

Precious is a timid little hen, a snow-white Cochin bantam; her feathers curl backwards, which hinder her from flying— even up to the roost. Thus, I made her a small, wooden canopy bed inside the coop. One day, Martha noticed some purple bruises on her body. We guessed that a hawk had tried to snatch her. Martha, bathed her, rubbed her bruises with Desitin, and kept a close eye on her. Precious came through fine.

Sweetie Pie is a tiny Quail Antwerp Belgian, like Itsy Bitsy, and weighs less than a pound. She got sick right before we were to take a trip to Oklahoma, where I was speaking at

---

[77] According to our poultry sources, a hen has two ovaries, but only one functions. When it is injured, the hen stops laying eggs.

Itsy Bitsy's Gang with Martha

a Bible conference. Martha feared that Sweetie Pie might die while we were gone and be turned into *hors d'œuvres* for her peers. Knowing that chickens are cannibals, I agreed!

After debating the issue, we decided to take her along to Oklahoma. We called my relatives who were hosting us and asked them if we might bring Sweetie Pie along. All of them went along with our crazy idea. They probably thought that the chicken would die before we arrived. We took food and water along, and she traveled first-class in a pet taxi lined with fresh hay.

By the time we arrived at my nephew's house, Sweetie Pie had perked up quite a bit. We assured Dan that Sweetie Pie was sleeping in the barn. However, Jean, Dan's wife, refused such a notion! The spoiled chicken spent the night in their kitchen, inside her taxi, of course. They had two cats and a golden retriever. Their gentle golden retriever, a gracious host, lay by the cage and tried to lick her. Since she was unable to play chase with the cats, they ignored her completely.

By the time we had visited Fran and Bill (my sister and her husband) and Paul and Velma (my brother and his wife), Sweetie Pie was feeling like a brand new Quail Antwerp Belgian hen. On the way back to Iowa, she entertained us with her soft clucking. Then, halfway through the trip, she started cackling at the top of her little beak.

Sensitive to female matters, Martha exclaimed, "It sounds like the crazy hen has laid an egg!" Martha looked into the cage, and sure enough! Sweetie Pie had laid her usual tiny-light-tan egg—her thank you token for keeping her alive. It had been a while since she had laid an egg. She certainly wanted the world to know it!

98

Edelweiss

"What do you think about going to Austria for spring break?" This is how I greeted Martha that day when I came home for lunch.

"Sure!" Martha replied without turning around and interrupting her work. She was in the kitchen washing vegetables for a salad—her favorite part of the meal.

"Great!" I continued, "I'll tell Emanuel."

Martha forgot all about the veggie salad, and did an about face with knife in hand. "What is this about Emanuel?"

"I'm going to tell him that you want to go to Austria for spring break!" I answered.

"Oh! I thought you were joking! Is this for real?" I couldn't get a word in so I just nodded. Martha was excited. When she is, she talks faster and her Spanish accent gets heavier. "Of course I would love to go to Austria! That's wonderful!" Martha exclaimed. A big smile lit her whole face, and I told her the whole story.

This is what happened: Spring break was a week away, and students were eager to go home. That day, I had just finished teaching one of my classes when Emanuel, one of my students, approached me. He asked if I might excuse him from class the following Thursday and Friday—the last two days before spring break was to start. I asked Emanuel the reason. He replied, "I'm going to Austria to visit my family, and I'm flying out on Thursday."

"Oh!" I said, "My wife hopes to go to Austria some day. She grew up in Guatemala and misses the mountains." I also explained to Emanuel that, as a young bride, Martha had seen *The Sound of Music*; and ever since, she had dreamed of visiting the Alps.

"Then, come with me," Emanuel said grinning. I thought he was teasing me. But, after visiting with him, it became evident that he meant it. I told him that I would check with Martha and get back to him ASAP. That's how our unexpected trip to Austria came about.

Now, with Martha's enthusiastic consent, I called Emanuel and told him the good news, "We are going with you!" Since spring break was only a week away, we had to move fast and work out the details already on my list: get substitute teachers for both of us; contact our neighbors who usually took care of our homestead, including the animals; pack; and buy our plane tickets.

When I returned to school after lunch, I found Emanuel at a library computer. He was already trying to find airline tickets. With our updated passports and my credit card on hand, Emanuel secured some cheap tickets for us, quicker than we thought possible. Soon it became evident that God had provided a personal travel agent and an expert and gracious guide. God used Emanuel to be with us all the way!

By the time we left Ankeny the next Thursday, Emanuel had already laid out our itinerary. He took into account some of my suggestions and wishes. Martha, as usual, left the general planning of the trip up to me and was happy to tag along wherever we went. Her adventuresome spirit adds spice to our travels.

On my atlas I found Innsbruck and south of it, Mieders, Emanuel's hometown. I noticed that it was in the narrow section of Austria that borders Switzerland, Liechtenstein, Italy, and Germany. I asked our kind guide if it would be possible for us to drive up to these countries and spend a few hours in each. He said, "Sure, I'll drive us there!" And he smiled.

Emanuel went right to work and made all the necessary arrangements. Seven days later, Martha and I were buckled on our airplane seats, beside each other, on our way to the Alps! Emanuel was nearby. I had a window seat by an emergency exit door; a stewardess stopped by and offered to find me another seat.

I gave her a *"Why?"* look. She responded with an impatient *"Because"* look and gave this reason: "In an emergency, the person sitting in your seat needs to be strong enough to take down the emergency exit door and help people get off the plane."

My quick reply to her long explanation was, "I am strong enough! I could throw every one on this plane out of this window!" Martha and Emanuel turned to me and snickered. The stewardess looked a little startled, but allowed me to stay in my seat.

After a long, trans-Atlantic flight, we landed in Munich on Friday. From here, Emanuel's father drove us to his home in Mieders. A luscious lunch, prepared by Emanuel's mother, was awaiting us. This is how our special treat of generous Austrian hospitality began.

Emanuel planned our home base in Mieders. This was his family's "chalet"—a big house where his grandparents lived. It was within walking distance from the center of town. They let us stay free in an upstairs apartment, which they rented during the skiing season; it had a private bathroom, a kitchenette and a spacious living room area. Mountains surrounded us; the view from our balcony was breath-taking. The small chapel on a hill top was a photographer's dream.

Emanuel's parents spoke English; however, his grandparents did not. Although we didn't speak any German, the four of us connected right away, especially Martha and Grandma. One evening when Emanuel was visiting his sister and Austrian friends, he arranged for us to have dinner with his grandparents.

As we ate his grandmother's yummy meal, Martha and I spoke English and grandpa and grandma spoke German. With my Dutch background, sometimes I could get the gist of what they were saying. Hand motions also helped, and we also drew pictures to describe what we were trying to say, and laughed a lot. It certainly turned out to be an entertaining evening.

On Saturday morning, before we drove to Germany, Emanuel knocked on our door and said, "Come with me I want to show you something." We went downstairs with him and followed him through a door off the first-floor hallway.

Surprise! Surprise! We stepped into a barn where some cows were munching hay. They looked up with their big, brown eyes and stared at us in wonderment. Then, Emanuel directed our attention to the floor. There, lying by her mother was a tiny, cute calf that had been born during the night. Our home base had a barn attached to it. It was an old-fashioned house-barn!

In Germany we visited some of my former students in Bad Heilbrunn, Erlangen, and Blairsdorff. At the last place, I preached in English at a German church where a former student was the pastor, and Emanuel translated my sermon into Austrian German, which is a little different than German. The pastor then re-translated parts of my sermon when necessary.

Afterwards, I learned that a group of Chinese believers was present in the service; and their Chinese pastor re-translated my message into Chinese. A four-language sermon turned the service into a first-century church charismatic service. Once in a while, because of the people's puzzled countenances, I had to wonder about the accuracy of the translation!

On the way back to Austria, we stopped at Nuremberg and visited some of its famous places, like the stadium where the Nazi party held massive rallies. Then we walked through the city, which was nearly destroyed by the Allies in World War II. However following the war, the city was reconstructed, including some of its beautiful medieval buildings.

Tired, but happy, after a full week-end, we arrived at our cozy apartment. The next morning and every morning that week, Emanuel came by early and took us to the places according to his itinerary. We visited castles and museums; went through an old silver mine, an Alpine zoo, and a beautiful crystal exhibition.

He took us to a quaint town in Italy, and we treated him to an authentic pizza lunch. In Switzerland we sampled Alpine Ice cream. To help their economy, we bought postage stamps in Liechtenstein, which is the smallest country in Europe. Part of the finances to run the country come from the sale of postage stamps!

The itinerary also included a dress-up dinner at a fancy restaurant owned by a friend of Emanuel's sister. We did as our Austrian hosts did to make sure that we used the right utensil—we had several to choose from.

The highlight of our trip for Martha was the climb by car to majestic, snow-covered mountains. It was cold, but the view was worth it all! For me, it was the Austrian German chocolate. Emanuel's aunt and her family loaded us down with a lot of the delicious, dark brown delicacies.

In addition, I decided that chocolate was one of the best souvenirs to take back to family and friends. Before we left, we went shopping in Mieders and bought what Martha thought was enough. However, right then and there, I made a mental note of who was worthy of receiving my favorite souvenirs. My plan was to store in our home freezer a good number of the chocolate delicacies—which I did!

The week went by quickly, but the memories will last a lifetime. Martha and I had never taken a trip abroad that took so much planning in such a short notice. However, it was one of the most enjoyable and relaxed trips we have ever taken. Emanuel and his family made this grand vacation possible.

God blessed us with Emanuel: a gracious host, a patient guide, and an excellent driver. Because of him, Martha's dream of visiting Austria came true at last!

*Now that I know Christ,
I'm happier when I'm sad
Than I was before when I was glad.*

—John C. Wheeler

99

Are All Things Possible?

One of Iowa's enjoyable features is its changing seasons, which is closely connected with one of my favorite hobbies—gardening. During the cold winters, I look through my seed catalogs and plan my gardens. Cool spring days are perfect for planting the seeds and the tender starters. Weeding and watering fill up the long, hot summer days; toward summer's end, my gardens reward me with their first-fruits. Surrounded by beautiful yellows, oranges, and reds of fall, I complete the harvest, and then I prepare the soil for next year's plants.

God used my love for gardening and changing seasons, with their various tasks, to prepare me for an unexpected duty. In April 1995, the state representative of our Iowa fellowship of Baptist churches approached me and said, "We would like you to start a church in Grimes."[78] And he asked me to pray about it.

He added that the Next Towns Evangelism (NTE) team of our fellowship thought that Grimes was ready for a church plant and that this project was tailor-made for a full-time, Bible college teacher who lived nearby. Like the Apostle Paul, this church planter had to be a tent-maker (have another job). It was spring, and I was in garden-planting-season mode, but church planting seemed like an impossible undertaking at the time.

---

[78] Grimes is a growing bedroom community near Des Moines.

My reply to his challenge was, "I'll have to think and pray about it."

Planting a church takes great commitment. I made no decision on the matter at the time, but shared it with Martha. Swamped with end-of-school responsibilities, the issue sat temporarily in the back burner.

After graduation, God helped me remember the need in Grimes, and I prayed as I planted my gardens. Often, when Martha looked through the back window and saw me working, she also thought about God's will and the church plant in Grimes.

In May, I met with the State Representative and the NTE team. To my questions about available funds, possible meeting locations, and a core of people to help us get started, their answer was, "We have none."

I thought to myself, "No money. No people! No place to meet!"

However, a few years back, the team had surveyed Grimes, and they said they planned to share the information with me. Most importantly, they promised to pray for the church-plant effort and to encourage our sister churches to pray also. Oh, and they told me that they had some used hymnals available for us.

At the end of the meeting, they asked me if I was willing to take on the task. I replied, "I can't give you an answer now. I have to discuss this with my wife and with the Bible college president." I needed the backing of both of them. Also, I wanted to pray more about it.

Before leaving, I told them, "If we start a church, our first Bible study will be in September when people's vacations are over." They looked encouraged.

But I went home discouraged. Like Elijah the prophet, I felt I was alone in this effort. When I arrived home and shared the news with Martha, she said, "I'll help you!" God used her daring spirit to lift me up. Our core group doubled in one day. Now we were two.

Soon after Martha offered to help me, God helped us with the finances as well. I preached at a small church in Missouri and received $75 for an honorarium. I put the money back in the envelope and set it aside for the church plant. Now, with a core group of two and a $75-monetary seed, we started to plow the field.

The next month, Grimes produced its first two residents—Rich and Dorothy Skinner. They had been praying for a Baptist church in their home town, and they were ready to be part of God's answer. The core group doubled again! Hot summer days, brought in more fruit, Ron and Carol Williams joined us in July.

The long summer days afforded me time to work on my gardens and also on my church planting tasks. I contacted pastors of area sister churches and asked them if I might present our future Grimes' ministry. This groundwork produced an early crop. All the churches promised to pray for us. From three of the churches came six adults and three children who planed to stay with us. A few others said we could enlist their help temporarily—they wanted to help us get going!

Since our first meeting was set for September, I knew that a few college students might join us. At the most, we figured that a total of fifteen people would show up. The Skinners had offered their home, but we realized that in time their living room would not be big enough. We had not even started meeting, and we were already facing the possibility of crowded conditions!

After weeding out the potential but not available locations, Rich found us a meeting place. Because he was a Grimes resident, Rich was acquainted with the school officials. They granted us permission to meet at the Dallas Center-Grimes

Junior High School for our Thursday night Bible studies. The rent was $12 a week.

On Thursday, September 7, 1995, we began as a fellowship with our first Bible study. Instead of fifteen, twenty-two people showed up! Jeff Ray, our temporary song leader, led us on our first song, "To God Be the Glory!" This became our theme song for Maranatha Baptist Church. During the first weeks, in the midst of beautiful fall colors, God continued to yield more fruit.

Our first monthly budget was $330.00. In order to acclimatize the new, tender fellowship to a mature environment, the people began paying me a salary of $25 a month; and we also established a building fund. In addition, it was important for this young plant to start thinking about branching out. Thus, about a month following our first Bible study, we began to support our first missionary at $15 a month. To meet expenses, we took up weekly offerings. After several months, two sister churches gave us a total of $1,000.00.

During the fall and the beginning of winter of 1995, we plowed the field in preparation for the planting of a full-fledged independent Baptist church in Grimes. Rich Skinner proposed the name of Maranatha Baptist Church. By December, we had formulated our church constitution and corporation articles. Qualified fellowship members voted to adopt our constitution, elected deacons, and called me to be the pastor.

Usually on the cold evenings of December, I look through seed catalogs and plan my next year's gardens. With God's help, that frigid December in 1995, we jump-started the spring planting season, and set on the snow-covered ground a small, tender sprout—

Maranatha Baptist Church of Grimes!

100

All Things Are Possible!

On Sunday, January 7, 1996, the Dallas Center-Grimes Junior High School band room resonated with "To God Be the Glory!" About forty-four people attended our first worship service. Moreover, several classrooms that were used to quiet, peaceful Sundays became alive with the cheerful buzzing of Sunday school teachers and students. Some ladies rearranged slightly the furniture in a school office and squeezed in a port-a-crib. Lo and behold! We had a nursery!

That first Sunday, we also started children's church and evening worship service. On Wednesday, January 10, we held our first regular mid-week service, which included Bible study and prayer time for adults and a children's meeting. Up to this point, our people had attended two mid-week services: Wednesday and Thursday. As a result, attendance at all our services was consistent.

Growth and change resulted in higher expenses and more work. Our rent went up five-fold, and we had to set up and move furniture around before every service, then tear down and set things back in place afterwards.

Several people volunteered to transport the things we needed; such as bulletins, hymnals, Sunday school materials, offering plates, port-a-crib, collapsible pulpit, Lord's Supper set, and two signs—one to put by Main Street and one by the school. Jerry and Kathy Grimes took the signs in their old,

All Things Are Possible!

orange van. My list alone contained 48 items. Soon I got tired of having to check them off before leaving home.

I tore up my list and crammed all the stuff in the "portable-church-storage-bin"—our car trunk. It was a practical way to keep track of all the church things. Then, one beautiful spring Saturday, I took everything out of the trunk, gave it a good cleaning, and crammed the stuff back into it again. The next morning, Martha and I left merrily on our way to church, assured that we had everything. When we arrived, the people helped us unload the trunk; then we set up for church.

The service was about to begin, when an usher came to me and whispered, "We can't find the offering plates." "Oh! No!" I exclaimed softly. He knew I had forgotten them. He replied with a "That's okay!" nod and walked out. As the pianist struck the first offertory note, the ushers walked down smiling confidently, carrying tin pie plates in their hands. The resourceful ushers had foraged through the school kitchen and had found what they needed. Our people were generous givers, and that day they were also cheerful givers!

We experienced amusing growing pains as well. One Lord's Supper Sunday, after the deacons passed out the grape juice cups, they walked down with uneasy countenances and empty trays. They had passed out every single cup of grape juice and had none left for me or them. One of the deacons reached discretely over to the piano, grabbed the pianist's cup, and gave it to me. When I said, "Let's all drink it together," all of us did, except the deacons!

While grateful for our temporary facilities, we eagerly looked forward to building our own permanent "home." At the end of December 1996, our building fund had reached $30,000. At this point, I asked the deacons what building-fund goal we should set for the end of 1997. Enthusiastically, they proposed $100,000!

Pleased but a little hesitant, I did not want to throw a cold blanket on their great faith. My response to their proposal was, "We will trust God, pray about it, and do our part."

In the spring of 1997, we purchased six acres for $75,000. Actually, we bought five at $15,000 per acre, but I asked the seller if he would throw in a free acre. And he did! We bought the property on a land contract at 10% interest that was to start when the land closed. It took the seller more than a year to clear problems with land covenants. All this delayed the closing.

Early on, we had decided to allocate the offerings of every fifth Sunday to the building fund. December 31, 1997, landed on a Sunday. When the deacons counted the offering, our building fund reached $100,065.28! God had helped us meet our 1997 goal through the faithful giving of His people. At closing time, we had the cash to pay for the land and did not have to pay any interest—not even one cent!

Our plans called for a 10,000-square-foot structure. Of course, the building cost more than we could pay for with cash; we had to acquire loans from various sources. Banks do not like to give loans to new church plants. After being turned down by six banks, we finally found one in Waukee, a neighboring town. This bank had opened for business at the same time we had started our church plant.

In those days, the construction of a 10,000-square-foot building cost about $600,000, but we took a different route. We submitted a request for assistance to Continental Baptist Missions. They agreed to help us and sent nine professional builders and their families.

By now, our church membership was up to eighty-four. Under the leadership of CBM and their invaluable help, our church people and volunteers from other churches put in many hours. Consequently, we reduced the building cost by 40%—from $600,000 to $350,000. Since our land was paid in full,

All Things Are Possible!

Waukee State Bank was willing to lend us the $350,000 at 9%.

The loan would have been sufficient to complete our building project, but we ran into an expensive, *dirty* snag. The city of Grimes refused to issue a building permit until we raised the back three acres by a foot and a half. This entailed hauling 450 truck loads of dirt at the cost of about $27,000; to this, we had to add the site work expenses, bringing up the cost to $55,000 for *dirt*.

Then one day, as Martha and I were taking a Sunday afternoon joy ride, we drove by the church's six acres. A six-foot hill behind them caught my attention. Thinking out loud, I said to Martha, "I wonder if the land owner is willing to sell us three more acres. We could get the dirt from that hill." About two years had passed since we had bought our six acres from him, and land prices had gone higher than $15,000 an acre.

When I approached the owner and asked him, "Would you be willing to sell us the three acres behind us," he looked willing. But before any words had come out of his mouth, I continued with my request, "for the reduced price of $12,500 an acre?"

Amazingly, he agreed with no qualms whatsoever. Bolstered by his response and knowing that closings take precious time, I asked him if we might have his permission to start moving dirt from his land if we paid him $5,000 down. Again, he agreed. Clearly, God was involved in this real estate transaction!

However, before we could close the deal, the issue had to go to the church for a vote. Two members were not in favor of buying more property. Before we held the business meeting, I built my case.

(1) I sought guidance from two pastors who were facing overcrowded conditions in their churches. They needed to

build but were land-locked. Their advice was, "Buy the land. You will need it!"

(2) A third pastor provided counsel by recounting his church situation. Twenty years earlier, the church could have bought an adjoining ten-acre piece for $30,000. Thinking that it was too much money, the people voted down the recommendation to buy it. Recently, they had bought the last undeveloped acre. This one-acre piece cost $30,000. I got the point!

(3) After visiting with our banker about the issue, he didn't tell me any stories. Bluntly he said, "I agree. Buy the land. You will not be sorry if you do. Land will go up in value."

(4) Then I went to our lawyer. He gave me the following "legal opinion": "It's a no brainer." To make sure I understood his legal jargon, he repeated his opinion three times during our conversation.

After completing my research, I presented my findings to the Maranatha Baptist Church members at the "Dirt Business Meeting." The recommendation was to purchase the three adjoining acres. Everyone voted, "Yes," except two members who abstained from voting.

Now, we encountered a new financial problem. The bank had lent us the maximum that the state of Iowa allowed a new bank to lend to one borrower. We needed to borrow $37,500 more for the new acres and $17,500 for the site labor—to bring the dirt across the line. The dirt seemed expensive; but, since it came attached to land, it was pretty cheap dirt after all!

One of the deacons suggested that we take out promissory notes. These went directly to lenders at a set interest rate and for various time limits: three, five, ten, and fifteen years, with interest paid quarterly, yearly, or at maturity. We offered the notes to other churches and church members and received loans to cover the $55,000 we needed.

We were ready to move dirt! Our land came alive with huge earthmoving equipment. CBM missionary builders were expert excavators and moved 450 truck loads of dirt across the line and built up the area specified by city code; then Grimes issued us a building permit. We were ready to build! The missionary builders opened their tool truck, and they got down to the business they had been called to do initially.

We had broken ground in May 1998, and we dedicated the building to our faithful God in July 1999. When we moved into our facilities, the congregation began to grow even faster; the giving increased; and we were able to pay the interest on the promissory notes every time they were due. At the same time, we were building up a fund to pay off the first notes that were coming due in three years.

Several months before our first notes were due, we had $9,000 on hand. As I considered our financial situation, it became obvious that we had taken too many three-year notes. I did not want to default on our promissory notes—that was the worst thing that could happen. I pled with the church people to covenant with me to pray every day for two months. I asked them to pray specifically for God to help us meet our promissory-note obligations.

Our people prayed faithfully and earnestly, and God began to work in people's hearts. A sister church, much larger than we were, responded bigheartedly. They promised to give us the whole offering from a particular Sunday, which happened to be a week before the notes were due. That Sunday, the generous people of this church gave twice the usual amount—$21,000!

That same week, an anonymous giver, a modern-day Barnabas, gave us $25,000! Within one week, our $9,000-promissory-note fund increased to $55,000! We were able to pay off, not only the three-year notes, but all of the five-year, ten-year, and fifteen-year notes and interest. Once again, God answered our prayers and provided our needs—far beyond our expectations!

I served as pastor of Maranatha for ten years. During that time, more believers joined the church, and a number of people trusted Christ as their personal Savior and were baptized. It was a blessing for Martha and me to grow spiritually through this experience and to see the people grow as well.

Numerically, the congregation numbered 200. We were at the point of outgrowing our building. Thus, in 2002 we began a new construction project, which we dedicated to the Lord in May 2005. The new facilities included a gymnasium, shower rooms, multiple Sunday school rooms, and a prophet's chamber.[79]

It was time for me to retire. I retired in December 2005. Maranatha Baptist Church of Grimes had matured into a full-fledged independent Baptist church. When its planting was first suggested to me, it seemed like an impossible task.

But "the things which are impossible with men are possible with God."[80] "To God Be the Glory!"

---

[79] A place to house guest speakers.
[80] Luke 18:27.

101

Rest in Peace

As the world anxiously anticipated Y2K, a glorious peace awaited Mamá Sarita, Martha's mother. On Saturday, January 1, 2000, she came to the end of her earthly journey and entered her heavenly home. We had to take some unexpected measures to attend her memorial services, which were scheduled in Guatemala City for Tuesday and Wednesday, January 4 and 5.

We needed passports to travel, and they were locked up in our safety deposit box. Since it was January 1, the banks were closed. Pat Duer, the college bookkeeper, knew a bank executive and called her to tell her about our dilemma. The executive, escorted by a policeman, let me in the bank. I went straight to my "bank business" and opened our safety deposit box.

With passports in hand, we arranged our flight to Guatemala. On Sunday, we drove to Chicago, spent the night there, and flew out the next day. Monday night, our flight landed in Guatemala. Upon arrival, Papá Toñito, Martha's dad, assured us that their church and a funeral home were carrying out all of Sarita's plans.

Years earlier, Sarita had convinced Toñito to plan their funerals since their children lived in the States. By taking care of these end-of life issues, Martha's parents were thinking of us. Their plans spared us from having to make difficult decisions when we were sorrowing and weary. Also, we were able to focus on Toñito and be a great comfort to him. He and Sarita had been married for fifty-seven years!

On our flight back, Martha brought up the issue of preparing for the inevitable, just like her parents had done. I did not pursue the matter for several years. Then, a peaceful scenery inspired me to think seriously about preparing for death. A nice, little cemetery, a half mile from our house, lies on the route I take daily on my way to and from work. Finally, I became convinced that it was wise to plan our memorial services. This way, if I died first, Martha would not have to make decisions at a difficult time.

One afternoon after teaching my last class, I got into my old, red pickup and drove merrily home. A few minutes into my route, the peaceful landscape caught my eye. Without stopping to think about it, I turned my old truck into the parking lot of the little cemetery. I went into the director's office, visited briefly with him, and picked out a nice burial plot near a tree—an ideal location since I love trees. I then put down the required money and drove merrily the rest of the way home.

As soon as I arrived home and before I confessed to Martha what I had just done, she jumped into the pickup and said, "Let's go!" We had to go to Menards for building materials. (Not for a coffin!)

From Martha's perspective, trips to Menards have replaced our Sunday joy rides. We had barely left our driveway, when I told her, "I have a surprise for you!"

Don't ever tell a woman that you have a surprise for her and are unable to reveal it immediately. She'll bug you to death until you disclose it to her. For three miles, Martha begged, "Please, tell me right now!" Her pleas went in and out of my stubborn Dutchman's ears.

At an intersection, three miles from home, I asked her, "Why do you want to know the surprise so badly?"

"Because," she replied soberly, "A drunk driver might run this red light right now and hit us! Then, I would die without knowing what it was!"

In line with my Dutch disposition, I still did not tell her the surprise. The rest of the way, Martha gave me looks that could kill! It's a good thing Menards was only about two miles away, or I would have been dead myself. Once we arrived at the store full of interesting gadgets, Martha forgot the whole matter.

She doesn't like to shop and rarely goes shopping alone, but when we are together, she goes crazy, not shopping crazy but silly crazy. She finds humor in the most ordinary things. Of course, I egg her on. When she starts laughing I'm afraid we might get kicked out of the store, or that she might drop dead right there. That day, I had serious things on my mind, and she just followed me around as I found the building supplies.

Then on the way home, I took a different route—my daily route from work. As I approached the peaceful landscape, I slowed down my old truck and was about to turn it into the driveway, when Martha's sixth sense alerted her that something was up. She spun around and exclaimed, "I know what the surprise is! You bought a cemetery plot!" Martha and I have been married for almost fifty years, and I have yet to figure out her sixth sense.

I simply nodded my head. She was eager to see my latest real-estate purchase. When she saw it, the location pleased her immensely, but her excitement about the plot made me a little uneasy! During the next few weeks, we had meetings with a cemetery staff lady to work out the other details, like the coffins, the kind of memorial services, the headstone, and the engraved wording on it.

Our last meeting involved a visit to the plot. On the way there, Martha, my directionally impaired wife, told the staff lady, "I want to know exactly how to get there, so I don't get lost on my way there." Then, Martha added, "Oh! I guess I won't have to worry about that! They'll carry me there!" We all laughed.

Then, we returned to the office to sign papers. Before we stood up to leave, Martha told the lady, "Thank you for your kindness. May I have ten minutes of your time? You may have noticed that we're not afraid to die. I'd like to tell you why."

I knew what Martha was up to, and I prayed silently for her. Martha explained to the lady why she was not afraid to die by telling her about the gospel: All of us are sinners and deserve condemnation in hell, but Jesus died to pay for our sins' penalty. Moreover, He rose again from the dead after three days, and this assures the future resurrection of our bodies from the grave. Trusting in Jesus Christ as our Savior guarantees us everlasting life with Him in heaven.

The lady did not respond to the glorious gospel that day, but Martha encouraged her to contact us if she had any questions. "You have our number!" Martha reminded her, and then added kindly, "Please call us."

Martha had learned from her mother to turn an ordinary event into an opportunity to share the gospel with others. At her mother's funeral, many people told Martha that they had trusted Jesus as their Savior because of Sarita. While on earth, she spoke of Jesus faithfully, and her soul is now in heaven with Him.

Her body is resting peacefully in the grave, just as she and Toñito had planned it. But, Sarita's body will not remain there forever. Soon, at His coming, her Savior will raise it from the dead!

Mother and I

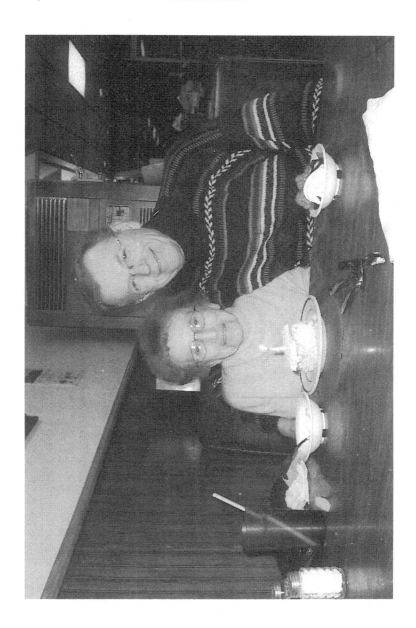

Appendix

Heaven is a wonderful place!

The house on 2nd Street in Orange City was not merely the home where I grew up; it was also a secure, godly haven. Loyal to her Dutch heritage, my widowed mother read the Bible to us three times daily, after every meal. More importantly, she motivated us to live godly lives by her example and by disciplining us when we disobeyed her.

She also took us to church every Sunday. Orange City was a remarkably religious town. During my boyhood days, its population was about 2,000. But on Sunday mornings, when the families of the surrounding farms congregated for worship, the population increased to 5,000.

Church every Sunday was not enough; Mother also sent us to catechism on Tuesday afternoons. The pastor drilled us on our church's Bible teachings. All this was good for my character development, but there was one big problem: though I tried to live a morally upright life, I was still a sinner. I did not always tell the truth, and I did not always obey my mother. However, no one confronted me with the crucial fact that as a sinner I needed to trust Jesus as my *own* personal Savior.

All that changed the summer of 1955, when I was eighteen years old. The young people of a small church in Orange City were going to a Bible camp near Maxwell, Nebraska. I was not a member of that church, but when some of its young people invited me to go, I jumped at the opportunity and went!

The speaker that week at Maranatha Bible Camp was an evangelist named Paul Levine. He preached the gospel clearly every day: We all are sinners deserving judgment in hell; but Christ died on the cross for our sins; then He gloriously rose from the dead on the third day, thus securing everlasting life to all who believe in Him.

God used the gospel to convict me of my sinful condition. One night that week, I trusted Jesus as my personal Savior. Mr. Levine then reminded me of these truths found in the Bible:

"As it is written: 'There is none righteous, no, not one; there is none who understands; there is none who seeks after God. They have all turned aside; they have together become unprofitable; there is none who does good, no, not one'" (Romans 3:10-12).

"For all have sinned and fall short of the glory of God" (Romans 3:23).

"But God demonstrates His own love toward us, in that while we were still sinners, Christ died for us" (Romans 5:8).

"For the wages of sin is death, but the gift of God is eternal life in Christ Jesus our Lord" (Romans 6:23).[81]

"Whoever calls on the name of the Lord shall be saved" (Romans 10:13).

The moment I trusted Jesus, God granted me ever-lasting life—a secure life with Him. While I live on this earth, God enables me to know Him by reading the Bible and obeying what it says. When my earthly life comes to and end, I have the certainty of an everlasting life in heaven with God.

I am so thankful that my Mother made sure that our childhood home was a secure, godly haven. My heart also overflows with thanksgiving to God for saving me and securing me a place with Him in Heaven.

Heaven is a wonderful place! Won't you come and go with me? Trust Jesus Christ as your Savior today!

---

[81] Bible quotations are from the NKJV™.

Made in the USA
Lexington, KY
26 November 2016